MIURA!

Acclaim for Nicholas Anderson

'Due to censorship restrictions, a veteran of Britain's MI6 intelligence service tells a fictionalized version of his covert action experiences'

Publishers Weekly

'Nicholas Anderson has rare insight knowledge'

Daily Mail

'Licence to Thrill: gritty spy novel'

The Scotsman

'While MI6 did not have a specific department to deal with assassinations it did have access to the necessary expertise through its 'Q' Ops section of the Technical Services Division, and to qualified personnel in the SPA (Special Political Action) section. It could also call upon the SAS, whose NATO remit included undertaking special operations and assassinations'

MI6: 50 Years of Special Operations

Nicholas Anderson

NOC Twice

More UK Non-Official Cover Operations

– the middle part of an intelligence officer's autobiography –

"There is often in the circumstances that betrays the most cunning scoundrels something so unexpected, so surprising, so unforeseeable that men who follow this kind of affair come to believe that human justice is not entirely without some supernatural assistance in seeking out the guilty."

— Joseph de Maistre, philosopher, following the aftermath of the
French Revolution

Copyright © 2014 by Nicholas Anderson

Second Book, Second Edition

Part Two of *The NOC Trilogy*

ISBN 978-1-7329661-2-3

Library of Congress Cataloguing in Publication

Foreword

Don't romanticise it.
There was never anything Byronic about it.
This is brutal dirt-down real shit.
Reality is just before going beyond into imagination.
Melancholy is a bastardisation just before that…

When I read the first third of my trilogy of fictionalised autobiographies (*NOC – Non-Official Cover: British Secret Operations*), it showed the subject to be a much finer chap than perhaps I truly am. I allowed everybody to think they knew me well: when, in fact, they didn't know me at all. I can be an absolutely stinking rotter when I have to be, especially if it had to be on behalf of Her Majesty Queen Elizabeth II of England's British Secret Intelligence Service, the SIS, MI6, the Firm – they all meant the same thing: protecting the Establishment, *then*.

Publishing my memoir in the form of 'a documentary thriller' novel was a fierce counter-invasion of the battles in my life. To briefly respond to criticism of it, my only tongue-in-cheek comment is: "Well, yes, it *is* a tale without an end though it wags a bit in the middle. But it is *based on truth*, like it or not, except I can't completely say that it is true for legal reasons I'm sure you understand."

I have to admit that when I finally completed writing my very first book-length composition, I thought, 'Well, at the very least my children will know something about their father.' But having that manuscript and seeing it published, I have the strange sensation that I am just awakening from a dream to find myself lying alone on a bed. And the first thing that comes to my head is to think about writing the next one, because I had only told a third on my life's story thus far.

So here is my next book – the follow-up second – warts and all: *NOC Twice: More UK Non-Official Cover Operations* – the story behind the other story in front of it (with another story to come). It should have been categorised as "nonpareil friction", sic – read that as code for "non-fiction", if what the label-conscious international literary industry put me through is anything to go by with continuous rejections. But the never-ending game continues: Where one side's story ends; the other side starts – and vice versa. I hope the ping-pong ends one day soon…with a compromise. Readers will find out what I mean after completion of my trilogy.

Still here we go round the Mulberry Bush again in a ballet with the forbidden…

It is the wisdom of those who think of themselves as experts
…is why things get screwed up royally.

* * * * * * * * *

The chapters that unfold herein are selected writings mostly presented in chronological order and are really a series of stand-alone short stories plus a couple of longer ones. There is no main story or central theme other than that I was involved or was a witness to the events. This is not a disclaimer, more an explanation of what you are about to read.

YOU CAN'T JUDGE A BOOK BY LOOKING AT ITS COVER: THE HISTORY OF THIS BOOK COVER'S ARTWORK

The image has long been etched into my memory. I had already started writing the manuscript for my second book. In my mind I had already decided on the one country where the narrative would start and where it would end. And then one day as I was strolling along a deserted pavement in Dubai, United Arab Emirates, I saw the image almost magically reappear in front of my eyes. It was a life-sized replica standing there just outside an art gallery but nobody was sitting in it. It was not for sale but just an advertisement. A real Lebanese jalopy parked there with household belongings piled up on top. In peacetime a sight such as this might look odd and perhaps even comical but the reality is that in any place about to be invaded, families must evacuate on a moment's notice. Being prepared is the warped survival instinct and modus operandi of the moment. By-any-means-possible, and pronto were operative words for a successful abandonment with all lives kept and some cherished items intact. I had witnessed this madness in Beirut, Lebanon, 1982-1983.

Then a year later after that trip to the Persian Gulf while attending the Frankfurt Book Fair, I met the minister of culture for Lebanon and asked him if he had access to photographic archives from Lebanon's civil war. He cheerfully told me he did, and promised to mail me some pictures of the type I had in mind once he got back home from Germany. To my utter disappointment these proved to be big words that ended up being a typical waste of time and energy. And in spite of my repeated follow ups, the minister did not deliver on his promise. For me it was Lebanon revisited in Europe decades later. Some things never change.

Finally, another year goes by and I am now in an Irish pub in Nice, France, watching my football club, Sunderland, live on telly, when the woman sitting next to me tells me she is an American artist based in Paris. I get home, view her artwork on her website and one image captivates me at once. It is the perfect piece to complete the jigsaw puzzle. Linda McCluskey's art is a deliberately distorted view of the world but for me it represents the artistic version of how beat-up Beirut was then and is an apt presentation of this book...*because at that wacky time mostly everything defied logic.*

Thank goodness you are spared then the pain in the faces of the family sitting in the car.

* * * * * * * * *

AUTHOR'S NOTE

In addition to my first person style of writing, you will find that from time to time I insert prose in *italics* to describe a secondary thought I had.

This is a form of poetry – the Japanese call it *haiku* – that uses unrhymed iambic pentameter, usually in dramatic or narrative verse, e.g.: the lines don't rhyme but do follow a certain rhythmic pattern of thinking. It's an insight to the way my mind works: Where I could intermittently foresee ahead with a wee bit of karma; visualising how I wanted the outcome to be and it would often materialise.

Alternatively, it is also a written form of *kōan*, the meaning in Zen Buddhism in which it cannot be understood by rational thought but may be accessible through intuition.

I grew up the child of British parents in the Far East among people of this deep form of thinking so it's an integral part of me, a part of my being and a built-in protective instinct that allowed me as an adult to survive the dangers that I encountered throughout. So please accept this occasional textual intrusion.

Others may eat, read, sleep, talk, listen to music, create art, dance, and watch birds or whatever else makes them tick. Instead, I spent much of my downtime during operations in the field putting pencil to paper, then committing it to memory before destroying the physical evidence (because it would incriminate me for being in the wrong place at the wrong time):

For this man
the infinitely tinted meanings of psychology
vanish without the symphony of language.
It is what I am.

* * * * * * * * *

I will always remain grateful for the unswerving support of "d", Fiona, Jimmy and Kenny.

NOC Twice
More UK Non-
Official Cover Operations

Prologue

When stuck in a blast furnace yet feeling strangely cool,
don't let it cook over you as you will start to melt, you fool.
Death's first move is a sucking illusion,
you must dupe its delusion.

God and the Devil got together once, in the form of the Jews' clandestine but insufficient provision of arms to the Persians in the latter's war against the Arabians. True. Ariel Sharon's hypocritical Zionist rationale being that if Mohammed's chosen man, Saddam Hussein, won the battle against Iran then Iraq would have the most powerful army in the Middle East and Israel could not allow that possibility even if their original Christian weaponry supplier was on the opposing side...

I had long left the veiled marshland Arab who had canoed me across the inky still water wonder where the Tigris and Euphrates rivers calmly merge. For a while we stayed midstream on the *thalweg* (centre line border between Iraq and Iran). It was dawn when he had dropped me but now the orange ball above was growing dangerously hot with the suffocating dust kicking up to boot.

The extreme weather conditions now required me to cover my head with my own chequered olive and black *shemagh*. It is the same Arabic head scarf often worn by SIS officers on quasi-paramilitary deep cover ops as well as the Special Air Service (SAS), the UK's élite soldiers. I rechecked that the real (unused) condom was securely around my Browning Hi-Power 9mm pistol's nozzle to prevent dirt from jamming it. I'd kept the metal in my shadow, so it wouldn't get too hot to handle. If needed, a fired bullet would easily pierce the rubber. I had to be back an hour after dusk for the return journey as the old leather-faced man of few words would be waiting all day under the date trees for me. I imagined he would most probably be snacking on dates along with nature's free olives. Not knowing what his real moniker was, I'd nicknamed him "Sinbad" as the hero of legend who was thought to hail from this part of the world. I was assigned to monitor this specific situation so that's what I was doing. A wad of dinars would be his reward for delivering me back to where I belonged later that night. He already had some safely deposited in his pocket.

Out here in the shimmering desert I had been warned to be particularly careful of "sand sea", a bizarre kind of quicksand that didn't whirlpool you down whole but more or less floated you to a middle spot where you would simply be unable to move. It was either super-glued at the ankles or trapped thigh-deep.

I'd just passed one dead Iranian combatant who looked like an integral part of the landscape caked there. He must've got stuck knee-high and his upper body eventually keeled over face down snorting the muck with his palms held outward in fervent prayer. Bloody bastard died in an ignominious bent over position with his arse up in the air almost like an ostrich does with its head hiding in the silt. His upside down badge had read *Sepah-e-Pasdaran*, a member of the so-called élite Revolutionary Guards – rendering it an irony, to atheist me, to die while in the process of praising one's god.

Actually I hadn't realised it was a corpse until I came alongside him and my nostrils were whammed by a peculiar warm bad pork stench. At the same time, I noticed the green plastic key lying there as if it had been placed flat like a prayer mat on the brown floor. My gaze had followed the chain hanging from his upside down bloated head that turned slightly sideways. His face twisted in agony revealed the empty eye sockets that the insects must have feasted on not long ago. I'd gagged but couldn't exactly run away from this frightful sight. *"Bismillah-ir-Rahman-ir-Rahim*, in the name of Allah, the kind and merciful," I had muttered to myself. "This isn't what you thought Paradise was, is it poor sod? Welcome to Hell." [The Ayatollah Ruhollah Musavi Khomeini had promised Iranian fighters that if they wore these plastic keys and died in battle it would give them entry into their version of Heaven. *Nida-ul-Momineen*, the call of the faithful, resulted in almost a million of dead *baseeji* (paramilitary volunteers with no formal training in using weapons). And just like spawning salmon racing against the tide, these hapless warriors perished in the mistaken belief that ending one's life is proof of their nationalistic fervour. Sadly, this confusion between patriotism and religious conviction continues in mistaken glory in some medieval lands to this very day.

It was like walking in a field of land mines lurking beneath someplace except the earth itself was the sneak doing the same killer job in reverse motion, pulling victims down instead of blowing them up. Getting through the area was painful as I had to do it in the "British slow march" (or "technique Ulu Tiram" or TUT a term we sometimes liked to use. Ulu Tiram was the base of the British Jungle Warfare School, a covert training facility in Malaysia that closed in the late-sixties but the terminology lives on). The technique involved putting one foot down at a time slowly, stopping every five or ten unhurried steps. Eventually one develops a measured rhythm all the while feeling and listening for danger. Though I wished my satellite phone and three "ATOM"'s* I had left on me weren't so heavy as to drown me out here.

My own antenna signalled a presence that I couldn't see yet. Somewhere up ahead over the brow I could "smell" the murmur of war that was in progress. The Persians and the Muslims had been at each other's throats since late-September earlier this same year. Like two blind men fighting over eye drops, they would keep it up for eight more years over this territorial dispute. Personally I couldn't wait to go home to the UK in a few days' time. I had arrived to the region just one week after the conflict had erupted and I was now stuck in this messy Iran-Iraq War for a grimy stinking long one month. That was incidentally the maximum duration for assignments such as this one.

An hour later, I finally reached the other side of the brown patch where the greenery was and tumbled down through a bank of tall reeds, making a fair splash. A wide muddy stream was flowing and I stood in it with my boots on letting the cool water relieve the outside of my steaming feet. As I remained kneeled there motionless, I reached for my miniature field glasses and scanned around.

Suddenly against the backdrop of the sky I witnesses what could be best described as several grotesque dances of darkness whiz across. "Zulu time, this is Zagros, come in please, over," I'd said urgently into the phone unit's mouthpiece. The controlling station came on pretty quickly. "Zagros, this is home zero meridian receiving," replied the slightly static voice sitting at Greenwich Mean Time responding with the op's standard call back sign. "Go ahead Zagros, transmit, over." That was this mission's code of the day, spoken on a specially encrypted waveband, and it also happened to be the name of the nearest mountain range to the desert region I was alone in the centre of. He sounded as though he was just a few hundred yards away upstream and not the thousands of miles back in the more civilised world of Hanslope Park in rural English Buckinghamshire.

As I stood up slowly I was a bit off balance, "You wouldn't believe what I've just seen…jeez…" Then the full panorama presented itself in front of me.

"Try telling me," echoed the Welsh accent, sounding caustically bored with his continuous global radio traffic co-ordinates. "Zagros, you are ordered to revert to your special language protocol on this live recorded line, boyo, that is to say use no swear words, over."

"Wilco, sorry, sir, but they're chucking the dead over at their enemy as a method of engagement, over."

"Say that again? Repeat. Over."

"Not trying to be funny, sir, I said the Iraqis are catapulting Iranian carcasses back at them. I can't believe my eyes. Looks very surreal. The field medics are spreading powder onto the *shuhada* (Farsi for deceased heroes or martyrs) as fast as the firing party can load 'em on a wooden contraption that resembles a huge slingshot the height of a three-story building. Miles and piles of bodies everywhere. It's an amazing fucking sight! Sorry…over."

"Roger that. Wow, sounds like they ran out of TOW's. Once again, be careful on your street jargon on this taped band, boyo. So what's your location, Zagros? Over." (He was being sarcastic. TOW's are US-made Tube-launched, Optically-tracked, Wire-guided missiles often used to destroy tanks.) I gave them my grid zone identifier, the geographical position as I knew it to be. As the crow flies I wasn't all that far from the designated entry-exit point in the wetlands, despite the hours it had taken to get here.

There was a gap of a few seconds. Then a clipped very educated English voice came on, "Zagros? They're using a trebuchet to hurl unwanted items when they don't have enough ammo handy and they're probably contaminating them to spread plague. Plague comes from rodents and spread by fleas. Both sides have already poisoned each other's water supply, a common military practice. Over."

I happened to be scratching myself incessantly all over at the time he said it and had nearly been tempted to dip my bare hands into the water more than a few times. Upon closer inspection I had also become the doormat of suburbia for a community of tiny ant-like creatures crawling on and around the trees of hairs planted in my flesh. I identified for the first time what it was like for the raunchy mutt standing on all three while the hind leg rotated forth. As I bent to look closer at the wet, it did glint an oily film that I wouldn't have put my lips to. I was standing in half a foot of meandering miasma's as I talked to home base.

As I waded the few steps up to dry land I accidentally slipped and a squishy feeling crept in between the bottom of my elasticated trousers with the top of the boots. I continued to talk nevertheless, "Well, Zulu, the cadavers they're bowling over there are smattering into many pieces at the other end, about 150 yards into what looks like a utilities installation with a high wire fence…"

"Tell me, are they botched in a lime colour? Over."

"Blimey," I said, "I was just going to say that. Kind of looks like Martians flying around in space, over."

The doctor's voice sounded like he was on the verge of laughing. "It's bloody disinfectant they're using! They use it to prevent disease. Besides mutilation is a traditional way in some Muslim lands to deal with the stiffs of its political enemies. When they have the other side's dead they obviously don't need them anymore and lob them back at them. The cleaning material also seeps into and softens hardened remains innards just under the skin, which makes for an effective messy explosive upon impact. Quite ingenious I'd say…"

The man from Wales was back on, interrupting us. "Zagros, one mistake and you could be winging your merry way out of your life too, boyo. The Iranians would do the same to you for being an enemy of their God, think they call 'em something like *mohareb*. Airtime lacking now, sorry! Teatime is over ladies and gentlemen. Proceed with caution. Check-in at next signals log-in. See you when you get home, lad. Oh, Zagros, try and take a bleach shower at base tonight to decontaminate yourself, OK. Over and out." The line clicked dead.

"Sarky bugger, he was," I said to nobody in particular as I pressed the 'push' button off.

His shower statement puzzled me for the rest of the assignment. How could he know the need to decontaminate myself? I never told him I was standing in shit.

When I met that stoic Welshman in London a fortnight or so later, from a 10-digit numbered FULCRUM file sub-marked 'Images from Khorramshahr, Arabstan, Iran' – during the Iran-Iraq War the occupied town was renamed by the Iraqis as Khuninshahr, which means City of

Blood, in the newly created province of Khuzestan – and dated '29 October 1980', he produced a series of high-resolution colourised 12" x 18"'s pixelated blow-ups of a blurred stagnant me in that river, which indicated and identified the multiple kinds toxicity and its potency that I was surrounded by. Not that dissimilar from a wall chart of abstract paintings. (Fulcrum means "one that supplies capabilities for actions" was the US CIA's own satellite operated by its Directorate of Science and Technology. The Americans and British fully supported the invading Iraqis at that time while Israel elected to furnish Iran with its benefactor's weaponry to be used against it, its backer – the US – being one and the same entity…who had their own American-made guns fired *at them*.)

No wonder I suffered severe blotches and slight burns on my feet and arms for weeks after that episode. He was visiting me in a military hospital ward where I was being treated. The hair on parts of my legs and hands never did grow back again after that either.

"When you gave your location, we switched the Yankee's tin can 'feed' on," he said, smiling fleetingly, referring to the American spy satellite and its pictures that were in his grasp.

Of all the barmy things that could have happened to me in the strangest of circumstances, it was the least expected that did me in with the bosses sitting comfortably at home having a cup of tea watching me do it, too.

Modern technology has come a long way since. Over and out.

* * * * * * * * * *

* The "ATOM" was an ingenious invention by SIS' UK-based technologists at its Operational Research Department that had no actual label name but clandestine operatives like me temporarily coined it "A Thinking Operational Mine". While on reconnaissance on this op I was simultaneously placing several "ATOM"'s in strategic locations. An "ATOM" was a camouflage-coloured multi-purpose unit the size and shape of an average toiletry bag and was much lighter than a normal cake (slang for mine). Inside each was a powerful amplifier, which could transmit to and from on automatic pilot from a portable radio station that was already positioned covertly in the mountains. Subsequently psychological broadcast of propaganda alternated in the main Persian languages of Farsi and Dari that could be heard by the Iranians. The sophisticated little box also had an in-built two-way fibre optics frequency-hopping transmitter that

communications could be briefly burst undetected along a chain of other "ATOM"'s. If one link in the chain was lost it could still hop to the next though clarity was reduced. At a signal and/or if handled incorrectly by non-authorised personnel its booby-trap would detonate but not like an ordinary exploding mine. It contained a small wheel in its head that operated like a revolving mini-machine gun, of which its ammunition contained a phosphorous charge that once one of its 36 bullets lodged in any ground vehicle, it would act like an incendiary device and blow itself up at a later time causing death in some cases. Later models that were introduced had noise sensors as well as listening posts inside them. These little all-purpose devices were only in the developmental stage and were never fully integrated into the mainstream, apparently, due to government funding delays.

* * * * * * * * *

The Iran-Iraq War (also known as the First Persian Gulf War) began on 22 September 1980 when the world's sixth largest air force, Iraq's French-built Mirage fighter-bombers, hit 10 Iranian air stations. Iran subsequently undertook a counter-offensive. The closest Iranian town along the Shatt el-Arab waterway was Khorramshahr, was called the "City of Blood" because up to that time with only a month passing since the war started 7,000 Iranians had died. By 1982 Iraq had 1,200 casualties a month. By 1984 Iraq suffered a statistic of 65,000 dead with 60,000 prisoners. Iran, in the same period, reported 180,000 killed with half a million wounded. All because of a long history of border disputes. It ended in August 1988. Where the central line begins and ends mid-water is still not resolved and, likely never will be, even though Iraq means "shore of the great river and the fertile plains surrounding it" while Iran's old Persian etymology doesn't mean anything resembling it!

* * * * * * * * *

Chapter One

Prokofiev blazing in my ears,
in the dark a thousand years ran by.
Even the statues walk, dear Lord.
Claim me for the cause I die for
to end its addiction to insanity.
Amen.

The blizzard's howling winds suddenly died. Everything was deathly silent around me. It was so quiet that I felt as if I had entered into a deaf world. Almost like being sequestered under a heavy blanket of a porcelain colour with flickers of dull light seabirds gliding past beyond. Only the laborious rhythm of breathing around me reminded me that my hearing was still intact, that it was me standing here in the drizzle.

I never heard the pastor's farewell made on behalf of all the mourners. So preoccupied was I. The earth was being shovelled noiselessly into the Cimmerian hole where she lay serenely. "Goodbye my love, have a safe journey yonder," I heard myself whisper, as I dropped my white rose into her final resting place. Then I turned to leave her forever. My footsteps' scrunched gently on the icy powder sprinkled on the path towards my car. The double click of the front doors' closing became gradually amplified like a scratched record. Sitting there I felt like my world was moving in slow motion.

I had said my real goodbyes already, on the days leading up to the funeral. When I'd arrived from South Africa I never expected her to die in my arms amid the frozen sand dunes on the deserted North Sea beach so soon after coming. It was as if she had held on, waiting for me so she could pass away peacefully. "Did you hear the panic in my writing?" she had smiled with her bright eyes when I had bent to kiss her hardening skin. She had looked scared. She didn't want to think about expiring. Vibeke had wanted me to sleep with her that last night at her Mum and Dad's farm house. We never made love – she couldn't. She was so wasted with pain, spending her twilight days in the wheelchair that I hated with a passion. This accumulation of bones wasn't the *bon vivant* girl I'd met almost nine years before.

Her last words to me were, "You must learn to live without the sound of my voice but I'll try to be near you. Don't ever feel alone, Nicholas. I will always love you." Her spirit had glided on sometime during my restless sleep with her body left behind pressed against mine. She was only 30. Her body ravaged with a debilitating disease nobody recognised at the time. It was January 1982 and I was only six months older than her. All my crying had already been done in the cold emptiness of her room when I awoke.

Her family had known I would be leaving early straight after the service. I had been summoned to HQ urgently a few days prior but had ignored the order and delayed my trip out of respect for my beloved. It seemed she decided to end her life on cue, so that I wouldn't have to return there. Not that my employer cared about such trivialities. Dying was an everyday occurrence in our line of work…except this one was all mine; it would wither away slowly inside me, my unheard rotting soul screaming for mercy. She was the only woman I had ever loved, until then.

My ashen world remained pallid around me, my light breath slightly steamy. I sat fixedly for a few minutes more, inside the dim frostiness of "the Firm"'s Audi, then heaved a broken hearted sigh, removing my tartan scarf and black silk tie. The engine rumbled into life, barely audible above the staccato in my head. As I pulled out of the cemetery's gate, I switched on the radio. The bass bars of *"Under Pressure"* by Queen was just bursting into static life and my own internal audio came alive with it then – though the dimness around me remained, strangely, in sepia – and I allowed the music to drown out my adrenaline. What an appropriate title for the record I mused darkly then as I wiped a teardrop, not for the last time today. #
"Pressure pushing down on me"

The soaked Danish motorway zoomed south away from the soggy town of Thisted towards dank Esbjerg, the dull western port of Denmark. I knew this route so well. It was the first time I'd sobbed freely on it though.

Soon the Copenhagen commuter traffic, looking forward to the weekend, joined me streaming in the direction I was heading. # *"It never rains but it pours"*

The ferry owned by DFDS opened its mouth and swallowed my car in it. And the remaining and fading daylight hours from this rough trip became shrouded in the miserable fog of a netherworld. As the shores of Denmark disappeared from view, I whispered then, "Goodbye my darling." I haven't been back since not even to visit the grave.

There was a hell of a lot to think about during 11 hours of solitary confinement on the buffering boat but I tried to block it out. I usually did so for a living. Her death had been a repayment for all the many misdeeds I had undertaken for this miserable lot of an employer. I was sure of it. What went around; came around. I'll explain myself later as best as I can. You'll understand me eventually. I'm a good lad really. I bear remorse most of the time. I owe it to a Danish girl to cure me from my malady once and for all. # *"It's the terror of knowing what this world is about"*

We docked at Harwich on a bleak midday. The weather was grimmer than usual. 'Welcome to England' the huge speckled sign announced unenthusiastically in the dim light. As I headed towards Colchester and then onto London the radio broadcast repeated storm warnings. I drove straight through The City, across the Thames following the signs to Elephant & Castle in the pouring rain, flooded roads and all, in swish-swash silence on the 'wrong' side of the road in my left-hand drive Swiss registered racer. I had been based for the past five years at our secret spy station in Berne.

The robotic-looking plain-clothed night shift parking attendant in SIS' HQ's at Century House had mechanically saluted tired old me. I could see the bulgy outline where his machinated metal was under his raincoat. I think I forced a stiff smile in return, who knows what I did in my anguished state. Then the other fresh-faced night security guard inside the door repeated the same arm-waving ritual following the standard entry procedure. I noticed the new one-inch of shatterproof Plexiglas mounted behind the standard-issue normal glass, making it bullet-and bomb-proof. Looked like this lot expected trouble, most probably from the IRA. # *"People on the edge of the night"*

I wasn't a regular daily worker but a returning non-official cover officer from overseas who was recalled home every now and then for briefings. Most people here had no clue of what I really did, though I noted a certain distant reverence in their cleanly shaved facial responses to me and my unkempt stubble tonight. My six-numbered security card that carried no visual link to SIS, whenever it was inserted in the box, followed by my four-digit PIN code (that made the green light flash) told them something nice about me on their monitors…or it may have read 'don't fuck with him' in easy-to-understand legalese. Certainly at this particular moment I felt like bashing someone's face in and those feelings probably were betrayed by my scowl at the camera.

The entire building was a rumpled bed of activity, even at this late-afternoon hour and a Saturday at that. Obviously something must have happened to warrant this mayhem on this weekend, only I didn't know yet what it was. I would soon find out.

I clipped on my ID badge and stood in the ascending lift feeling absolutely buggered. For some reason my vision returned to 20/20 (6/6 metric) at that very moment while I walked down the endless corridor to the farthest door beckoning. This time my footsteps were audible, a full colour had finally flickered and replaced my blurry vision. I smirked to myself; I was becoming focused in the nick of time.

I remember he hadn't offered any condolences. Why should he? After all he had been a withdrawn widower himself for several years. In any event as a P case officer – for Production, the unit that was responsible for collection of intelligence by operators in the field – at the London Controlling Station, he had no interest in hearing my feeble excuses for abandoning my post in the middle of darkest white Africa to travel to pale dismal northern Denmark, and then arriving a full 72 hours later after they'd tracked me down. I should have left my car there and flown in to save time. I was being irresponsible as usual. I deserved the latest Staff Appraisal Form admonition. He dished out the crap expected from a disgruntled slave to his job who spent his time either mourning his own privately deceased at the Baptist church across the street or inside the Horse & Groom a.k.a. the 'Doom & Gloom' pub further down the road, coined because of the poor glow of its inner recesses; when he claimed to have been at the admin training school opposite Southwark police station.

I didn't attempt to defend myself. My studied silence told him everything he needed to know about what I thought of him. The unseeing blows to his psyche intended to hurt more than any physical words that I could have spat. I'd always preferred the slow neurotic delivery over a quick punch – it would sting more that way at the receiving end.

He had helped me make up my mind therewith that I was going to get out of this nasty business soon; *very soon*, 365 days from now would do fine. I didn't want to mutate into a murkier version of that miserable bastard; a too calm man that projected a stillness of a person who had seen much madness…still in progress as well as being emotionally absent. I just had to give them a reason for letting me go, hopefully without strings being attached around me like a rubber band…snapping me back into their grasps at will. Such was the powerful aim of Britain's Secret Intelligence Service, which monitored the world for gain on behalf of its manipulating masters across the pond and in turn our own meek mandarins, those guardians of UK government standards and intentions (who are senior civil servants thinking they're maintaining the status quo while also ignorantly vetoing elected ministers decisions). From inside the machinery you understood that SIS' intel officers were slowly becoming Washington's tool, the undercover boot boys of corporate America and its global tentacles, in return for our country getting a piece of the pie. In this quiet army I was nothing more than an expendable longbow soldier at the far unseen front line, the first ordered to spit the arrows and then left to dodge the return strafe alone. They didn't teach us how to deal with that ducking-the-blows part either as it was active duty on-the-job training. The pay was good but it wasn't worth dying for. I found knowing the cause and effect of the end result objectionable: Money over morality was the bottom line.

When the man in grey had finished talking, it was hard to know what was so incredible – what he said, or what his words meant in the implied sense. It was a harvest of white-knuckled war-producing words. Even his own lengthy pauses assaulted my senses with their penetrating silence. A veteran of psychological manoeuvring he was playing my game back on me. *When he sometimes repeated my words it didn't come as a question mark but more as a final full-stop; end of the subject statement.* As an experienced SIS "deep cover in the black" officer I was supposed to have got used to it…but I never did. Even though I was a team member of the first eleven that is those designated "ticking bomb" assignments, which meant dealing on-site with those cases deemed "extremely urgent to be solved before they blew up" – one before "smoking gun" meaning the bullets had already been fired. What it also loudly translated into was the hierarchy admitting that there was something indefinably wrong at the outset, which would require a dependable disruptive action soldier like me on the spot to correct the problem – whatever it may entail – and to undertake the op as fast as humanly possible, preferably without the loss of my life. That didn't include everybody else's lives, mind you. It just went to prove my bow and arrow theory once again plus using one's own noddle and wits to get away.

I recall next that I had signed for and then left his office with the usual file of papery elocution to digest. This one's heading was UNIFIL (United Nations Interim Force in Lebanon) 1982 Deployment of Republic of Ireland Contingent. So I was going to get a real green Eireann passport that was knowingly issued by the Irish government in order to serve in a "false flag op" (covert mission conducted by a government to deceive and appear as if it was carried out by another entity). I headed to the reading room in the library that was gratefully empty at this time to debate the operational assessment in the drama of my mind. The assignment, as expected, was classified starkly there boldly stamped in red as "BEYOND CRITICAL" and I was going to be in the theatre of Beirut in a few days time.

I flipped off my still damp shoes and socks and put them on the seat of the chair opposite the heater. The wall clock gravely told me it was still less than 24 hours ago that Vibeke had been buried, though the day's full cycle was going to be completed in just a few minutes time. The time's curtain was about to finally close and mark a sad time that would be etched forever in the trenches of my fertile brain.

Try as I might, I couldn't concentrate on the files. I could hear her voice whispering as I tried reading the silent diction. It was as if she had relocated into the living quarters of my mind, permanently, a ghost-like figurine flitting around inside there, talking to my inner ear. I had even glanced over at the next chair but there was nothing there. As the clock chimed at five, I had thought grimly to myself, 'I'm all alone within these four walls with someone in my head.' "Goodbye my darling, I loved you dearly." I had murmured again. The deeply enjoyable chapter entitled "Vibeke Brink" in the book of my life had finally closed. # *"And love dares you to change our way...this is our last dance..."*

* * * * * * * * *

I was able to visualise myself as if from afar. I'd known from my SIS training that after the loss of a beloved one I would go through the conventional five stages of the grieving process: *Denial* (Would I have trouble accepting the fact? – I didn't think so): *Anger* (Would I blame somebody? – I blamed myself already): *Bargaining* (Fix things around me? – I knew I had to get myself out of this lousy employment. I had decided that exactly one year plus one day from now it would be more or less over): *Depression* (Wasn't I already desensitised from being on this job too long? – I conceded, maybe it was burnout): and *Acceptance* (We'd see on that fifth one.

– I was only human but I was to find out later that the girl curiously didn't permit me to easily accept her untimely departure).

I put the documents down to think. It was down that same hallway but painted in a different colour that I'd walked in a decade ago when I'd returned from attending my first Laban Notation special seminar not that far away in New Cross, East London. Apparently the concept was developed before the last World War by a Czechoslovak ballet choreographer called Rudolph Van Laban, who had died in England in 1958. Some bright spark in clandestine operations had seen the similarity between classical ballet and our kind of subversive manoeuvring minus the music. The next thing we know is that a bunch of us likely lads were studying it in the classrooms with one of Van Laban's British disciples, either Ms Ullman or Ms North…in simple terms the theory stated that when the mind is occupied with undertaking a new task then the body subconsciously copies it – i.e.: linking mental and movement to each other.

I have to admit it was damn interesting though. The behavioural connection was then thoroughly studied – yourself looking at yourself as a stranger on 8-mm film – when a posture or a gesture combines in an integrated physical action. By scrutinising oneself like that, we would then be worked hard by the two senior acting coaches to adopt stances which were the *opposite* of all described. That way we couldn't be easily "read" by others, as in not noticed by those enemy observers wishing to seek us out.

The end result was precisely that: Blokes getting around without being seen, usually in countries that didn't want our presence among them – almost illusionary, performing essentially a high-octane method while using low-key technique. In a sentence you moved with deliberation in a fast-moving environment. *The quicker the action speeded up; the slower the frame went by in my mind's eye.* A chameleon-like Pyrrhic victory at SIS' famed "London School of Metamorphoses", as it was then dubbed by us newer recruits.

Next was being told to read a book with an ancient dog-eared brown-paper cover that had been first published in-between the World Wars, *How to Analyse People on Sight Through the Science of Human Analysis: The Five Human Types* by an American man and wife named Benedict, complete with diagrams. What you really learnt from it was about *yourself.*

Then I'd been among a select few that had not completed university that were seconded (a government term meaning transferred) on to a form of philosophical studies for the Firm at a university abroad, while still on the job. Specifically, the art of dialectical thought – the process of reasoning correctly – the establishment of a theoretical model of thinking, which had not yet been put into practice. SIS even selected my doctorate's thesis: *"Communist States and Social Revolutions: A Comparative Analysis and their Critical Theory."* So very smart of them, you know, looking back. My years burrowed into the books of Pierre Bourdieu, Clifford Gertz and others, memorising their *"Outline of a Theory of Practice"*, *"The Interpretation of Cultures"* and *"SPSS: Statistical Package for the Social Sciences"*, could only benefit them in the strategy of *where* to stab the sharp western dagger into the hearts of the Soviet Union and its satellites and choose *when to do so.*

My musing into the past drifted down the hallway back into today's empty room at SIS headquarters, where I still sat thankfully alone. All that wondrous training years ago combined with my natural athletic ability made me what I was now. I was born in the Chinese year of the hare during the rotation of the bull, blessing me with the ability to bulldoze through the bullshit swiftly. I had considered I was going to be 32 on my next birthday. By January 1983, as I'd already promised myself, it would all be a memory. I'd start a new life, somewhere, somehow. My deceased dearest would probably endorse a new woman in my soul by then, if I was lucky enough to find somebody who wanted me someplace. I would have wished the same destiny on her too, had I been the one who died.

Buoyed then somewhat by the start of a new day, in my mind, I had glanced around the gloominess of the room – the light bulbs seemed to flicker livelier already – and had taken a few bare-foot steps across to the double-glazed triple-reinforced shatter-proof windows, built to withstand a blast. This area of town was within the radius of the Irish Republican Army's favourite firing range after all, the financial district. I can still vividly remember that inspiring few seconds then, of realisation – as I was always aware of telepathy and mental connections – as the few London black cabs were weaving their way down there in a curious slow moving left-turning formation around a junction and they had held my attention momentarily that I could make out a clear positive tick of a confirming visual "yes" message in their pattern, confirming agreement of my own future target: *Go, do it!* There are times a bit of ju-ju helps the inner self. Even the traffic lights were green. The pavements had a double shine to them from reflections of the wet lampposts bouncing off the floor up into my eyes like blurred mini-spotlights in front of the stage. I blinked back at the beams that were seemingly fixed instantly on me, and then looked away. *After only one day gone, I had surprised myself on how already I had accepted her early death as a warning sign to stop going headlong into my own premature demise.* I nodded then in understanding and heeded the karmic transference of acquiescence.

My decision came on that lonely day, all those years ago in London and minutes following the closure of my 24 hours of private mourning. It was after my fiancée's funeral that I had first considered on putting my hard-gained expertise for the benefit humanitarian and other worthy causes dear to me…instead of just continuing keeping the controlling powers in the position they were and had been for staid centuries. It had been as good a time to evaluate my life. If I didn't make plans to escape SIS then, was I going at this rate to see the score years from then?

Subconsciously, looking back, I was trying to comprehend where I was coming from before understanding also where I was heading to. It was the beginning of the end of the circle for me on this path at that time. But every end must have a beginning. Well I'm happy to report that I did abort myself and lived to tell the tale, and I'm going to tell you all about it hereinafter in chronological order to the end of this book.

* * * * * * * * *

F. Scott Fitzgerald was on record as saying, "The test of a first-rate intelligence officer is the ability to hold two opposed ideas in mind at the same time and still retain the ability to function."

Looking back, at the onset of my career at SIS, what I was earmarked for involved a lot of things I am not allowed to make public, so I won't. *But what I can divulge, I will.*

What SIS sought to fast-forward in a prospective covert action operator is a person that ticks all of the select boxes of the following (in no particular order), and more: Macro thinker (as opposed to micro). Innovative. Loyal. Professional. Leader. Positive. Empowered. Elite. Ingenious. Juxtapositional. Multi-cultured. Pioneering. Crosses borders. Out of the box. Original. No copycats. Dependable under pressure. Recognises that *if you dance with the devil you may have to factor the fiddler.*

A man or woman that had a personality who didn't get too high about the highs or too low about the lows, and tried to stay on an even keel, who reasons logically that there are many versions of the truth – all of them elastic.

I had foresight, always did and will have – with some other gifts from the heavens that I later took advantage of – but it's born from understanding anticipation in all its forms, low, high, left, right, inside and outside, even under the ground and over the clouds.

Comprehending the default reflex of various societies was paramount;

what the hot button was in terms of reaction and response to a good or bad issue to one culture was seen entirely differently in another. So getting a handle on the pulse of a situation was the key to destiny. A lot depended on one man's take on it…and to then relate it either verbally or in writing.

I appreciated full well, too, that I analysed mostly in a straight line while many others thought in circles, some in squares, a few even are blank and occasionally going backwards – to avoid altogether those that were a waste of space and all take. To beware those that do so in dots and worse the dashes as they didn't know where they were going to or coming from. You had to give to get but the get didn't always come immediately. To focus intently on what was happening down the lens of the binoculars but to also look away peripherally and perpendicularly, even the posterior, to observe in every conceivable direction from where you are while simultaneously imagining how others are looking at you, too…in the event you need to make an escape. *You don't make mistakes when you pay for it with your life.*

A large majority of questions asked by people are, in fact, disguised as statements of their own opinions. It is often a straight projection of their own thinking that they are trying to impose on you. You at once recognise the transference though they may not know it themselves. It usually comes about when they say something in the third person about a subject but relating it to yourself. The SIS calls it psychogramming, part-psychology and part-programming. We do it, too, only we know full well we are doing it. It's a conversation starter towards information gathering.

Most people are mirrors reflecting who they really are. Winners have winners' lobes and losers have losers' lobes – it's a gut feeling you get quite quickly from talking to them. Bull-shitters don't have ears, only mouths. Those are the kinds that don't allow you to finish the sentences you are speaking because they are not interested in what you have to say…only want to listen to themselves. We used to call them talking heads, slang.

Then there's also what I labelled EES, it stands for empty eye sockets, which are those individuals with no eye contact, ignoring everybody, showing no acknowledgement of your presence, perhaps holier than thou, maybe introverted, and they don't know you one time to the next requiring a reintroduction, that is if you can be bothered to. It could mean empty space syndrome as well. It's my own little joke to myself. See 'em a lot at functions.

Tactical behaviour assessment is also required: Verbal and body clues with unnecessary qualifying statements such as "indeed", "honestly", "frankly", "oh really" plus other obvious words specifically chosen in an attempt of dominance and superiority over you. Then there are the unspoken clues and the body language like overly fidgeting, hands on hip straddle stance, power grip handshake, air hand gesticulations, befuddled scratch of neck, lower lip corner crease and avoidance of eye contact. My favourite clue is the glance to the floor or the invisible object to the side just before the lie is delivered with absolute conviction.

You process what you see with your eye to make an informal judgement. There is some information gleaned from hearing and even less from a feeling. Thus the overwhelming amount is gained visually from observation and you must have the ability to process it by communicating it verbally most of the time. In some cases, you must also be able to present the facts and presumptions in a written report to allow readers to equally comprehend the situation even though they weren't present there like you were. *I was rebuked once by a superior officer for furnishing too much information when he said that he didn't wish to know what colour eyes the guy had.*

A lot of people subconsciously work on the theory that a problem can have only one of two correct answers or a combination thereof, even if it can in reality have multiple answers. There is no simple explanation. I expected the abnormal as normal. The cream eventually floats to the surface. It's a learning curve, like a squeezed in the middle letter H (that has no discernible camber):

It would arrive at me.
Never the What.
Not Who.
The Why.
BINGO!
Initiation.
Then intuition.
Delivering instinct.
Bringing me to the door.

There are spoken words to use and not use to avoid conflict and to keep the door open for gleaning information:

"But" – (replace with) "and at the same time".

"No" should always be avoided – substitute with a valid reason why it ought to be something else more preferable than the supreme negative of shutting the door in one's face (which is the physical version of same).

"Never" is in same category as "no" obviously – prefer to use "it may be possible" to keep the door open…but don't use "let me think about it" or "get back to me" or "I'll call you" as those statements are grey area side-trackers (the physical version of looking at the floor before you tell a lie).

"Should" – "what I prefer is…"

"You" – (reverse it and put the onus on yourself) "I".

"Problem" (yikes, it's a red flag word!) – choose "a challenge is welcomed, I will try my best".

In non-Arab countries and the western world, the beard is stigmatised as a sign of introversion, being non-social, a failure and laziness. Not always true, mind you because Muslim cultures regard a shaved face as un-Islamic – the reverse.

Many foreigners upon hearing someone speaking in English automatically assume that the person is from the world where Freedom exists. In many underdeveloped societies what sounds right *is right* and it is that which guides their thinking. They are the ones that are manipulated the most by their governments. (Older societies have evolved over centuries to recognise this.)

In tradecraft the more experienced operators from the other side know that when you place them under surveillance, the movement of your eye will also slightly shift your body in the same direction. So when not looking at them on purpose try not to let your body language give the game away.

When on surveillance in pairs if you observe the person going left, remember to turn right. And vice versa. Let your colleague following behind go in their direction and you take their place by backtracking around. Use doors and reflections, cross streets. I did the unusual by managing to do so from in front of them where I'm sure they never foresaw that. It took a while to get it down pat I admit.

The experts that tail you in foreign countries will know you're a spy if you use professional methods to shake them off…*when you knew* you were being tailed to not shake them off. SIS preferred you to abort till another day.

A sacred tenet of the intelligence game: *Don't become intimate with your source.*

We were taught to apply Newton's third law of motion in our job: For every action there may be an equal and opposite reaction by the other side.

No answer was also an answer.

The rule of thumb is: If I am selling I speak your language but if I am buying you speak mine.

People in positions of power think by saying it, it then becomes true.

All government agencies and departments switch sources of information to maximise the possibility of reaching the results they have pre-set before seeking the data to fit them. Most intelligence worldwide is purposefully politicised and a creature of partisanship, beholden to its governments' wishes. (Further down the totem pole maturing civilisations have received wisdom to suspect this but can't prove the shenanigans because it's not documented, therefore legalities can be deliberately circumvented.)

In the business of espionage, the higher the priority the lesser the number of people that know about it as it is an extremely compartmented world.

At training school, the class instructor once memorably stated, "When certain elements instantaneously and simultaneously deny a statement, there is a greater chance of it actually being true."

Some internal documents had a disclaimer that would make me smile: "The authenticity of this content cannot be verified, therefore it cannot be trusted." *This warning coming from our own side!*

Intelligence from the streets is like playing dominoes, a cascade of meaningless statements ensure that you have to sieve the information to mine anything useful. A lot of cultures' mentality is: What I do for you is for me; and what you do for me is for us. Anecdotal evidence, conclusions deduced from generalisations, is rife and wrong. Propaganda needs filtering constantly.

The eight-week paramilitary training course for new intel officers designated for covert action included: map reading, compass navigation, weapons practice, clandestine movement, sketching, miniature photography, electronic communications, extreme environment survival, and more.

And then you are sent out to survive your hostile environment, act like you belong where you are and not be detected, and to snoop.

The intel officer's principal role as an NOC abroad is to be a one-man spy station. He or she reads the "local tea leaves", measures the ripples while treading water with the enemy, foresees trends, events, feelings and to detect plausible associations, which means perception and deception management. Often I found I was focused on the day that comes after or the horizon ahead. I also discovered this about myself: While I appear stoic

I know myself to be Panglossian; but I know nothing is what it seems on the face of it.

In conclusion, if you are sceptical that your government has the capacity to lie to you then you are naïve because intelligence is really, at the end of the day, informed conjecture.

* * * * * * * * *

Chapter Two

Often the test of courage is not to die but to live.

After passing out from Dartmouth's Royal Britannic naval college and stringent training as a junior flight officer in RNAS Yeovilton (a Royal Navy Air Station located in Somerset in the southwest corner of England), I gained my first operational experience flying for 18 months on routine domestic 'copter sorties. For the most part these were sea search and rescue (SAR) operations originating from RNAS Lossiemouth in Scotland to patrol the British Isles' northern shipping lanes and locate ships or yachts in distress plus in extreme cases extract mariners from shipwrecks. All seagoing crafts, when moving at right angles to the wind, will experience a drift leeway that will pull them a little downwind off their intended course. These vessels often get into trouble when the pull of the tide combines with the crosswinds to ground the trawlers or worse, high waves tip hulls. This is the water version of when a small aircraft like my bright red Westland Wessex gets the same sudden cross-winds that can send boats down below to the unkind jagged rocks waiting to scuttle them. I'd smile warily to myself thinking I was going through both problems at the same time, up here watching them down there below – and having to factor each nasty sucking element into my aerial manoeuvres.

At least twice a month in winter, we'd winch aboard mariners and salvage select loads from marooned cargo ships and from smaller boats smashed against the country's life-threatening rocky shores as a result of insanely high seas. The more dangerous currents occur in the area where the Atlantic Ocean, the Norwegian Sea and the North Sea all meet. The sparse outposts of the Scottish islands of Orkney and Shetland were notorious for attracting those destined to drown. A mile-long tanker in yaw movement – when hampered by low ceiling and day-long periods of zero visibility – becomes a quivering dot which disappears behind a ten-story wall of seething water on the breakneck move, in the second it takes to blink. The regular exposure to these air patrols gave me the invaluable presence of mind to consider all the possibilities. No matter what the speck was you thought you saw, you guide the whining and intransigent chopper to it. Even peering directly down you could miss what you were searching for in the howling and vicious wind, dense fog and heavy rain. Radar told you it was there but you couldn't see it. I was often amazed to miss something so big so easily. As we returned to base, I'd wonder how an angry Mother Nature could certainly play nasty tricks on your mind when she wanted to.

My next deployment was to participate in a short but unusual training programme to prepare us for another mission. Over land above the inhospitable landscape of Dartmoor back in Devon, we all took turns in a one-of-kind revamped whirlybird – to practise steep spiral descents, rapid climb-outs and various evasive action (EA) procedures.

This is the time when we were given our first designated "special operations" Royal Navy Fleet Air Arm overseas posting "to the Far East (location unspecified)". The minimum one month-long assignment was deemed as *fairly* routine with "moderate risk" and was to last until the mission was successfully completed. I took notice of the word "fairly" that preceded the "routine" term in the telegram. All the lads selected for the mission were excited at the prospects of some overseas duties. For some, it was the first time abroad even though we didn't know yet where we were going to.

But it did not take long for us to find out our destination. Our British aircraft carrier would be cruising the Andaman Sea, due south of the Burmese capital of Rangoon, in the Gulf of Martaban. Inside the cavernous hull there were far less aircraft (AC) on board and more choppers than normal. We were assigned to two formations of five specially equipped Sikorsky's, otherwise known as HLH (Heavy Lift Helicopters). These choppers had no markings on them – the fact that we were told it contravened Geneva Conventions went over our inexperienced heads at the time – and had a 340-nautical mile range. We were randomly assigned by draw to all-day sorties to either the "north" or the "east" areas of operations. What that meant was you got either the Burma-Laos-Thailand trip or the Cambodia-Laos-Vietnam one, which we duly coined them as the BLT or the CLV team.

The BLT route consisted of a 400-mile one-way journey in "critically deficient airspace" – meaning no air traffic control. The CLV route was 500 miles long that required a 15-minute refuelling stop on friendly ground in both directions. All transport had been fitted with XL drop tanks to store extra fuel. We intended to file our flight plans only up to where the friendly borders ended. Aerial refuelling was a "no-no". While over enemy territory we would spend between two and three hours to carry out our clandestine mission and then head back to ship.

The times were the early-70's and I was in my early-20's. I was already a mean old hand at tricky helicopter manoeuvres but on this trip I would swap the Scottish no-man's land grey, watery, cold, moving mountains for lush green carpeted jungles on steep ravines in the shimmering heat of southeast Asia.

To get a better understanding of the geopolitical reality of the region one has to remember that the underdeveloped colonies were, in general, politically aligned with one of their old colonial patrons. Burma and Malaysia were British; the Americans supported Thailand; while Cambodia, Laos and Vietnam were formerly Indo-China and still under the influence of the French. Meanwhile the northern peripheries were completely controlled by Red China. In a sense it was an intense kinetic kaleidoscope, which had and was to dominate international news for years to come. *The white, black and brown man's spirited defence of the yellow man.* Also in the region at that time the Soviets had their navy base in North Vietnam at Cam Ranh while American war ships were docked at Subic Bay in the Philippines. The US-Vietnam War was, at the time, in full demonic flow in "Big Muddy" (as Vietnam was known to some) and so was the tide of the Cold War overlapping. It was battle zones everywhere in that area of the world. In short: *A total bloody mess.*

As we sailed around the Horn of India from the junction of the Gulf of Oman and the Arabian Sea (the point where we had joined the ship), we practised daily on the way east. In accordance with our five-day brief we were tasked to seek and destroy the poppy crop with a newly developed mycoherbicide (fungus derived herbicide called *oxysporum Fusarium*) by spraying the agent on the opium fields. The specially designed helicopters had a 12,500-pound payload and its interior fitted with large alloy tanks containing liquid chemicals with sprinklers to deliver the herbicides to the targeted fields. It was to be a hit-and-run low-intensity operation, to get in, do the job, get out, and move on to the next designated spot, so on and so forth. The visual pesticide drop area was 30-by-30 nautical miles, even though it was to be over land, and it was changed on a daily basis in order to reduce any detection by the enemy.

I was assigned to the "north" team while Dave Brennan was attached to the "east". Young two-stripe lieutenants we were, and we were to age quickly. Though I'd been friendly with him at the naval academy, it was on this secret operation that I really got to know him well. After the pre-dinner daily football match in the hangar with two upright ground pulley devices serving as temporary goalposts, we spent our evenings comparing notes taken at the briefing rooms in our bunks in the cramped carrier's lower deck.

The dangers were duly observed. There were the 10,000-strong Mong Tai guerrilla forces, also known as Shan soldiers, under the opium warlord Khun Sa. Real name: Chiang Chifu. Then age: 43. A series of photographs were provided. It seemed he liked dressing in military fatigues. There were other photos of drug traffickers, mainly of one named Lo Hsing Han. (In typical ironic British humour a wit once remarked from the back of the briefing room, "That it was highly unlikely we'd see these blokes from up in the air, sir!" So true!) Area of operation: The Shan state of eastern *Myanmar*, the local name for Burma; the far northern section of *Muang Thai*, otherwise known as Thailand; and the extreme western part of Laos – the isolated mountainous jungle area popularly known as the Golden Triangle. The village of Hmong where Kuhn Sa may have been headquartered was a specific area to avoid due to suspected concentration of armaments. I recall still, that the information was provided to the British Royal Navy by a character from the Burmese intelligence that went by the name of Kyaw Thein and cleared by General Ne Win himself, the then ruler of Burma. Other documents bore the cleared stamp of a US government unit based in Bangkok, Thailand, called BNDD (Bureau of Narcotics and Dangerous Drugs).

Brennan's report also focused on Pol Pot, the leader of Cambodia who was in effect the warlord of a nation known to the locals as *Kampuchea*. Real name: Saloth Sar. Then age: 45. He headed an outfit called *Kateak* or *Khmer Rouge*. His brother was his right-hand man and was named: Saloth Nget. Another man was identified as: Khieu Samphan. Their centre of operations was in Anlong Veng, Northern Cambodia – another place to avoid due to heavy concentration of weapons. Photographs of all the named individuals

were also attached, including one rather poignant stiff presentation of Pol
Pot with his wife Son Sen as they stood to attention beside each other; arms
non-lovingly untouchably straight down in what some jokers coined "a
Soviet-style portrait". The regime's killing fields were already in full swing as
accounts circulated of shooting of innocent civilians for just wearing glasses
or simply for appearing as lazy. "I would imagine, they had to keep the
maggots well fed," said Brennan deftly, in a moment of mock mordancy. I
got used to his deadpan Irish farcical fare from then on – it sometimes left
me gawking at him.

The contrasts between Khun Sa and Pol Pot were stark but also
illusory.

The former described himself as a capitalist while the latter thought of
himself as an avowed communist. Brennan and I would have rather chosen
words such as "drug greedy fucking fascist" and a "shithead Maoist mass
murderer", but opinions such as ours lacked political correctness and
therefore were not encouraged in the theatre of operations. As events
unfolded, one was to become the world's largest producer of heroin and the
other was to be the world's most ruthless exterminator of his own
countrymen, killing as many as 2 million of his people or 20% of them.

The main thread running through all of this was that Laos became the
centrepiece in both configurations of the BLT and CLV acronyms. It was in
reality one of the world's poorest countries and it had to make money any
which way it could. As a result, it had massive poppy fields at both ends of
its nation, aided and abetted by their wonderful nice neighbours who
needed nice easy incomes from it – claimed to be from rice – while they ran
their respective destructive campaigns. Khun Sa and Pol Pot – the terrible
twins were factually: The scourge of Laos.

The US had officially ended their air war in Laos the year before we
had arrived. The north of Laos' topography consists of mountain forests
that sloped down gradually eastwards to the dry plains around North
Vietnam's Hanoi. The southern part of Laos is essentially pure jungle and
where the old Ho Chi Minh trail was, which the Vietcong strategic supply
route that ran along the border of Laos-South Vietnam towards Saigon
(now renamed Ho Chi Minh City) was. Ignominiously the Laotians were
known to be the "most bombed population in history". The country was
littered with landmines and was nicknamed "Me Laos" by us, making it
sound more like "My Lice" as we scratched our bodies in jest. Technically
Laos was a neutral country during the US-Vietnam War, serving as a buffer
between North Vietnam, which was supported by the communists, and the

capitalists-backed Thailand. The US government saw Laos as part of the "domino" theory and feared that the Pathet Lao rebels would eventually take over the country, as they actually did. They eventually seized power with the help of the victorious communist Vietnamese who became emboldened after the American pull-out from Vietnam.

Every time we began preparation to fly into the war zone, there was an unspoken sense of it being the last trip and a degree of fatalistic premonition came and went. Not a comfortable feeling, as I felt I had most of my life still to live, and that I would have missed life had I died…

I used to marvel at one particular *chedi* every time we roared over it – a Buddhist tower shaped like a bell. Every time I went past it, the dome had changed its colour from my angle on a different new day. It was situated just east of the Burmese town of Hawng Tuk, the last outpost before entering Laotian air space on a low altitude incursion. A request for permission to enter Laos airspace was never sought as it would have never been granted anyway. This was now our fifth illegal entry with the previous incursions having ended "routinely" and without incidents. Whenever we crossed the invisible to-the-eye demarcation line, radio silence was strictly observed with radio contact to be initiated only in the event of an emergency. Since all operations were planned for daytime hours, infrared, radar, sophisticated sensors and night vision goggles had been removed from the aircrafts' fuselage ostensibly to economise on space and weight.

It was standard procedure that after relaying our new radio frequency, the 10-minute regulation count down was timed at 60-second intervals. The last full minute always did seem twice as long, at least to me. During that final minute, the commanding officer's voice would communicate calmly in his Yorkshire accent, "Fifteen seconds to 'hot zone.' Good luck everybody. See you at fourteen hundred hours at designated locale. Cut out starting…now." Then it would be a "deafening silence" for hours down in the weeds, just your own silent voice talking to yourself, devoid of intercom chatter, and the clatter of the machine.

Up to that time all chemical spraying of the poppies had gone according to plan and with very little sighting of the natives. In fact, the forays were routine and plain boring. Just like my sorties in Scotland, no matter what I thought I saw, I would divert from my ops and go and check it out. It took a while for me to get used to having to look at the ceiling as well instead of just at the floor, as the enemy could sneak up on you the way a bird snags a dragonfly. On my second ever reconnaissance I did see a single wild elephant and found reason to investigate it, even on the rather lame pretext of discovering nature. To hell with the fuel-saving directive! Well the elephant turned out to be a malevolent looking old male, doubtless banned from the rest of the family. He saluted me rudely a few times straight up with his trunk. That late afternoon, when I finally made eye contact with the other birds over the Laos-Burma divide and with commo re-established, I brought attention to an unexplained streak of light in the sky several miles away. The flight commander radioed in response that it most probably was part of a meteor shower.

On this current trip into Laos, the boredom set in early, probably as I was navigating over flat terrain for the first time. The flight pattern was a simple straight up, turn, and head back parallel following the same route. It felt much like lawn mowing on a grander scale.

Right at the designated rendezvous time, three hours later, I joined the four other birds to return "home" along the same route we came. The re-entry point was set at just north of Ban Houayxay, Laos. We hadn't crossed the border yet and radio contact hadn't been established, but I could see the marker of the Buddhist tower looming towards us on the horizon. Once again, with my natural far-sightedness, I spotted something high in the distance, but held off for the estimated few more seconds waiting for the connect command to come in. The object looked like a telegraph pole and was certainly moving faster than the meteor shower that I had observed before. It was like a perfect straight chalk mark drawn on the blue blackboard of the sky. Had there been glare, I don't think I would have seen it. Based on a training film I'd seen, I guessed it *had* to be a heat-seeking air-to-air missile (AAM) locked on us and fired from a fighter jet miles away!

I could not wait any longer so I quickly plugged my radio and spoke: "Butterfly oh-three to Chrysalis, captain, two o' clock high, unknown object coming in fast, I think we are painted sir." The CO crackled on immediately with an urgent tone, reminding us of training procedures to deal with in such an eventuality. We immediately initiated our newly-learned EA tactics as our heightened situational awareness kicked in. There was no time to get scared. The CO issued us clear instructions in a calmly steady but authoritative voice. He could have been reading a bedtime story to his children for all I knew.

Today pilots call it 'viffing', a swivel effect manoeuvre, a slang word for thrust Vector In Forward Flight, but back then there wasn't a non-swearing word for it. The trick was to shrink our collective size as a target or in our jargon: Go from five wide bulky to one speckle thin (from the missile's perspective). The manoeuvre was accomplished by rapidly forming a queue behind each other and proceeding on an exact pre-designated wavy flight path, like a snake if you will, and flying head on towards the oncoming object then performing a "corkscrew up and away" exercise upon the command. I was internally cursing then at the sorely missed high-intensity flares, which would have been ejected to divert the AAM's "eye" that was zeroing in on our aggregated mass of hot turbine engines. Unfortunately, the tools for distraction had been dispensed with to save space. *They would have surely helped us now.*

The deliberate elusive weaving started and I followed in unison from my third and middle position in the pack. I was straining at my tachometer, doing my own concentrated countdown as we proceeded into another twist. This was the final sway coming up. Moment of impact or not. 'Good-bye cruel world. Steady Anderson, steady boy,' I found I was lip-synching to myself. We performed the perfect coil, sharply climbing up and around to the assured safety altitude of 10,000 feet like a cobra on the flat blue canvas. A trickle of sweat ran across my Adam's apple. Had we still carried our chemical load, due to the imbalance shifting against gravity, it would have been an altogether impossible move.

The CO slightly nervous stutter came on, "See it there, at six behind us, see it go. Looks like it may have been a Chinese-made M-9 AAM. Well done everybody. Good team work! Maintain flight path until further command. Thank you for your resiliency." That bloke was so cool.

Then there was a click, and then another clack, "Thank you too, good work Lieutenant Anderson."

I found time to peer back and could see the temple behind us going away in the slipstream. The bubble beyond it burst into tiny wet splashes like fireworks in the now light green sky, as the hunter rocket smashed into a mountain peak. The CO had cleverly misled the missile to hit something before it could turn around and scream back towards us. Privately I was so proud of myself. Until that moment I'd never felt such a tremendous rush of excitement. I found myself breathless, clenching my fist in swift punches while the body took its time to unfreeze from its tautness of stress and the numbing terror. The feeling was better than scoring a goal in the last minute of a cup final, by far. Up to then, it was the highest "high" of my life.

By succeeding – I felt like I'd gone where the dinosaurs died, out into the wild, falling off the edge of the world, and clawing back over the side by the torn nails of my bleeding fingers. When you play games with your life you have no choice but to win; victory is the only option.

Back at base on Her Majesty's Ship I took a great deal of good-natured ribbing from everybody. Even the "removed concept" (Brennan's droll description) of the normally unseen captain of the carrier climbed down from his conning tower and shook my hand in the officer's mess. That was a novelty that got even more nice fun poked at me after he left.

But the celebration would not last long. Three weeks later, as we approached the end of our tour in Asia, we took the same flight pattern as we did on the day we escaped that missile. Only this time I was assigned the hilly section along the *Menam Khong*, the Mekong River, where the terrain went from 1,500 feet to flat within seconds. On that level there, there were plenty of rice paddies to keep the nation well fed indeed, if only the stuff could be distributed to the starving people. There was plenty of time to philosophise on world affairs.

The CO suddenly broke air contact with a short burst of command and then returned to uncomfortable silence. I stared at the intercom. It was the first time ever he had undertaken a break of the "no chat" link behind enemy lines. He had read me my helicopter's coded call letters of the day. What he just did was authorise me to proceed to an issued SOS (save our souls) at a specific grid and to LZ, set down in the landing zone, as I saw fit, and pick-up a platoon of friendly soldiers. At an altitude of two hundred feet flying just above the trees at hundred and twenty knots ground speed I again broke into a cold sweat at the prospects of what he had just dictated. I shuddered in disbelief.

Actually I didn't have to wait long for further commo to be established. A flare almost hit my belly as I winded around a bend in the river. I circled back around, coming in slower and lower, almost touching the clumps of green tops. Sure enough there was a single non-helmeted camouflaged individual standing at the edge of the river banks, waving frantically with his two arms to the opening behind him, as he ran backwards hand-signalling me to follow him.

The situation seemed acutely abnormal triggering in me a clear red hot alert status. I was beginning to get nervous and felt a need to scan the surroundings, so I lifted her and went around again for a quick recce (reconnaissance) but saw nothing of note, then came back down right over dead centre of the clearing. The trees were bending furiously from the force of my Sikorsky's rotors wind-blasting within fifteen-feet of the nearest palm, a tight fit. I set down perfectly with a gentle bump.

To my great surprise, around two-dozen white, black and brown-faced American-clad troops were scrambling across the tall grass towards me.

Certainly I could carry them all out but I first had to go back up to dump my remaining load of chemicals.

Leaving the engines on, I unbuckled myself and ran down the helicopter's body to the ramp's door. I was screaming at them to go back. But they couldn't hear me. It was against unmanned pilot regulations to do so but I dropped down to the soft grass to explain my predicament. The first soldier was a young white man in mud camouflage and wearing a helmet. I was yelling in his ear and he understood my instructions immediately. He turned to his comrades who were advancing towards the helicopter and relayed my plans. They started running back to their positions and I returned to my bird. My heart was pumping louder than the racket of the helicopter and I made the open doorway in one leap.

Seconds later I was aloft again and starting the standard emergency jettisoning procedures into the water itself, trusting the herbicide would dissolve rapidly in the water. In our numerous pre-flight briefings nobody had previously addressed the issue of *where* to dump more than 12,500 pounds of highly toxic liquids in such a situation, and I suppose nobody cared as we were eventually disposing of them anyway. I had been stationary at this location far longer than the maximum allotted 45 seconds for a helicopter to remain stationary on the ground during war-time manoeuvres. I was attracting attention way too long and in broad daylight. *I felt like a newly hatched brood in a nest with a hungry hawk eyeing me.*

Within seventeen long minutes I was back where I started, cursing quietly.

Exactly twenty-five heavily armed men made that mad dash from the bush towards me like a rugby kick-off scramble at the man with the ball. They were boarding in a cumbersome fashion because the doorframes of this specially adapted Sikorsky were not designed for airlifting troops. The machine had been outfitted to hold chemical tanks as big as possible thus leaving limited area to accommodate two-dozen or so able-bodied men with their clunky equipment to boot. It was taking way too long as the minutes became ten. I was shrieking internally; like my shrilling engine.

Finally, an American officer-type slammed me on the back thumbing to go up. We only went a couple of feet, when the HELMS (Helicopter Malfunction System) light blinked rapidly as she hit the ground in an all-but-uncontrolled landing. Something was terribly wrong. I had no power to lift her again. The sound of loud popcorn penetrated the screaming mix of engines and men. A thunderous brilliant flash bloomed just above me to the right of the cockpit. I flew out of my seat and madly tore off my helmet, dropping it to the floor, so I could rub my aching head feverishly. Then a wind-tunnel hollow metal sound followed. She toppled slowly over to port, as if she was wounded in the leg. From my angle there was no more green to see, only mostly blue.

The brown water in a gully from the river mixed with dirt flew up everywhere, like a wallowing elephant in mud spitting it. The sky darkened and the pinching wind began to howl, piercing the tin box's alloy we were stuck inside. Then the blades whined and died. It looked like all hell had been ripped up and let loose. The same army commander who had stationed himself behind my seat was now hollering repetitions to abort. The profanities flapped while everybody got out. I had to be last; I couldn't get past the mass of bodies ahead of me. There was another bang of metal outside. Finally, I scrambled out of the sardine can – the door was almost at floor level now – into the dazzling sun and ran like a blind man for the nearest cover.

As I caromed into the shrub some twenty-five yards from my helicopter, I glimpsed the Sikorsky leaning on her side facing me. The number one tyre (left side) had burst. Next to her was a shambolic crater with a single large candle flame aglow in the centre.

I began to realise that I was lying in a swampy muck. It was like quicksand swallowing; it didn't have a bottom. With a sloppy tasteless hollow suck, I pulled myself out and crawled to behind a beckoning tree for fleeting safety. I looked back at my chopper again; the stuff around her wasn't anything from the bowels of her body, more the droppings of the troop in their wild dash for cover. From my vantage point, it appeared that only the tyre was damaged and that the chopper did not sustain any structural damage.

My ears were ringing; the spasms of hurt made me crouch over foetal-style and hold my head as I rocked to the beat of pain. I loosened my restrictive and bulky survival vest so I could have more freedom of movement. For a few wobbly seconds I didn't care about anything, just a wish to be quickly put out of my misery with a bullet to the brain.

But the throbbing subsided slowly, then came back, then went down again. I got used to the coming and going of sound. You don't know you are listening to noise until it stops. Logical thinking returned to me thankfully and I abandoned my temporary plea to meet death itself. I stumbled to my feet and detected some movement on my right side. Suddenly the motion stopped and standing there was a single American soldier, facing away from the perimeter of our panic, scouring the dense jungle from the edge of a clearing, some fifty yards away from me to my starboard. I'd wondered how he could have got so far away from here in such a short time, but maybe he was first to eject out of the hot tub. He was clearly Hispanic and finally turned around to look at me, grinning with loss of breath, indicating for me to stay put. Then he hand signalled again to me to look behind myself.

I turned and my heart pumped at the sight of a single uniformed Asian combatant treading warily approximately a hundred yards away, his lighter clothes stark against the dark green. He held a rifle in his left hand as he slowly parted the head-high vegetation. His movements reminded me of a stork standing on one leg in the marsh with the other held aloft, waiting to nab the unlucky frog for its next meal.

I rotated again and in an instant my new brown American friend had disappeared at the most inopportune of blurred times. I cussed for his availability at a time when I needed his visual assistance. I was frightened. Despite my obvious hearing loss, I was still hearing a cacophony of bazookas, shots and bullets. But all this time, I did not leave sight of the bird-like Chink in front of me. I mentally tried to dampen my loud heartbeat by in-taking deep breaths through my nose to calm myself and hoping to hell that he couldn't hear me as I couldn't hear myself at that point. I yawned a few times. I don't know now if this was an attempt to pop my ears or it was simply my reaction to fear or a combination of both. I remained transfixed to my spot while intently watching that yellow man slowly advancing toward me.

I removed my Browning service pistol from its holster as quietly as I could. I reminded myself that I had to sign for it every morning. They would issue it at the ship's gunnery on the way to the aircraft hangar beneath deck. I'd never even bothered to check that its contents were in working order on this day, as it became a standard procedure for three and half weeks straight. As I sat there, I thought I would never forget to undertake any brainless ordinance for as long as I live. That is, if I survived this impending calamity. It had better be functioning properly. Too late to examine it now. Fuck.

Time began to feel like a countdown akin to the ten-minute routine when entering enemy air space. He was coming closer by the minute, at about an average of ten yards per. As usual, his last ten yards seemed longer. I was certain he could hear me and I was holding my breath in rapt concentration. I was hoping he wouldn't pepper the stalks in front of him. I kept sitting there pointing at the spot I thought he would come through.

My world went into slow motion as frames glided by delayed degrees filtered through my viewfinder.

The seconds' burn inside an icebox feeling, a coldness before the blaze.

His skinny leg in a sandal appeared first. This is how it must be for the frog before being devoured. Then the wooden butt of his rifle came into view held by an arm. The other hand was off to the side slightly dividing the reeds.

At a surreal snail's pace I found myself staring up into the tight perspiring Oriental face of a man about the same age as me, only thinner and smaller. He wore no helmet or hat and his black eyes popped wide at the sight of me sitting on my bottom directly down in front of him. He betrayed an animalistic fear – and I have no doubt I did too – his pupils pulsated in and out as if they were breathing, like savouring the seconds before committing a killing act or being killed. I could smell his sweat. For what felt like an eternity we faced each other. He exhibited more surprise than I did and he uttered a profanity under his breath. Then a jagged third eye appeared in the centre of his forehead. Then a part of his skull cracked and he did a quick split flip-flop backwards to whence he came. All that I was looking at was the same leg lolling over its other leg, level with my nose. I never even heard my own single shot leaving the chamber but the sulphuric snort lingered.

It was the first time I'd ever killed anybody, and I felt fine. Regardless, I still wasn't out of here and it didn't solve my lingering problem of how to extricate myself from this hellish place. Eliminating his presence was only one component towards my survival. It was either him or me, and that's all there was to it. It could have been my legs dangling unceremoniously there instead. *If it takes many more actions: so be it.* My response proved to me that I wanted to outlive him more than he wanted to outlive me. All I could think of, at that defining moment, was that I wanted to be a father one day and to see my children grow up, as irrational as that may sound. I would never know nor cared if he had now left behind fatherless babies, peculiar reasons that they may be on hindsight as my breathing returned to normal speed after the high of remaining alive...

Much like the frog's own life if the insects around it don't move then it could die of starvation itself surrounded by food, so during the course of the next quarter of an hour I remained transfixed there, frozen in fear perhaps. I was convinced my shot had alerted others to my position. My adrenaline level slowly reduced. It was difficult for me to think about finding another location other than refocusing at the slightly dangling and distorted leg a foot from my nose. It wasn't a sandal he was wearing; it was fashioned by hand from an old tyre. I was hearing klaxon-like shouts around me and within perhaps a fifty yards radius. The noises and sounds reverberated in my ears from all directions.

My ears were ringing loudly once again and I doubled up in pain for the umpteenth time. Phantasmagorical flashes rhymed to the combat in progress. Brown blotches appeared as if they were burnt holes in old film. I must have fainted from the dizziness and I felt like wanting to vomit as my equilibrium betrayed me. Suddenly a snippety nightmare of fitful brief sleep descended over me.

I came to; I don't know in how many seconds or minutes. It could have even been an hour or hours later, no! I started to half-crawl with my bottom in the air. I was covered in filth. When I wiped my brow, I felt blood and some coarse sand-like grains. Then I realised these were in fact bone fragments that had ricocheted from the other man's head on to my face in a rather macabre spurt. I was silently sobbing inside. This wasn't how I wanted to die! I thought it would be more glamorous than this. They never told us that it would be this scary, lonely, heart-pounding – liars! Nobody would even have the foggiest idea of my pathetic stinking demise, melded to the earth. Where in the flying hell were my whirly bird compatriots?

I collapsed exhausted beneath another tree trunk. I suddenly realised that silence had fallen around the area. The only sound I could hear was my own breathing. This is how I knew my ears weren't playing tricks on me. No birds, no leaves rustling, no voices, no nothing. So this is really what is called deathly silence I thought morbidly. I was crying softly now, as though my tears were speaking as they were streaming down my cheeks while I conveyed taciturn words of encouragement to my own outer physical being.

Then the devil's revolving door flung open again and there was a familiar sound of afterburning turbofans, looming louder. They were definitely coming around again this way. I stared up at the empty blueness. A tingle went down my back. A pair of British Phantom FG.1's must have been catapulted from the ship and were circling the skies providing us an umbrella! The Sikorsky's needed cover to come in. The AC's up there were giving us protection. So that's what they were waiting for! I half stood up teetering against the bark so I could get a better view of my surroundings. Still no Americans. I began a slow crouch around, confidence motivated by the illusory and out of range firepower above me.

I tripped over slimy remains of something that was once alive. Lumps of dead flesh, producing an unfamiliar stench of raw meat to my nostrils. Pink parts were protruding from the small branch-less tree. It would be nibbled on later by the returning bantam creatures of this celestial body of hell called earth. There was no telling what nationality it used to be.

I came to a clearing and a sigh of relief came over me. A dozen US soldiers who looked like marines were standing over a series of mangled very dead Asian peasants; a kill count of sorts. I was wading through enough bloodshed it seems to float a ship from here to the ocean. It was the most bizarre scene, as tomato ketchup redness covered everything. A strong sickly acidic stench permeated my nostrils. But those guys treated my appearance walking across the surface of this sea of carnage as a common event and I got a couple of "hi's". This is far from bloody normal I muttered to myself, it was barmy.

A sergeant in a mid-western drawl blithely said, "Commies, they're from up the road. There's another wave coming. We bagged about twenty-seven so far today. They're hopelessly weak in weaponry on the ground against us. Though their air support is good, the rockets and stuff." He hesitated to light a cigarette and extended his hand, "I'd introduce myself, sir, but the use of names is forbidden. You know how it is with all these undercover ops." I could only nod aimlessly as I was in the same boat as him, drifting on this foreign land in the middle of nowhere, feeling as dead as the ones at my feet. It wasn't really me standing there.

A corporal handed me a piece of tasty fruit from a queer-shaped fleshy object that looked like a thing from space. "Durian, locally grown. We only have nine hours to eat it in," was all he offered. I took it and savoured it. Years later I was to learn durian indeed could only be eaten in that time before it would go bad and become quite pungent. Tasty as hell though. Who would think to want to be so hungry in hell? But I was.

The friendly corporal contradicted the more formal sergeant somewhat by volunteering to me that the expired enemy were specifically guerrillas called the Hmong. Then in his sunny California disposition, he added, "We are SGU's, sir. Special Guerrilla Unit." I suppose in his mind that explained all the blood being shed as we munched our food in peace. Years later I was to learn that these boys were actually a small élite unit of Green Berets from the US Army 10th Special Forces' Studies &

Observations Group (SOG)[1] who were attached to Military Assistance Command, Vietnam. These guys were as tough as heck.

There was a definite rationale of a lull before the next storm came. There was still no sign of my helicopter squadron. I was puzzled; then it dawned on me that the hurtling war planes up above were perhaps waiting for me to wake up! I scanned my surroundings and could now see the tip of a rotor from my prone craft peeking up over a clump of low trees a couple of hundred yards away. I started a fast walk towards her. My feet weren't that steady as I had problems with balance. I'd have to check to see if she was airworthy and to get into radio contact with the fighter plane pilots up there, to hell with the no commo directives.

Two Yank soldiers were sifting through the debris where the hole was blown in the ground, next to the Sikorsky. She seemed unscathed, a couple of burns on her skin here and there, plus a hole torn through a rotor blade. The tyre's rubber had completely melted off the metal. I clambered in and sat in the cockpit, and threw on my fallen helmet which was still there but amid all the chaos it had only acquired a wee dent and a scratch. She fired straight away with not a hiccup. I could feel the nervous sweat meander down the middle of my spine.

I mentally performed quick technical check-ups and everything was unbelievably in order. No malfunctions that I knew of! This was like Cologne cathedral standing alone within the flatness of the obliterated German city after the blitz of World War II. One of the soldiers outside had appeared alongside me in the cabin talking. "Sorry, I can't hear that well. Shell shock I think. Listen, I'm going to try and take her up. From what I can see, she looks fine. Give me five minutes. But get the company ready to go, just in case. OK?" He understood immediately and disappeared astern. I yelled at him to return. He did promptly. "Do us all a favour and spend the time looking for a good flat log about the size of a tyre. When you see me coming down into the designated LZ, I want you to try jamming it under what's left of the wheel so the helicopter's launching pad can be somewhat stabilised. Got it?" He thumbed me and took off again.

The modified Sikorsky tottered, as she was already leaning on her side, but I managed to coax her up. She had the same struggling balance problems as me. There was a slight occasional odd clanking going on but she made it aloft admirably. I was stroking her like a purring kitten. I kept

---

[1] This SOG no longer exists, as of the end of the Vietnam War. The modern day SOG is the Special Operations Group, which is the CIA's own paramilitary unit. The two were and are

re-checking the dials. Everything was functioning; even the fuel gauge was at the levels where it should be. An absolute fucking miracle! I felt emboldened, again!

From my lofty lookout I could see a small army advancing a mile away! I started my descent and on cue two marines were down there holding the required "spare tyre". After a couple of attempts to jamb the wood piece under it, we got it right, and I signalled from the open window to urgently commence boarding again. They did so minus the already dispersed army equipment they'd discarded to save on weight. It saved a few minutes of loading men as well. They wanted to get out of there as much as I did.

As soon we were airborne the ROC (Rate of Climb) was fine as we cleared over the fence of the trees, the two-hundred-strong enemy opened fire with their outdated guns. To my dismay two AAA (Anti-Aircraft Artillery) units were hurriedly prepping a launch of hand-held ground-to-air missiles. A short burst from my turrets saw one group drop like flies. It reminded me of a fairground stalls' sideshow. I had to come around again to aim at the other unit 500 yards away, dead ahead, who were ready to fire by now. Like the Chink before, it was either them or me; depending on who hit the button first. The orange glow of an explosion ruptured from their maelstrom and a handful of matchstick men were spiralling upside down in the air, as I climbed away to safety.

Then my delayed anger kicked in admittedly for the first time. I wilfully and unnecessarily returned to the scene to release another barrage of .50-calibre machine gun fire at those running specks. Expended shells spat out in a white spume; falling like knocked out teeth to the floor. The twin lines of my aim "walked" up to them like railway tracks and tore up the ground as I wantonly massacred them. A grim remorseless lust for living as the pins below continued to fall at the end of my tracers in twisted grins, revolving arms and reverse long jumps, slammed to their destiny with death. Former humans were charred to blackened forms in piles scattered across the mosaic carpet. The acrid odour of burnt gunpowder filled the cabin as I calmed down.

The cutting off of life was easier than I thought, just to gently press the button of carnage, and an unspoken hiss from my unused cutlass clips through the wounded air like an uncouth game at a real amusement arcade. It was as simple as that.

That period of madness is now an isolated incident within the temple of my skull and is mainly blocked from my verbal memory, today. I think

completely unrelated to each other.

about it a lot but don't feel like discussing it much with anybody. It's a strange personal thing that I don't expect listeners to understand, only because it was me there and not them. But I will confess to a perverse pleasure in doing my duty. *This chapter has become my closure; I am understanding this slowly while I weep internally with pain writing this.*

The other choppers never did show up. With alternate roof cover from altogether four different Phantom fighter AC, I was ordered by the squadron leader to limp my way to a United States Air Force base in Chiang Rai, northern Thailand. It wasn't easy, as somewhere along the way the hydraulics flight control system stopped functioning, and then the shuddering got worse. Soon after entering the MATZ (Military Aerodrome Traffic Zone) the AC jet noise dissipated as they went on home to wherever base was to be because I doubt they had enough fuel to make it back to the ship. Upon arrival at the destination, a temporary flying station was under construction with a single MATS (USAF Military Air Transport Service) C-137C (Boeing 707) sitting idle on the freshly-laid tarmac. An antique British-made Bedford Green Goddess fire engine also patiently awaited our set-down with mostly yellow anxious faces at the ready. Once down a half a dozen of those American servicemen shook my hands in anonymity before leaving the confines of my battered specially fitted aerial eradication Sikorsky, though the officer, who was last to leave, saluted with his only words being, "If there is a UK need to know…tell them we were coded 'WATER PUMP'[2] and this place is Lima Site **, OK?" (** I do not recall the two numbers anymore.)

"It wasn't designed for combat and the weaponry looked like it had been added to this HLH as an afterthought", volunteered a USAF mechanic, who helped me off my aircraft. He'd already inspected what was left of her severely damaged undercarriage.

It was just over a year later when the US lost its conflict in Vietnam, a confirmed war zone. The United Kingdom too will deny any involvement in such battles in the region, including Vietnam, but we were under 'British Commonwealth command structures', i.e.: Aussies, Kiwis, South Africans and (then) Rhodesians led by Britons – "Not quite the same thing, you know, old chap so it'll be vehemently rebuffed," I can imagine an indignant but dictatorial voice from the UK's Ministry of Defence (MOD) saying. Somewhere out there are men who were involved who may step forward and confirm the unofficial warmongering by their respective beloved countries in the nations neighbouring Vietnam. Sixty minutes of insignificant death in the clock of the world, which was probably removed forever when the powers that be arbitrarily put the hour hand back in daylight savings time measures.

Another significant point is: those Americans were making sure that the dead were unidentifiable by shooting into the faces and disfiguring them beyond recognition. Perhaps few know what I know. Based on the background of my childhood, I know the difference between a Burmese, a Lao, a Thai and a Vietnamese. That large group of so called "Hmong" invaders were as Chinese as they come – as in Red China, excuse the pun. I know so, because one of them was right in my face and I couldn't mistake him to save my life. The dead man had also uttered a mouth-read obscenity to me before he was obliterated. I'd understood enough to know in Hong Kong as a kid (even though I wasn't so fluent in Cantonese); it was the language of the Chinese mainland region of Guangdong. He said to me *hen*, which essentially means "hatred" of me, and a slang word which translated as "anti-aircraft", another way of saying male masturbation or "fuck you". How obvious was that to me to think otherwise?

I never flew again. My battered Sikorsky of scrap metal never left that Thai base, for all I know. And if it did it was not flown by me. The telex sent from home by AARE (Aeroplane and Armament Research Establishment, Boscombe Down, Wiltshire, UK – the MOD's airworthiness assessors) confirms my suspicion. The pretence was that it would endanger the ship upon landing in the open sea. There is some truth to that because it would never had made it that far anyway.

Within a few days I returned home to Britain via Bangkok and was certified as having sustained a 50% loss of hearing in my right ear. Following a bomb or shell blast a pressure wave leads to a rapid expansion and contraction of blood vessels in the ear canal. The air embolism causes tremendous damage, sometimes death, after the effect of the actual explosion itself. I was luckier than my helicopter though.

For the record, when I was asked in London how many persons were killed in that massacre in Laos, I responded "one-one-one" because the time on the naval debriefing office's electronic wall clock behind him was 1:11 in the afternoon. So it was officially logged as 111. Since then

---

[2] A book published in 2005, "Spymaster" by Ted Shackley with Richard A. Finney, on page 137 states "...the Water Pump project started in April 1964 in which the United States agreed

whenever I do look at the time, it is invariably that same figure or 11:11, AM or PM, to remind me for a split second of my day of unpunished guilt.

The initial Thai hospital check-up had determined that I had been grazed by a bullet a quarter of an inch over my right eye. That explained why it had been totally bloodshot all that time, like a vampire's crazed gaze. I truly thought it was the result of undergoing a rare form of temporary insanity as the blood vessels burst from sheer pressure. Of course I was later to find out what had burst in my ear instead was a lot worse by comparison. But I still had my brain and wits about me in one piece for which I was thankful. It was my first of nine lives used. The scar remains visible to this day.

Reassignment came immediately – after a brief get-to-know you meeting in the British capital. Following this I attended several concentrated months of new training courses at the Secret Intelligence Service in Gosport and later its London HQ. Also came some therapeutic downtime spent on readjusting and rehabilitating my damaged right ear through the physical vibrations of music. No metaphor can ever describe the abject emptiness yearned in my ear today. From the loss and over the years I gained what I would describe as "developed instinctive relativity" – the ability to connect the dots of what is happening around me far better than anybody else – a kind of sixth sense of intuition when called upon or a situation presents itself. Sensory deprivation of one kind enhances other senses. A balancing in nature that rounds out. Instead I inherited good psychic awareness, strong perception and an increase in smell. Three for the price of one!

After all this time and with the physical sacrifices I have had to endure ever since, I would still like to know why the operations that I participated in were hushed up. Perhaps somebody out there can tell me?

It all seems like it was 845 years ago.

Today I telepathically hear the words now to my prose in the sound of the waves, in the whistling of the wind, from the birds who glide in the air, from the creatures who live in the sea, who tell me messages which I translate for us to read. Every pause has a meaning. Yet other places I visit strike me as peculiar without being possible, with no music to my ears and eyes, little sense of diction creeps through with absolutely no rhythm in the atmosphere. Still, at least I am now blessed with no fear.

---

to train Lao and Thai T-28 pilots…" presumably in the air war against Vietnam next door.

Nicholas Anderson
Let everything happen to you
Beauty and terror
Just keep going
No feeling is final.
— Rainer Maria Rilke

* * * * * * * * *

Chapter Three

Terrorism is warfare by the powerless,
warfare is terrorism by the powerful.

*A*s I age, a little chill creeps up my spine at the oddest of moments, whenever I think
about those three weeks in West Africa back in 1976. It was meant to be a
rather routine assignment as an emissary to collect a capsule containing a microfiche from
a local informant. But it turned out to be nothing but a wrenching experience that I
would never ever forget. These memories are etched deep into my being and never leave the
body and my soul within.

Black society has a long dark denial process.

Immediately after completing my training as a new intelligence officer,
I served a brief stint at HQ. My first overseas posting was to beautiful
Copenhagen but I was to return frequently to the UK for a variety of short
terms assignments.

When back in London I would board the underground's brown
Bakerloo line to Lambeth North. To get up to street level one had to take
the old-fashioned slow-gated lift, then it would be a left on Westminster
Bridge Road and in a few minutes along there I'd be the SIS offices at
Century House. Often SIS officers had to give verbal reports to senior
Members of Parliament and would do so a quarter of an hour in the
opposite direction at the Houses of Parliament (Westminster Palace was its

internal name) across the river. I know that way, too, because I once had to relate my findings from this story to an MP.

The majority of the in-house higher ranking SIS staff were settled in suburbia and worked a Monday-Friday, 9-5 schedule. They would commute daily by the main line railway trains into nearby Waterloo station and walk the short distance to the office with brollies in hand; black bowler hats no longer the norm. The most junior ones walked from their digs in nearby Pimlico, bicycled from Fulham or came by tube.

It was on one of these trips to London that I was briefed about a fortnight's assignment to West Africa. The trip had come up rather unexpectedly as the fellow who was the first designated became indisposed due to illness. After a thorough briefing (both oral and written), I was told to report daily for an unspecified period to Ghana National Bank located in London's financial district. Within a few days I was well versed in the routine of banking procedures and I was duly given a "GNB employee status" along with a valid chequebook and an official photo ID card.

By the end of the week I had flown in a Ghana Airways VC10 to Accra, Ghana's capital. I assumed the identity of a 24-year old British bank clerk called Alfred Slaney from the London office of GNB, sent on a training visit to the bank's headquarters. Ironically enough I didn't think I looked like an "Alf" nor did I talk like a Cockney from East London, as my "birth place" stated. Furthermore, I was not a Chelsea football club fan as my newly acquired character proviso demanded me to follow. Under that alias, my specific instructions were to make contact in Nigeria with a Nigerian national called Dano Daniyan and to receive an important microfiche from him for processing by SIS back in Britain. Apparently the intended courier was forbidden from leaving his country and had no one he could trust to deliver the microfiche to next door Ghana for pick-up. This is why I was asked to travel to Nigeria proper to collect the secret capsule. As originally planned, the key part of the op was only to be a long weekend journey – Friday out, Saturday night stay and Sunday back – to a land in the midst of a civil war. It involved overland travel and covering a one-way distance of some 400-mile as-the-crow-flies.

I enjoyed a few light-hearted moments during the days I'd spent at GNB's HQ in Kumasi, a town north of Accra, to establish my cover. I learned that African men prefer ladies that are considered "big" by western standards. To the Africans fat signified wealth and prestige. During my time serving with the local male employees of GNB, I would occasionally turn around to gaze at skimpily clad women that to me looked as would-be Miss

World contestants. The men in the office would immediately "pooh-pooh" my poor taste in women! Meanwhile they in turn would all gawk in astonishment at very heavy-set girls waddling along in their *batakaris*, the woven garment worn by nomads. I understood then why no black African country had won an international beauty pageant up to that time.

Despite these brief moments of levity, those weeks in December were to become the single bloodiest period of my life, by far exceeding and eclipsing anything I had experienced before. And that includes that fateful day on a month-long mission in southeast Asia just a year and a half earlier. As a result of my experience, I now think, without a doubt that the armpit of Africa and its people *are* the walking wounded of life, even to this day.

Even though Nigeria was also part of the British Commonwealth, the contrast between the thriving ex-British colony of Ghana and its eastern neighbour was stark. The nations of Nigeria, Togo and Benin as well as Burkino Faso and Niger to the north, were the collective basket case of subterranean Africa. These nations were poor beyond belief, making do on an annual income of US$200; at best, or much less. The towns were filled with the sorry sight of people eking out livings by dealing in trash.

Every usable remnant that may be tossed out is somebody else's gold. Re-straightened nails, ten pieces of cloth sewn together becomes something treasured to someone else. Anything wooden is a nugget of some kind. Every edible reptile and insect captured becomes a valued snack. Bank notes are a wealth unknown to most. Drinking water has more value than diamonds. A fortune is having a real roof over your head to shelter you and protect you from the glittering sun and the scorching heat.

Much has been written about the Biafra War between 1967 and 1970 with its "Ibo problem" and the international conspiracy to exterminate 14 million Biafrans who were seeking independence from Nigeria. At the time the West African country was on the cusp of discovering the value of black gold. It was itself an artificially created state, carved out by its British colonial master according to exigencies rather than sound rationale. Its three main ethnic groups were the largely Christian Ibo in the southeast, the nondenominational Yoruba in the southwest and the Muslim Husa-Fulani in the north. This latter group had historically produced most of the nation's current and past regimes. But the three largest factions comprised only 65% of the entire population, leaving a significant number of other minority groups mixed into the brewing melting pot of hatred and the killing of each other. *It was a neat trick by the white men to stir up the black men's blood; smartly side-tracking them by calling it the "war of the trees" (dividing of the provinces).* Britain's deliberate ethnic, cultural, political and economic manipulation by gerrymandering to kept the nation weak and unstable while their oil reserves were plundered from its southeast Ibo provinces, where the deltas glide into the Gulf of Guinea, is a book story all on its own. It's interesting what a few words of propaganda can generate among the gullible. As a result of the experience I have often wondered if the word native is actually derived from the word naïve.

The greedy so-called civilised nations of the west led by my country wanted the oil badly and the profits it gave them. So they supplied the emerging nation with arms and the undertrained Nigerian army grew from 6,000 to a quarter of a million in a flash. Much blood was spilled as the natives bumped each other off while the monies continued to flow to the coffers of the oil companies and their patrons, unknown to most at that time (but finally noticed now because they still haven't benefited exponentially from the revenues).

What early history books fail to mention that the conflict did not end until January 1970 making it a three-year war rather than originally being reported as a short-lived conflict. The less said the better. It is a fact that any disruption in the flow of oil from Nigeria would have shocked the world stock exchanges and adversely impacted the profit margins of the oil companies and reduced the dividend stream to shareholders.

It was consanguineous to their ancestors in the slave trade. They suffered the same fate in that their bodies continued to be piled up like black stuffed bin liners. Sadly, the dates etched into the ancient and freshly-dug wooden tombstones tell a story. All you had to do was read one of them, as I did have the singular opportunity to do and duly noted.

I was also to discover that in this region of the world it was easier to get guns then make a telephone call. Instead of sleeping with a woman, men cuddled up to a cocked rifle. Because it was an affront to their manhood, they also refused to wear condoms for sex so disease and unwanted babies became the norm. The level of hatred between the various ethnic groups created a charged atmosphere that eluded my comprehension. These were nations all bordering on economic chaos. Ghana had apparently experienced a relatively smooth transition to independence while Nigeria seemed ready now to capitalize on its new found black gold and enjoy its would-be wealth. Their in-between neighbours had only recently survived the turmoil of their own internal divisions. But all I could see were millions of Africans with immovable blinkers on, being led by some amazing leaps of faulty logic. I was often left gasping for a drink and grasping at short straws fallen inside nearly emptied soda bottles. Despite the difficulties

Coca-Cola's female-shaped glass bottles and its sister in the hoop petticoat, Fanta, were in plentiful supply but affordable to the richer elements only. Sitting on the musty bus, I kept drinking from the calorie-rich fructose drink that only made me thirstier, which was another clever capitalistic ploy. I realised I had been duped, which is more than I can say about my fellow travellers.

* * * * * * * **

After passing through the Slave Coast nations of Togo and Benin then crossing the border into Nigeria and just a couple of hours down the road between the towns of Abeokuta and Ibadan, I met the rotund Dano at the designated rendezvous. He was a white-haired orotund elderly man fluent in English. A man of God as the hanging wooden cross on his chest announced. We walked unhurriedly to his village along a dusty road from where the bus had stopped, a half-a-mile in the heat of the midday sun. His home was made of stone and was separated from a cluster of ramshackle huts made of straw, wood, mud or whatever could be taken from the land. From the bus window one soon understands that people can be quite enterprising at creating something from nothing.

There was no way to cool down during the day. You just mopped sweat nonstop during daylight hours. Quickly I went to his modest home's tin plated domain, which he described as a washroom, to clean up before lunch. When I saw my reflection in the small mirror, I realised I was the first white man I'd seen in two days, as I made that arduous bus trip through three different countries to reach this fourth one.

There was one slight problem. The courier had not shown up to deliver the pertinent capsule I'd come to get. We were to wait for him to show up. My only main concern was that it was sweltering here, five degrees latitude north of the Equator, and I constantly needed to drink fresh water in a place where there was no flowing tap supply. There was no way I was going to give myself cholera by drinking from the unclean water that had collected in the nearby jumbo-sized bomb craters that had been renamed as lakes. There was plenty of rain water gathered for washing yourself in them as many local inhabitants did. I could imagine that some of these ponds became depositories for body wastes as well. He took me to the back of his house and showed me oil drums containing purified water to which he added pure rainwater. It was also the main spot for the concentration of mosquitoes that I nicknamed the "Nigerian Air Force". Unfortunately, he didn't understand my British humour.

Out there, as we rested, I asked Mr. Daniyan, an ordained cleric it turned out, about the smaller crater-like holes in the ground a stone's throw from his fence. There were so many of them visible. "Smaller landmines were buried there," was all he said, bluntly. I knew that over 25,000 innocent people were killed or maimed by landmines worldwide every year. So I asked him if the area was still problematic. He looked at me gravely over his glasses, "Oh, yes, quite regularly. They built this village over the field the landmines were originally placed in. In fact, one went off a few days ago just down the road." His statement came across as if someone had committed wilful suicide in the middle of the street, a normal occurrence. Either that or he was completely desensitised. He continued to read the bible, trying to get a few inches closer to Jesus. I shook my head.

Being who I am, I decided to take a look around. Before I walked away to check out the neighbourhood, he looked up and said, "Mr Slaney, we have developed a culture of death in my lands. Be careful where you walk please and stay strictly on the paths." It was a kind of "Welcome to Nigeria" statement. My head dipped once blankly in acknowledgement.

It was during that first stroll I came across the graveyard with the wooden crosses and dates chiselled into them. Other nearby larger burial spots were like craters of a different kind, only instead of water filling it, there was dirt – lots of it, like inverted mounds.

Later I asked Dano Daniyan about those. Apparently they were mass tombs, not only from the Biafra War, but they dug them on a regular basis. Whenever the dictatorial genocidal generals who were fighting the rebels wished to make a point or two, they would order the soldiers to round up whole villages and wipe them out. His next profound statement, which came before dinner, really struck a chord with me. "Many die beyond their means so their naked lifeless bodies are buried without caskets in illegal graves, looking very much the same way they came into the world. Then the rain washes away both the burial place and the decaying remains of the deceased, leaving an organic juice with all kinds of bacteria swimming in the hollow." He did the sign of the cross then. Again my Noddy act came and went.

The food was unappetising after I heard all that and I turned in early to avoid the oncoming mosquito aerial invasion. Before I bade goodnight to him and to his nondescript quiet wife, he gave me another few memorable words of advice, "A screech at night is normal and is reasoned to be a reaction to a cockroach, never a throat slit. You understand me, I hope?" Again I nodded, not really fully comprehending. In the middle of my sleep I was indeed awoken alright – more jolted upright – by a blood-curdling scream, and it seemed to be coming from not more than a few houses across the way. I sat up ramrod straight under the netting with my body tense. *In the seconds after the peaceful silence is resumed while the standing hair on the neck recedes the rule of law in western civilisation is yearned.* I opened my eyes at dawn still in the same sitting up position, clutching my sweat-soaked pillow so I "wouldn't be suffocated and not see the knife plunging from an attacker". Then I wondered if some poor soul had been sacrificed at the altar the previous night. I could not detect any discernible response in the street, which was easily assessable next to my pane-less window. "And it's probably called free air conditioning here," I muttered darkly to myself.

The original few days of waiting stretched to exactly two weeks. This was the maximum time allocation for this entire African assignment. I quickly tired of having to wash the same three shirts, underpants and socks but the good side was they dried in an hour. Plus, I still needed to get back to Ghana, never mind on to the British Isles from there. Nevertheless, despite the dire living conditions, I had got to learn a lot about landmines and the human existence on its unseeing edge.

Dano wasn't kidding me about the frequency of landmines blasts. Two went off in the time I was there, ironically both of them on Sundays. Clearly anti-personnel landmines – large or small – cannot distinguish between an adult soldier advancing in combat and a child playing war games. Its cold mean exterior is just angry against anything that treads on it. *One day it would be nice to see the eventual elimination of these invisible floor bombs.* The sole problem is that most of the member nations of the UN Security Council, including the US, the country of largest manufacture, stands defiant against the rest of the world in wishing to keep using them, and wants to make sure that "eventual" is a long, long time, still. They have the steely indifferent mentality of landmines that are the same colour as their greyish bank notes.

With the singing of hymns and the church bells tolling in the background, I began my stroll on this peaceful Sunday morning around the village. Escorted by butterflies I was careful to stay on the tried and true trail encircling the village. Then the air was suddenly shattered by a single loud bang. Then it went quiet. *My hair was on end again.*

A young boy happily playing alone with a football in a field half way between the church and where I was walking was frightfully disembowelled into the parts. He was not yet in his teens as and his sooty foot fell seconds later on the dusty thoroughfare, bouncing several feet from me. This tragic incident is too horrific for me to write the despicable words that would adequately describe it. It was such a beautifully pristine a day, and I'd like to think the merry lad wasn't whom it was intended for. I caught myself just in time, and prevented a sprint across the way to his smoking remains. It was clear he had already gone on to a better life because I could see the blackened stump smouldering from where I stood, aghast and rooted to the spot.

When I finally rocketed the long few minutes around to the gates of the church grounds, the dark spatters on the pockmarked light wall resembled drying beans on a towel. The entire frightened hundred or so congregants had come out by now and were weeping uncontrollably outside. Reverend Daniyan was standing watching me as I stood emotionless, before he strolled alone into the confines of the church building to pray to the Lord. *Fuck, I wanted to scream that they needed experts to come and clear this land of minefields instead!* When they scuffed past me with what was left of the kid in a hammock used as a stretcher, I cried too, for I could see he was in a handful of unidentified dismembered parts but large enough not to fall through the spaces.

I cannot now walk across an open patch without a wretched feeling that death lurks beneath the tranquillity. The sound of a mere pebble kicked may send me high like a volcano into the ashen trees, strewn among the twigs as morsels for the crows.

Perhaps it was just as well that the nine-year old sports loving lad didn't make it. During the following week, I learned that they didn't have any prosthetics close to his size in stock at the small hospital nearby. The Nigerian doctor there looked at me as if the answer was a no-brainer. His emotionless voice struck me hard when he said, "But the young ones *never* survive the blasts, so we don't bother keeping 'small' in the inventory." One can only force a weak smile at a paradox such as that, a small step further forward from the usual mute nod of the head routine. *It was then that I realised an idea was formulating in my head in that I am one day supposed to relate this horror to others.*

The next Sunday I stayed in the house as the Daniyans had gone to the comfort of the oft-frequented church. Some quarter of a mile over the ridge in the opposite direction, I heard the muffled sound of yet another bomb blast. I eventually found the spot 20 minutes later, which was just off the main road into the village. Amazingly the bomb had detonated underneath a house that was still under construction. From the doorway inside it looked like it had hailed glass and rained blood. The acrid smoke was still so thick you couldn't see your hand in front of you. The owner, who was working inside the building at the time of the blast, had already been taken away, alive but missing limbs. I seemed to be the only person concerned about his plight, while the few who mulled around inside, with hands over their noses, were "taking" any worthwhile "gifts" belonging to the unfortunate man. At the rate his few items were disappearing, he wasn't going to find anything left when he eventually limped home, if he ever did. A neighbourhood yard clearance sale without paying for it was in progress. The man had unfortunately built his future on top of a metal limpet and now he had no future. "I found it, it belongs to me now," being the most memorable quote I heard while observing the looting in progress.

Preys of landmines are victims of a crime, not the perpetrators of a crime. They lose more than just parts of their bodies; they lose parts of their lives, if they survive. Landmines prolong the war, long after the guns are silent.

...I cannot find words to describe people who go inside others homes uninvited then lift valuables and think it's their right to keep them, none...

I found myself mildly hallucinating by a natural lake. The godless Christian carnival-cum-season of rituals was upon us in faraway Europe with the snow-less desert-like heat replacing cosy hearths, surrounded by inviting invisible stockings, an imaginary repetition of the familiar. I cooled my feet in the warm water and shrugged. I'd always detested the cold but this was way *too* hot.

It was Christmas Eve and I stared down at my reflection. So many cherished friendships deteriorated over time; reduced to Christmas cards with obscure messages scribbled in the corner while I was forced to recall their faded images. I heaved another sigh. I'd always had a problem too with being nice about receiving presents I didn't want, or didn't need. I felt a fool forcing an artificial glee on my facial contortions when my real reaction was really nonplus at the stupidity of the contents. Being here bore out that thought – *these people needed the aid, not me, and an education, even old discarded cardboard, anything.*

I didn't expect my long-suffering Danish girlfriend, Vibeke, to understand my absence, then consoled myself knowing she was scheduled to work through the holidays anyway as it was double-pay time if you did. I imagined her swimming naked in front of me momentarily then snapped back to reality.

The next day, Christmas Day, I decided to go and find our missing man. Apparently he worked at the college of medicine at the University of Ibadan. It was ridiculous. I was rotting here. Reverend Dano said he was supposed to come from Iwo, north of Ibadan, which was less than a hundred miles away. It didn't take weeks to walk here, goddammit! He did add though that he'd heard there had been a massacre along the missing man's route a few days ago. "He may have been detained or was simply shot for being in the wrong place at the wrong time." He'd mentioned it as an afterthought, so harmlessly. Only now does he tell me this news. If you didn't ask, you weren't told. I had to at least go and find out more. *When someone disappears off the face of the earth, somebody must know something...no question mark inserted.*

On Boxing Day, the day after Christmas, at 4:00 AM, armed with directions, hard currency, the man's name, my false passport and common sense, I set out on my journey. The distance that I had to cover was about 25 miles if I stayed on the road. Even before dawn, I stood out like a beacon as I maintained a brisk walk in sharp contrast to the locals. Nobody walked fast there. My hat was over my face and I'd spread mud over my face and arms to be less of an unarmed white man in a black war "combat zone". It was a pity, too, I couldn't obtain a functioning bicycle from anyone. Assuming I'd get no lifts on the way, I'd calculated I'd be at my destination by 10 o' clock, at the latest. After that it would be too damn hot. On three separate occasions on the way, I hid in the ditches to avoid armed convoys, not knowing nor caring which side they rode and died for.

I beat my deadline by a quarter of an hour. Fortunately, in Nigeria, there were some well-educated individuals who spoke English. It wasn't long before I found the killing field with the help of a fine young lad with expressive eyes of about 14 years old, who took me right to it. He told me his uncle had managed to escape from being another grim addition to the two-dozen victims.

Unbelievably the corpses hadn't been buried yet and they were stacked on top of each other grotesquely inside a tight tin hut, the kind construction workers use as changing rooms. The murderous gang must have supervised the excavation of the large deep empty hole in the ground too, before they killed the diggers.

The stench was overpowering and the flies were thick in the air, flying in tight formations and buzzing loudly like diving fighter planes. In large numbers they feel like they are biting you whole, rubbing their hands together in glee at the feast of human flesh before them, and that included mine – dead or alive, same thing. Ooze seeped under the walls and formed a meandering river of an indescribable colour toward a gully. There was no lock on the door. I was gagging badly and had to recede upwind to figure out what to do next. Do I stay or do I leave?

The lad ran off without warning. For a moment I dreaded the possibility that he had gone to get the perpetrators of the crime but he came back leading a very wary but bright and good-looking fellow with a semi-dreadlock hairstyle who must have been in his mid-thirties. They had similar eyes. This was his uncle who had apparently survived this awful mess. We bade happy holiday greetings to each other. The man spoke excellent English and in fact he had been to college in Britain. He was a would-be poet and had studied literature. How does that help him here, I thought?

Despite his academic credentials, I gradually weaned it out of him that all murder victims were the better educated. Being educated was the reason why they were being singled out. The uneducated believed the bullshit that these deaths (sometimes labelled as "sacrifices to the gods") would eventually create a better society. Eliminating the academic class was thus viewed as a positive good. Certainly it wasn't regarded as a negative bad. Both sides, the army and the rebels, despised the academic as being part of the ruling class. Systematic victimisation was underway nationwide and he admitted that he expected to die soon "by virtue of only his education". I felt numb and helpless as I lay on the grass listening to his tragic tale of woe. *Never since then in my life have I ever admitted to myself that I have a problem with anything.*

The man's one main untitled prose he gave me to read will haunt me forever. At my request he gave me the handwritten copy to keep because it summed up Nigeria:

> "I am plagued by the same dream.
> My room is filled with water.
> I am fighting to get to the surface.
> I see the bodies of my mother and sister
> swirling past me in the current.
> I burst to the surface.
> I can always see it above me.
> The bridge from where I was pushed.
> The water stank of death."

I chose the right moment to ask them if there was a doctor in the area. The younger one nodded, pointing at a batch of concrete houses in the distance and eagerly pulled me with him. For an instant I thought about the lad that had stepped on the landmine playing football the week before. They both had pure innocence on their faces.

After banging on the door for what seemed like ages, an old hugely fat grandmother appeared, indicating that the doctor wasn't home as he had gone out. She didn't speak English, but as luck would have it, behind her was the bare interior of what resembled a physician's office.

With the help of my junior assistant and his uncle, who translated for the wary woman, we haggled backwards and forward for 10 minutes. We eventually left there with a pair of doctor's clear rubber gloves, a surgical mask, an already opened bottle of Vaseline and a rusty medical utensil, which I couldn't tell what it was used for. She was happy with the wad of English Pound Sterling notes I'd left her, staring at it like a priceless painting in her hands. On the way back I purchased three one-gallon plastic containers of distilled water and a lukewarm coke each for my African acquaintances and myself. *"American champagne for the world,"* I'd toasted, *"for the drug of money."* With a grim smile we clinked our glass bottles and wished each other a jollier new year than the one that had ended 11 months prior. The poet had written my own impromptu toast down for his own later meditation.

Alone, in the stifling heat of midday, I began the worse task of my entire life. Donning my mask and surgical gloves, I pulled open that dreaded door and a naked body of what was a child tumbled out brushing against my leg as I tried to jump aside. Bending on my knees I began a prolonged retching but nothing came up...just the spitting up of a purplish cola while I mumbled loudly to encourage myself.

You don't live here, it lives in you and it turns you inside out. What pisses me off deep down is to suffer through the madness of people that didn't democratically try constructively criticising the people that did try for a better life, only resorting to murder of them as a manner of anarchic response. This is the exact opposite of advancement. Nothing makes sense so you do nothing. Nothing plus nothing is nothing but here it is minus and lot of zeroes. Backwards and more backwards.

Within hours of death, no matter what the colour was in life, corpses left to cook in heat become a kind of dark yellow, even originally black ones. Dead bodies left for a few days also shrivel up like new-born babies. They don't look remotely like they were once a human being. Instead they appear like something with blotches and rashes from another planet, almost like a big dried prune with lots of blanched spots mixed with other unidentified objects stuck on it. Yes, there are former people's legs and arms and plenty of hard dark things that have fallen off and you don't have any idea from what section of the human anatomy it came from nor do you wish to know. Despite the mask and petroleum jelly plugged into my nostrils to block the stench, an odour of warm bad meat still penetrated through. My eyes were stinging continuously while the sweat poured out of my boiling body. I gave up attempting to swat away the bombarding flies as they engulfed me, constantly rubbing their hands with glee as they perched on my arms in clustered groups feeding on unseen goo.

As much as I tried not to look into the hardly-human faces, no two agonised contours were twisted into the same convolution. Ghoulish, scared, laughter and peace were all represented. Guessing an age was a foregone conclusion of impossibility. My mind played tricks on me: They all looked beyond old, or not born yet, sometimes a strange appearance of both, but not really dead, no. I never thought a person's body could depict such abstract ghastly delineations. It had also quickly dawned on me that these people were not shot but hacked to death, which explained the unidentified rotted bits and pieces of carcasses. Two women had both their breasts lopped off, the whiteness vividly stark holes like large moons. *Sick, sick, sick minds did this.* You have to force talk yourself through it, you know, you know, you know.

If there was a good side to my predicament – it's a survival instinct to find something – it was the fact their killers had the presence of mind to remove all their clothing. But they hadn't had the lime to spread over them though. Concentrating on males only, I began poking my fingers inside hardened mouths, having to pry some open. A couple of teeth cracked away as I levered them with the handy metal instrument I had. Some ears' hollows were large enough to contain a capsule as I peered in. Insects occasionally crawled out of the black caverns. My soiled fingers inquired into their clamped anuses. I avoided the few female's vaginas altogether.

Every other body performed a freakish inflexible stiff dance in death as I hauled them out. Many made me resort to a song of unrelenting vomit-suppressing sounds. Several had no heads attached, just a few dangling loose strands of an off-colour hard dark wool. Later at the back of the blood-stained hut I found a big black rubbish bag filled with half a dozen human heads. A gooey liquid of mixed warm juices from the bodies spilled from a splice in the plastic, flooding my foot through my sandals. I audibly said to myself it was "only Halloween masks thrown in a sack after the party was over." I ignored the glue-like feeling as my toes rubbed together like the flies were still doing.

My actions were attracting a flock of birds that began pecking the first few I'd dragged out. First few what? They could hardly be described as former humans. The dead usually lay serenely "asleep" in coffins. My mind kept me separated from the horrors of the insane labour the rest of me was undertaking. As crazy as things can get, you have to seek the humour to remain sane. Only today there was absolutely none, none, none.

Death is like no other lesson learned in life. By accepting death, you discover life. The end succeeds only in deepening one's emotional isolation. A calmness at last, a passage out. And a strange will takes over next: to always keep moving forward.

Meanwhile my duo of African friends were joined by a cross section of villagers staring aghast at the spectacle, hands over their mouths. I was struck by the sight of a group of brazen male teenagers sitting on the dirt enjoying my exhausting performance and arrogantly shouting toward me words of encouragement. To me this group felt much like the clutters of winged insects assaulting my body. I began to understand Dano Daniyan's comment about developing "a culture of death". Those boys were the future leaders of this sorry country.

The eighteenth anus felt different. This cadaver's face had a grinning smile as if he welcomed the Holy Ghost. After some exerted pulling and ripping with the doctor's tool I had, I finally recovered from the anus a half-inch long thin plastic capsule of the kind I was told to accept. I let out a deep pant as I bent down onto my knees, wiping my brow. Those teen boys applauded my act loudly. I in return acknowledged them by bending my head in an exaggerated manner with one hand extended up dramatically and holding an invisible bouquet of roses to express my appreciation. *I swear I don't know why I did that.* I guess it was a form of conveying my rancour towards them in a way that did not provoke.

Away from their view after washing the capsule carefully with spittle, I shook the contents. There was something inside it alright. I didn't think to open it and in any event I wasn't permitted to.

Even in times of unbelievable stress, the brain conjures up dementia. I thought seriously about putting the team of ghouls back neatly where I found them. Instead I waved in a fake curtain-call style – holding both arms high and then bowed the final bow – to that clapping group of loud obnoxious young men. Then I turned abruptly in the direction of the brown river, which I'd passed on the way in, a half a mile away – where I immediately vomited on its bank. It must have been the same river the literature academic mentioned. He too followed me meekly like a mellow dog. Those boys were just behind him chatting happily amongst themselves as if they'd attended a joyful garden party. I can't tell you how they stuck in my craw. *I instead wished: I were, the Pied Piper of Hamelin, leading the craven rats to the water to drown.*

I dropped exhausted into that welcoming hot bath, fully clothed, and used my hands as a flannel to rub the grime away. Who cared about crocodiles at a time like this. Several of those African children jumped in with me and splashed each other playfully. I didn't join in, in their fun, nor did I even smile at them as I would normally do.

As I lay in the water, the poet that would never be, dedicated a poem in English to all of us, as he crouched on the riverbanks looking at me only. In a sense I was baptising myself. My fellow bathers didn't understand his words thankfully:

"Our young men are killing each other.
You can't blame that on the white man.
You better take responsibility, black man.
It's time you woke up and shared the blame."

I've never forgot that. I clearly can still see him say that. I nodded in response in a way that he couldn't have noticed while memorising the poem and wiping my face in shame. I was weeping both inside and out for all of us. This trepidation of every day being the last must take its unbelievable toll on him and no sane man should have to do what I just did. *War creates that mad maddening madness.*

Minutes later we bade farewell and I dripped a wet trail down the road rapidly drying out. Fortunately, a lorry driver stopped for me and dropped me right to the entrance of the village where Daniyan lived. It was four in the afternoon when I stumbled in. It was decidedly the worst half-day of my life, but I was strangely proud I'd followed my intuition to obtain that half-inch capsule. *When an instinct speaks clearly, I am so grateful because too many are not.*

That night I had awoken in the dead of the night and had quietly tiptoed out on to the veranda. Dano was asleep out there in a makeshift swing of sorts. The moonlight cast a mask of death on the elderly fellow's face, a kind of impulsive prose cubism you had to get used to, to survive the haunting surroundings. Beneath his gnarled wisteria, worn Bible in veined hands, shadows playing across them, I stared hard at his lifeless-like form for many minutes. It was hard to know what to do to help these butchered people. "I think I understand you now, old man," I whispered to him. *When you are in an occupied nation, how you react is different to how you react in a free country. It is a nonstop blast furnace of pressure and emotional masturbation.*

You'd think the Almighty above had crammed enough terror into these people to last a lifetime. In those two and a half weeks in Nigeria, not counting my days in Ghana, Togo and Benin, you'd think that would have been more than enough blood shed.

Hell, He had one last trick up his sleeve.

The next morning, I bade my hosts, the Daniyans, a somewhat awkward good-bye. I feel uncomfortable and look away when anybody says "God Bless" to me. *If you don't believe like them then they don't understand they are insulting you.* On that sticky prickly return bus ride west towards the Benin border, we'd been stopped by an army patrol and everybody had been ordered out onto the side of the dusty road. They apparently knew what they were looking for and barely gave my papers a glance, and I was the only white man there. Apparently a rebel sympathiser was on that bus and when they identified him they dragged him away a few yards screaming at the top of his lungs then fired at him point blank, without explanation. I was only 10 feet away and nobody dared to move or make eye contact with those soldiers. *I hoped my face wouldn't crack a vein in reaction to the tension; otherwise the noise of the pop would have attracted attention on to me.* It was though it was just another day in the life for my fellow passengers, as they feigned a curious combination of disinterest, fear, calm, and wariness – the "pressure cooker look" I now call it.

I sneaked a glance at the victim. When a man is shot in the stomach, he makes a sound like a loud giggle, as if trying not to embarrass himself, as he falls slowly smilingly to his final resting place on to his knees. As he sat there upright twitching slightly, his face turned up to the heavens and the eyes slowly froze open. I knew he was gone for good to the skies. Almost naturally I gazed up too to see if I could naïvely glimpse his spirit winging away. But there was only oblivion beyond.

Everybody was then ordered to board again and we did so in singular silence. The sneering Nigerian army group had already taken off in their general purpose vehicle. We pulled away leaving the slain man squatting there by the side of the road where the bus had been halted. Fresh road kill. When I looked back at him as the vehicle drove off, from the distance he appeared to be praying. Nobody else dared looked back.

I knew from first-hand experience that a day later as he still sat poised there he would eventually develop a nondescript stiffness, like a large deformed dark yellow twig resembling a shape of a human. The flies and insects were already visiting.

On that bus I sat behind a woman reading a propagandist news circular, written in English. There was a photo printed of General Yakubu Gowon, the dictator of Nigeria, who had ruled through this bloodletting since 1966. He wore the worried look of a man too far removed from the action of the streets. He knew like I did that he could not fill empty tummies with meaty words of any quantity. Gesture politics can only survive so long on inedible newspaper headlines.

But amazingly some delusional people ate that while the paper profits were being cooked elsewhere. I began to explore the notion then that I was nothing more than a tool for the transition, just like the people I was among. I considered the idea of chucking the capsule I came for out of the window into the moving countryside but I didn't have the guts to do it. Not after what I had been through to get the damn thing.

I don't believe in a god, because I don't believe a god would permit such cowardly atrocities. Yet when I finally reached the relative safety of Ghana and *uhuru* – freedom, I stood for an unknown time at the border customs office staring out of the window in the direction of where I'd come from. I tried then to seriously comprehend that way of pietistic thinking.

A travel in space only to find yourself delivered back to the same spot in the universe before you left. There was still nothingness all around me, above and below, inside me; a stilled non-existence stayed inside my palms and my head.

The tormented angst remains with me, however.

Nigeria was a mad sad period when the gods must have been permanently out to lunch. When being so close to tasting genocide it makes you so aware of your own mortality that you can almost see it spread out on the table and dissected before your eyes.

…When I finally got back to London my immediate superior said to me, "Glad you're back in one piece but what took you so long?" I didn't know how to begin to answer him and could only shake my head…

War has no morality and no ideology.

* * * * * * * * *

Chapter Four

"If you are planning for a year, grow rice;
if you are planning for 20 years, grow trees;
if you are planning for a century, grow people."
— *Chinese proverb*

A heck of a lot goes into the execution of a covert action operation, from our side as well as their side. The planning phase is both painstakingly methodical and time consuming before the peeing in your pants scary parts arrive, if it ever gets to that and sometimes it doesn't. Sometimes like life in general what actually occurs only remotely resembles the original plan.

The Albanian account actually began in the principal city of Switzerland, Berne, where I was stationed at the time as the new number two and operating under the code name BEN/1. The head of station was a Barry Anderson (no relation) who had the code name H/BEN. I had suddenly been transferred there in 1976 from Denmark where I had been the third man, COP/2, on the totem pole. So I suppose it was a move up but geographically down to an island of land surrounded by mountains and endowed with remarkable technical gadgets of all kinds. The other Mr Anderson was an electronic eavesdropping expert and I was to assist him on field operations and analyses of all the data gathered from that country. It turned out that my resettlement was for a good reason.

The CRITIC/PRIORITY (CP) from London advising me of my promotion had read that it was "due to my understanding of Mandarin", which had made no immediate sense to me at the time. It should be noted that if added text appears in a CP encrypted telegram it will contain essential information about the operations currently in progress. What was written there was highly unusual and it understandably piqued my curiosity. A CP also meant I had to report immediately to my new post and I did. I was soon to learn that the Swiss capital was not only the world headquarters for hundreds of international banks but also the site of the Chinese Embassy *doubling as the largest centre of worldwide communist Chinese intelligence operations outside Beijing.* When you are there strolling in the tranquil hospitality of *Bern,* you just would never think in your wildest dream that the place was an important hotbed for the application of Red China's brand of communism.

To this day we still haven't recognised the power of the Bamboo Network – at least 60 million Chinese *not* living in China, who will generally answer that they are Chinese first and whatever their passport or land of residence comes second. I grew up among them – my parents had 17 helpers at their house in Hong Kong, where Cantonese is the local dialect, but my favourite person to hang-out with was the Mandarin-speaking gardener who taught me his native language reasonably well, as well as basic martial arts. So I had some grounded experience of their often inwardly self-serving and intricate thinking (compared to that of Caucasians) – with their closed mouths while the eyes smile contradictorily at you in bowing cordial mode. But when they stood upright with bright eyes and smiled boldly in your face my father used to warn me to be on the alert that some opportunity was about to be exploited. In all fairness there is some truth to that kind of body language in all cultures but the largely introverted Chinese are not generally outwardly affectionate in public places. They are a people that will choose to avoid eye contact, especially with strangers. Asking directions is not common, for example.

And very much like the well-educated intellectual Chinese mind, the structure of the Chinese intelligence services were set up in such a way that only the most wonderfully perceptive foreigner could figure out the identity, role and inter-relationships between the different units. The reason for that incongruity is due to the fact that the Ministry of State Security (*Guójiā Ānquán Bù,* or in short *Guóānbù*) was set up into different bureaus, each tasked with its own set of constantly evolving responsibilities. MSS was the equivalent to our own Ministry of Defence or the U.S.' Department of Defense with their respective agencies reporting to them. But unlike their Western counterparts, the Chinese institutions operated in a chameleon-like fashion. Having learnt something from the Chinese we began to increase the number of our own compartmented one-person overseas stations focused on accomplishing a micro undertaking within a macro game plan. I was to become such an operator myself later.

The Chinese version of the SIS and CIA is called simply the CSS, by us, for Chinese Secret Service (factually it's *Zhongnanhai Baiobiao*, which translates to The Bodyguards from Red Palace, but the terminology was too knotty to coherently explain so it was disregarded altogether).

The CELD (Central External Liaison Department) was a branch of the CSS and it was responsible for the analysis of their own foreign intelligence data. It was also the largest contributor to the Central Control of Intelligence that operated exclusively in Berne rather than from mainland China. *Cheng Pao K'o*, their Political Security Section, was also located within the same building in the city centre. The mandate of the latter Chinese counter-espionage service was to spy on forcigners deemed worth monitoring and at the same time to also keep watch on the Chinese overseas, including their own in-house staff. It was an internal affairs' spy unit to observe the spies within as well.

The engine room in the heart of all this machinery though was *Lin Luo Bu* (liaison department) who manipulated on three "soft warfare" fronts: media, political and psychological. Originally coined the Department of Enemy Work its core function was to present China as a non-threat militarily and commercially…*while it concentrated on the exact opposite of that, worldwide.*

But we at the British SIS were watching all of them, in turn, collectively and individually. Well, mostly listening to them actually. At first, the Chinese had the "technical means" of a multi-frequency simulator, a sophisticated phone tapping device, which made our original "bleep boxes" look positively archaic. But within a year of my arrival the technology lads back in the UK, fortunately, did a great job of scientific innovation to catch up with the Chinese and actually leap-frog over them with our newly developed expertise.

As a result of our superior devices there was an increase in intercepted cipher at Bletchley Park (the base of the code-breaking unit in Britain). In fact, I'd gone to Albania covertly a couple of times in that first year just to follow up on leads emanating from "chatter" from these sources in Switzerland. *To the best of my knowledge, before or since, I have never come across any public domain or consumer-orientated reference mentioning the fact that tiny impoverished Albania almost became a bona fide satellite state of China within Europe itself.*

While operating clandestinely in Albania I routinely observed pockets of Chinese troops at the nondescript small but very long one-runway of Gjadër-Lezhë-Zadrima airfield. An interesting aspect about this location was that from afar military aircraft in red star Chinese livery could be seen landing through the binoculars, would taxi behind some rocks and disappeared from sight altogether. The only conceivable hiding place had to be a natural hangar-like cave inside a mountain and big enough to hide a dozen large bombers and transport planes at any one time. A perfect hiding place for them and not so good for us because we did not know what else was stored inside there. It required constant surveillance to know, which we didn't do.

Meanwhile in the town of Shkodra, which was the nearest commercial centre north of the aerodrome, one could see businessmen from China often in their Mao suits going about their chores. They were beginning to swell in numbers much further to the south in the Albanian capital city of Tirana as well. It was becoming home away from home for them.

Chinese troops were mostly based at the country's main airport area that served both military and commercial AC's, which was approximately 20 kilometres northeast of Tirana. The second largest location was the aforementioned airfield south of Shkodra. The third in Vlorë, south of the country on the Adriatic Sea, had a regiment embedded. It was not known if any other location had significant units of the People's Liberation Army of China.

The Chinese influence was rapidly approaching dominance of the country. If it weren't for the likes of SIS and other intelligence services and the clever implementation of "symbolism reduction" (establishing by strategic pre-set designs an action whereupon the opposition's confidence declines or changes course in our favour); the outcome in Albania would have been a whole lot different. I'm quite sure it would have been an altered story on the maps and in the cultural development of today's European Union as well as the near Middle East. The episode is a classic case study of the creative dismantling of an enemy having numerical advantage by a small, effective and highly specialised team. *It was as if Buddha, Jesus, Mohammed and Moses co-starred in a bizarre science fiction special effects film about atheism entitled "Twisted History"...*

* * * * * * * * *

The new improved intercept capability was eventually honed to perfection and it made a huge impact on our total surveillance op. It included planting various contraptions inside the residences of the Chinese workforce, manning the listening post around the clock, installing 24-hour cameras around the perimeters and clamping tracking devices on all their vehicles. Other methods of surveillance involved the hiring of "cleared" Swiss informers on wages (mainly their internal cleaning and maintenance crew with "bugs" placed on them without their knowledge inside the linings of their clothes). Other infiltration methods were implemented targeting waiters inside restaurants and gardeners outside their homes, who also unknowingly carried miniature recording machines in their shoes' heels. All this on top of our own ELINT (electronic intelligence) and SIGENT (signals intelligence) in-house personnel; we were a total around-the-clock spy detachment.

We could hear the Chinese talking everywhere and anywhere at any time wherever there were telephones installed, whether or not that specific phone unit was actually in use with someone speaking into the mouthpiece or not. It came about when a sophisticated audio device was made to look like a Made in China security alarm and had been connected to the telephone cable lines *outside* their buildings. The hook up of these gadgets allowed us to listen via the interior unused phone units sitting still on desks in their cradles that doubled as instant microphones for the whole room. It made no difference whether the particular phone in use was automatically scrambled or not...provided, of course, that other phones in that same room were relaying the spoken sounds. So, in a sense their oral language smilingly produced our veracities for us, as I will summarily explain:

One of the first Chinese intercepts explicitly mentioning Albania by name, after it was translated and transcribed, was: *"We won't inbreed with them. We will help them and we will mix with them. But Chinese culture will stay with us. We won't place our culture onto Albanians as we don't want to start any friction."* That was the first time any link between the two countries was uncovered. We were curious what that was all about, to say the least!

Concurrently, an early Albanian "catch" specifically naming China's capital city that we had picked up from another source stated: *"We each are different, so if we can relate to Peking it's good. Between nations too, there should be that kind of social harmony. There must be cooperation; there must be union so that together we can confront and overcome common obstacles. I think their coming here should not be viewed as a hostile takeover of our poor country but rather as a welcoming of aid."*

Make what you may of this juxtaposition of double-speak meaning almost the same thing but *an intent of sorts* had duly been stated by both parties to join up and that really worried us. It was worthy of continued monitoring.

* * * * * * * * * *

One day in my second year in Switzerland I was urgently summoned to SIS' headquarters in London – the dreaded land of bombast, strop, bluster and stomp usually bossed by unctuous ruling class chaps who thought they knew more than we underlings. Over time, whenever I went to Century House, I got a sense that we only hunted for forensic evidence that fitted the hypothesis – squares going to squares and holes into holes – which I felt was borne out of erroneous thinking.

I left on the first available flight on a Dan-Air cargo jet directly from Berne into Gatwick airport, south of the British metropolis. I found myself strapped in the only seat on the aircraft just outside the cockpit's door, ominously going backwards.

Ready for a double dose of BS I was shown into the closeted office of P4, the SIS' Balkans section for production of intelligence, where I saw both the divisional controller and the man he reported to, the senior security officer for the entire ops in Eastern Europe. Both men stood up to shake my hand. Seeing them together and getting off their arses for me made the hair on my neck stand to attention like the rest of me did. *My, this was actually going to be important!*

Sitting down, less than a minute later, I got another case of goose-bumps when the SIS' in-house liaison officer for both the Special Air Service (SAS) and the Special Boat Service (SBS) joined us at the round table. This was the person responsible for activating our own paramilitary unit. No handshake was forthcoming from him as I had dealt with him before, somewhat acrimoniously I might add, so there was no love lost between us. In my humble opinion, he was too much of a straight suit to be in an office position that needed quicker decisions for those others functioning in the actual mad theatre of operation. A manager that once played out there understands the situation better. It was a case of a square peg in a round hole, as the saying goes, and upon his appointment I had been on record about it (and he knew full well my unvarnished opinion of him). SAS/SBS have a joint élite small cell who are handpicked from its already highly selective pool of special forces recruits that are on call to conduct covert military operations, exclusively for both SIS and its domestic sister, the Security Service (MI5). In other words, this lot were deployed to undertake rub-outs and similar covert high-risk disruptive actions to be officially denied if uncovered. Unfortunately, the group had a simpleton of a clerk with power overseeing them who also had a pig-arse attitude to boot.

So here we were, four knights to the Queen finding ourselves in an imperfect circle at a round table of a chessboard. Three slightly overweight administration types sitting closely on one side and slim fit me who was the lone active-in-the-field operator opposite them. It was my first time ever in their collective presence. Not only was I the most junior rank there but I was the youngest member by at least two decades to each of them. Sitting in silence I felt as if I was at the far end of an imaginary long wide table getting elongated and narrower by the second. I watched them intently shuffling paper loudly between them in some kind of show of bureaucratic officialdom. The dull sound of files shifting made me realise the usual hum of London traffic had vanished and that the walls around me were heavily layered with embedded white noise. This made the room absolutely secure from outside listening devices and even from the next room. We were inside P4's White Room.

"Time to act in Albania," finally proffered the most senior and eldest man present as they all nodded in unison as if party to a well-rehearsed game plan that the charmed circle club always did try onto those like me that didn't belong. He pushed across a folder for me to read, without glancing up. "Take a peek at that, Anderson. What do you suppose it's all about..."

I tried to examine his face-down eyes. I wasn't sure whether he was asking me or telling me, or he didn't have the foggiest notion about anything at all. I was surprised to detect a certain pensive burden within his hidden expressionless countenance and when he did glance at me his overly grey bushy eyebrows perhaps contributed to this vague air about him. Then I looked down and began to peruse the contents in my possession. While doing so I was acutely aware of six eyes burning into my skull and felt as if I was made of clear plastic as they studied the open mechanism of my brain's circuit wires fusing and fizzing. All of them were clearly sizing me up, no doubt.

I had to force myself hard to concentrate on the documentation in front of me. At first it blurred but then quickly came into focus. It was a bulletin from SIS' Asia section, transliterated from the Chinese to the

English with some mistakes. Apparently the material was directly "lifted" from the Hong Kong office of the Xinhua News Agency, the official Chinese communist government agency, in which a caveat stated, was "believed to be the centre of the Hong Kong Committee of the Chinese Communist Party". This information had come to HQ in much the same way we were currently getting ours in Berne, through telephones. However, the SIS lads in the Far East had also tapped into the electricity lines plugged to the typewriters and were getting lots of useful feedback coming down that added path of wire. I made a mental note of their innovation so we would implement the same when I got back. I was thinking at the time that since we all played for the same team, why were we not sharing the same systems between us?

The intercept's source was referring tediously about his or her holiday "where the Apricots tasted great" in the Soviet Republic of Kyrgyzstan at the Avrora resort on a lake called Issyk Kul. In Russian the country's name loosely means "Land of 40 Girls", which the translator had kindly gone to great lengths to explain, as if the information had any hidden intelligence value. The original writer was communicating a letter to a Chinese man who was known to us in Berne. Two connected sentences simply read, "There's a lot of Gold there too, I understand. The Kyrgyz people earn about thirty Switzerland Francs a month, you know." Then it was followed by a long paragraph about the Soviets using the lake as a testing ground for torpedoes and that uranium was mined for the Russian weapons programme in the Tien Shan. Another footnote explained that it meant the Celestial Mountains. I shook my head and re-examined some lines quickly again trying to pick up on some relevancy as to why I was studying these documents but couldn't fathom the link out…other than the fact Xinhua News Agency also had an active office in Switzerland, where I was stationed, and that the currency in the document had been referenced incorrectly plus a couple more typos.

Finally, I turned my gaze back to the three older blokes all staring across at me and shrugged, trying to prompt a response. The most senior, whitest-haired one who was sitting piggy-in-the-middle of the chubby trio smiled wisely to himself Buddha-like. "Just wanted you to peruse it, that's all, old chap. I did not expect you to figure it out on the spot. It's actually in encrypted numerical harmony. Each letter in all those place names carries a certain coded numerological value. The rest of it is mumbo-jumbo filler material. It's only the words that start with Roman capitals that internally count in this instance. As you may or may not know from your upbringing, the older traditional Chinese believe that in combination with a person's birth date it can affect their astrological destiny."

I did know that and I still wasn't grasping the point – was it another wasted exercise to express superior knowledge? – so I said nothing but appeared outwardly as if I fully understood. No sense in losing face. As a child growing up in Singapore and Hong Kong in the 60's and having visited Red China often with my father I had watched the mainland Chinese ruling class slowly evolve from the communist uniform colours of blue and grey back to the original brighter fare of their predecessors, the Koumintang, the right wing capitalists whom they'd defeated and who had fled to the island of Formosa (Taiwan). *"Falling leaves return to their roots," volunteered my master teacher Liang, the gardener, knowingly back then as I heard his words again.* It applied to the fallibility of both sides. Then his voice intoned again, *"Stop thinking too much, it's okay not to know the answers. They will come to you eventually. Be patient."* Still, I continued to remain silent to the three elderly Brits across from me and their studious observance of myself. Their appreciations had altered a bit and I had a strange feeling some unspoken consensus had been reached upon. Perhaps my file had spoken louder than I had thus far.

He continued: "Now that Chairman Mao is dead the new regime is expanding from the years of isolationism under him. Their stars are supposedly guiding them. As a result of this they are going to deploy 20,000 troops to Albania immediately with many more than that scheduled to join them within a year or so. Do you know what that means? It means that after they've set up shop they're going to branch out quickly, of that I have no doubt. The Chinese are finally going to use their little back door into Europe that's suddenly opened welcomingly wide. We have always known it was going to be a smoking gun. Agreed we should have done something about it before now but we simply didn't. Who would have thought that China would want to invade Europe? They are entering into a neighbourhood encircled by tribalism that they cannot remotely understand either… It'll take them an estimated 70 days to reach their destination."

The aged man realised then he was almost talking aloud to himself, arched over, in a concerned middle distance, because we were all sitting there like mute lambs offering no feedback. So he composed himself momentarily, took a deep breath, coughed then straightened his posture. "Like I said, it's time to act." The old bloke turned to the SAS/SBS liaison and nodded for him to proceed.

"Anderson, the wheels are already in motion," he blurted with authority. Our eyes acknowledged each other for a split second. I knew from past experience that his limited spontaneity was already exhausted and compressed my lips out of embarrassment for him, before he looked away and started to read verbatim from what was in front of him. "You will be assigned three of the best we have. Those we deem who are best suited for the roles we have in mind that is. You will meet them all tomorrow. They're on their way down here as I speak. Also the entire coordinating staff for this undertaking is being placed under the auspices of NATO's SHAPE (North Atlantic Treaty Organisation's Supreme Headquarters Allied Powers Europe). The West Germans are in with four that are in place in the field already from some previous op that just winded down. It looks like the Americans are designating the Israelis to take their place, same quota. And we are trying to enlist the services of the free Yugoslavs, the partisans fighting against communism that are also already actively operational in the area."

When he finished reading he looked into me at last. I still didn't know how to respond to all this startling mass of information. I was suddenly thunderstruck by the enormity of the job at hand and the picture being painted for me. Finally, to bring myself closer to them I said, almost half-absentmindedly, "Assuming the Yugoslavs come in with four faces too, what are we going to do, I mean us and the other groups. Sixteen of us to do what, take on a whole army?"

"Basically, yes, that *is* the general idea," came the reply from the Balkans section chief. It was the first time he'd spoken. I was gob-smacked again into silence. "But furtively so, and before the larger pack of Chinese cards arrive. For now, it'll be our small international group versus some 2,000 that are already in place. We're going to have to super-excite the Chinese to destabilize and abandon the state of Albania by whatever means possible. Have them fall victim to their own fears, if need be, anything and everything that'll count against them to achieve the purpose.

"You will lead up our contingent as you've been to Albania in, what, twice in the past year? An overall leader of the group will be chosen shortly by the American military chiefs in Brussels and you will, in turn, report to that appointed individual. I expect it to be somebody from Israel, mind you. Of course, they have absolutely nothing to do with maintaining peace in Europe under NATO's present political terms and conditions but nevertheless that's the U.S.' thinking, to them they're both one and the same. Everything in the world has to follow the leader, no matter under what banner they label it, and we must obey."

I noticed that he never once looked at me when he spoke, always at some object somewhere high off to my left ear as if an invisible somebody was standing to attention there. I even looked over once, and nobody was there.

Slithering over another sturdy file across the table to me – its slide spun perfectly in front of me that I could read the heading without touching it – the big suited one abruptly stood up then to end the meeting, while the others followed the majesty of the leader by creaking up to a stand too. "That will be all for today. That folder, Anderson, is your companion tonight. You will love it, hate it and digest everything that's in it by tomorrow morning. Think of it as the current lady in your life. You *have* to understand the beauty and the beast of what you will be living with until you kill the monster or it kills you. The other fellows will be here at nine hundred hours tomorrow. Good luck. May God be with you and the other young gentlemen. We shall need all of your utmost fortitudes to slay the dragon."

* * * * * * * * *

The folder was cleared to leave the building with me based on its low security colour code, meaning its contents weren't exactly top secret. I went by tube to my quiet flat in Stanmore in north London that I owned and always kept for my exclusive use, whenever I was home in Britain, which was infrequent at best. I could have rented it out but didn't as I never knew when I may need to stay there. Sitting there on the crowded underground, not reading nor taking in the straphangers, I mulled over the task ahead.

It was the most dystopian nation I had ever had the misfortune to see for myself. Having been to Albania I already knew what it was like: the starving little spotty kid in the village of Europe who lived in the poorest house that everybody beat up at will, and who had never learned to grow up to decide who he really was. Aptly in short: He was a born loser. And for some incredible quirk of personality always bit the hand that fed. The rest of the villagers in his street in Eastern Europe weren't that much brighter either: At this time and age Albanians amazingly still stopped to stare and point at jet planes flying high in the sky. That act of simple-mindedness told any other onlooker a lot about them already. I sighed. Now a wealthy foreign benefactor from Asia had moved in with his own ideas in mind. The impoverished Albanians were going to be the slaves in their own coliseum; the Chinese being the emperors in charge of the lions' gate feeding off them by necessity just to survive another day.

Soon after commencing my night's reading I had got the impression that the text, photographs and maps had been a long time in the making as everything was so neatly put together. It wasn't the usual rushed overnight compilation job where everything was in a jumbled order. I also inexplicably felt that I had always been in mind for this madcap op: the chosen one who could slice through the knot and solve the perceived complicated problem. At least that's how the written words and numbers seemed to talk to me.

The statistics that I didn't know shrieked from the page: A huge jump in arms sales to China had taken place, amounting to US$5.3 billion. Russia accounted for 72%, Israel 17% and the U.S. 11%. What on earth would the Chinese need so much bulk for, I mused, unless they intended to eventually use it?

Albania's official language was Shqiperi and the country's proper name was *Republika e Shqiperise*, which translated to "Land of the Eagle", and I had seen lots of the real ones like specks hovering above the mostly mountainous terrain. Their all-red ensign had a menacing black eagle dead centre, too, but it looked like it had died flying and then stuck to their flag as it fluttered in the wind. Black on red was artistically dark on the eye; some creative white would have made it a bit more attractive. In all of my 26 years of life it had been a staunch communist nation, perhaps the glue that held together its 26 districts, which were known as *rethes*. Religion was banned altogether. Two ethnic groups dominated: the Ghegs to the north and the Tosks in the south. We would primarily be dealing with the mind-set of the Ghegs, the majority. Of the 12 places that could barely be called towns, each of its total inhabitants never exceeded 20,000 since the west tried counting them. It was estimated there were two million *Shqiptarëts* (Albanians) in total in Albania, even though millions of ethnic Albanians where figured to live in the neighbouring countries to its east and north who had escaped to a perceived better life.

Only its biggest metropolis, Tirana, ranked as a real city by western standards. It had well under a half a million people, making it the hub-and-spoke centre of an ancient wooden cartwheel. There were notably low numbers of bicycles and whatever few transport they had were more than used-used-used cars. But they did have an extraordinary high count of donkeys and horses that solved the getting around problem, and an even higher number of concrete bunkers to gaze up at while sitting astride them. Amazingly there were *three quarters of a million* dull grey pillboxes staring back down the hills at them in a country the size of Belgium. They had been constructed by the country's paranoid leader to protect it against a nuclear attack. Ironically he had never thought that all anybody had to do was just walk in the door with some food to own the place…but would it be appreciated was another story.

Politically, from the end of the last world war to 1961, the Soviet Union considered Albania as one of its satellite states but they exasperatedly gave up on them probably for the reasons already explained. Then along came its neighbour to the north, Yugoslavia, and they soon dropped the idea of occupation too. I think both countries realised that Albania simply wasn't worth the effort, basically no return on investment and plenty of headaches. The rusty wrought iron shutters were subsequently left unlocked for China to walk in and as a result they began offering economic and technical assistance to the backs-to-the wall Albanians. To China, Albania *was* worth the trouble and effort ethereally. In return for China's largesse tiny Albania became China's only ally in Europe and it even played a major role in getting China admitted to the United Nations, a family adoption that was to spawn a giant baby in the making. It was not quite a marriage made in heaven but as a little and large couple they tolerated each other despite being almost exact opposites in just about everything one could imagine. It was the improbable kind of liaison that ends in a noisy disturbance of the peace of some sort.

Some bright spark in the SIS research department was thoughtful enough to paste two pages in the file from a recent edition of the Albanian daily newspaper, *Zeri I Popullit* (Voice of the People), with the translations duly alongside them: When Mao had died on 9 September 1976 there was a three-day period of real emotional mourning in Albania, synchronised with a drum-beating corporate-type propaganda piece to demonstrate that China was now Albania's main economic partner. But the western press had concluded none of it was worth a mention so nobody knew. *Not so this young lady compiler in our London office.*

The main player in Mao's absence was now the hardliner Hua Guofeng who pulled the strings. He was the main chap behind all things to do with the crazy idea of economically invading Europe via its poorest country. Two years in charge already.

I also noticed a small ad tucked to the side of the neatly cut-out page that wasn't translated but it clearly diagrammed the important fact that there was a weekly commercial flight from Peking-Beijing into Tirana via Tehran and Bucharest, returning the same way. The first link to a future European air network system, perhaps? And from that central core spanning out to somewhere else, if everything went according to plan…

The whole report could have been a page in the world's history books that inadvertently remained stuck to the page before plus the one following, after recording dramatic changes in Albania's own events. It was absentmindedly flipped over and missed by the historians and readers globally none the wiser for the omission. That is until now. A *sudden large-scale movement of troops and materials half way around to the other side of the planet made a massive political statement to the rest of the world's intelligence communities.* And if you knew anything about the military, since it took a long time to organise a bulk shift of manpower, there had to be a long-term distant goal and with a certain level of permanence in mind. Otherwise logic dictates why even bother to start with such immense plans?

The most telling document of all in the file was the hand-written summary in English from SIS' newly-formed MASINT (measurement and signature intelligence) unit that was rubber-banded around a batch of one-month old photocopies of Bills of Lading in Chinese. It clearly spelt out that ships that had recently left Shanghai en route to various Albanian ports were carrying refrigerated containers with 900,000 kilograms (900 metric tons) of fresh food – mainly of the provisions eaten exclusively by the Chinese military, and not the dishes the locals would bother with. The arithmetic then further showed that if a soldier of medium build of Asian culture ate not more than three-quarters of a pound or about 350 grams a day it meant that they were freighting enough rations for an extraordinarily large number of people for a third of a years' supply. Obviously then many more troops were on the way soon: One big accident already in motion and we were more than aware of it looming large towards us in Europe. And these numbers were only a first trial run that could be repeated.

"He's not planning on opening a Chinese take-out to go in downtown Tirana is he!" I said out loud to myself in summary when I closed the folder. It was the day the earth screamed back at me, "NO!"

* * * * * * * * *

Upon my return to Century House the next morning the head of P4 led me to a different meeting room where three robust lads, all slightly younger-faced than me, were seated. Also sitting in an adjoining cubicle was an obviously retired but very dignified man with much snowier hair than theirs, and considerably less so when he later removed his well-to-do country gentleman cap. No introductions were made. For probably the cost of his train ticket up into London and a free lunch, the elderly bloke then spent an hour chatting while he both reminisced and educated us on his cloak-and-dagger time in Albania during World War II and the years of upheaval afterwards. He had served in the Special Operations Executive, which specialised in sabotage and was the forerunner to the SAS. His foresight into the psychology of Yugoslavs and Albanians was quite helpful and could be summarised in one sentence: *He didn't trust any of them at all.*

"Lots of unnecessary perspiration and necessary inspiration is needed in the Balkans. Like their neighbours, the Albanians seem hell-bent on taking revenge among themselves in tightly-held grievances and you can easily be caught up in the middle of their own mess for the slightest provocation. Their contempt for anybody that isn't from there is earned the old fashioned way, believe you me. In my opinion, Albania might be better off being known as it spells backwards, Ainabla, because they shake their heads for 'yes' and nod for 'no' – that true, I'm serious! Always remember, too, that while we write left to right and the Chinese top to bottom – and the Muslims in the region from right to left – you have to wonder about those few who can write and read in Albanian, whether they do it by some unknown other variation as they burst forth to confront you verbally, always in an agitated manner that our brand of civilisation finds most baffling," was his final mocking quote while shaking his head, which made us all smile in appreciation of his odd sense of humour. When he stood up to depart, we all got up out of respect for him though there was still no shaking of hands. The old fart then rather smartly offered a brief stiff half-salute as he turned on his heels and marched out. The glass door half closed on him as the head of P4 escorted him out.

The best we quartet could do was stand there patiently fidgeting while continuing to glance politely at each other. It was only then that I realised that not only did we all had dark hair but we each had brown eyes as well, with almost the same build and height. I got to learn later that that was purposeful.

I smiled to myself at the delayed observation and looked across at them closer, who each made an effort to acknowledge me with a brief nod or a raised eye movement to the free info emanating from the next room. We were all standing around quietly waiting to be formally introduced, while the goodbyes between the two older men ran its awkward course of civility just outside the half-open door and within earshot of us. We could see their blurred outlines through the bubbly glass panel and hear the "plummy" accented niceties quite clearly. "The SOE office in Baker Street at 64 was much nicer than this place, you know…well I'm off back to my farm in Spain now, much more preferable to Somerset, hey what! Well, good luck with the job, old boy."

It's interesting what one can learn from openings. He, in fact, was a very famous icon in the history of the SIS and I regret now not spending more time talking to him.

"Right then, chaps, sit down," P4 pronounced when he strode back in, "as you can gather that was indeed Colonel David de Crespigny Smiley, who was awarded a military division OBE (Order of the British Empire). Pretty certain le Carré used his name in his stories, nudge." After a brief wink he lost his thread momentarily, then a sense of urgency resumed in him. "Okay where were we. Seeing all of you speak fluent Russian, which government-level Albanians understand, this mission will now be known as Operation SCANDERBEG, after Albania's national hero who led the resistance against the Ottoman Turks in the 1400's…"

It was the start of an equally mind-boggling but ultimately successful field op. But before leaving I went to see some creative people in London's West End. As I was given an unlimited budget I immediately began to use it so I set them a special project.

* * * * * * * * * *

"People sleep peacefully in their beds at night only because rough men stand ready to do violence on their behalf." – George Orwell

For the mission the assembled unit consisted of 16 persons handpicked by SHAPE for Operation SCANDERBEG in Albania. Unbelievably but true the following are the original cryptonyms of the clandestine crew of Israelis, British, West Germans and Yugoslav locals. They were collectively known internally as members of Group IBGY (see later for explanation) working within the framework of said covert operation. The individual codenames assigned to the 12 Israelis, British and West Germans from the task force were laughably based on the signs of the horoscope in the Albanian language while the four local partisans assumed ordinary persons names (I have no idea if they were their real monikers or not). Verbalised abbreviations of specific codes, as is common in covert military missions, are next shown inside quotations marks, along with our nationalities and other relevant details. But this I confess was getting into the realm of the ridiculous, especially for radioed commo, and we were all hard pushed to remember the Albanian names (though not so much the English translation of it or the military codes):

1	AKREPI	(Scorpio)	"Alpha-One"	Israeli	Op Commander
2	BINJAKËT	(Gemini)	"Bravo-Two"	Israeli	No recollection
3	BRICJAPI	(Capricorn)	"Bravo-Three"	Israeli	No recollection
4	DASHI	(Aries)	"Delta-Four"	Israeli	Navy Specialist
1	DEMI	(Taurus)	"Delta-One"	British	Team Leader
2	GAFORJA	(Cancer)	"Golf-Two"	British	Army Intel
3	LUANI	(Leo)	"Lima-Three"	British	SAS
4	PERSHOJA	(Pisces)	"Papa-Four"	British	SBS/Navy Spec
1	PESHQIT	(Sagittarius)	"Papa-One"	W. German	Team Leader
2	SHIGJETARI	(Aquarius)	"Sierra-Two"	W. German	German Army
3	UJORI	(Virgo)	"Uniform-Three"	W. German	Navy Specialist
4	VAJZA	-	"Victor-Four"	W. German	No recollection
1	BASIC	-	"Bravo-One"	Yugoslav	Team Leader
2	MUSIC	-	"Mike-Two"	Yugoslav	No recollection
3	MUSIC	-	"Romeo-Three"	Yugoslav	No recollection
4	TOMÁS	-	"Tango-Four"	Yugoslav	Medical Doctor

Due to the multinational character of the task force perhaps Albanian was reasoned to be a neutral choice by SHAPES's bureaucrats in Brussels. But I couldn't quite fathom why we needed them. For security reasons we never got to know each other's real names, even if the Yugoslavs names were ersatz or not, and nobody could ask either as a matter of strict policy. I was assigned DEMI (my codename in Albanian) but I soon reverted to introducing myself as Taurus. I was our Team Leader, with the obvious corps designation of B. (Israel was Team I, Britain was Team B, West Germany was Team G and Team Y were the Yugoslavs – hence the Group being known as IBGY.) We Brits addressed each other at all times as: "Delta-One", "Golf-Two", "Lima-Three" and "Papa-Four". Here we were an ensemble of four British lads, ranging from 22 to 26, I was one young SIS officer stationed in Switzerland. The second team member was an even younger junior officer in the assessment staff who was in-training at G2, the British Army's intelligence component, and was based in Wolverhampton. The last two were a survival specialist soldier from the SAS' camp in Hereford and an SBS frogman from their base in Poole. Each one of us was selected to represent our country in a serious Olympic-size war game of sorts.

Other than the same hair and eye colour, we were all Englishmen too – no sainted Andrews, Ivors and Patricks present among us – so instead of saying Britain we could actually claim the mission was represented by St George only, meaning just England with no Scots, Welsh and Northern Irish! Soon thereafter, after a joking discussion among ourselves about why they'd always been two England's but we'd reduced it down that we were actually only from the north and not the south. Then later we again nicknamed ourselves as *"grupi muzikor"* – Albanian for "pop group" – as The Beatles from the north of England were quite big at the time. Anyway, silly stuff to indulge ourselves in, to while away the excessive Oprep downtime, but at least we had an early camaraderie going and that was important – the corporate memory if you wish.

Once preparation for this operation was over, three of us flew as Lunn-Poly package tour travellers from Luton into Ljubljana, northern Yugoslavia, on a thundering old Jugoslovenski Aero Transport Boeing 707. I noticed JAT must have purchased it second-hand from Pan Am because its blue logo was burned into the seat in front of me. Whenever a low-budget holiday cover was required for covert ops, the SIS always seemed to use Lunn-Poly, a privately owned travel agent that had retail shops all over Britain's high streets at that time. As the inside legend goes, a senior member of the Lunn family, Peter, had been a top flight SIS intelligence officer during and since World War II. This may explain how that arrangement transpired. I suspect certain priorities were finagled behind the scenes in the name of national security.

We were expected to meet PESHOJA/"Papa-Four" from the SBS there later who would be travelling by sea. For me it was a repeat journey much like an exfiltration from Poland years earlier except our false British passports stated we all had the same family name, which we were in a way. Upon arrival, the tour company bussed some fifty Britons of all ages and sizes down to Pula (sometimes spelt Pola) on the Istrian peninsula and housed us in a newly built modern hotel with all the mods 'n' cons that didn't work. Technically, Yugoslavia was quasi-communist – read that as part-time capitalists – and they permitted us triad of "family members" to rent what could barely be described as a car the next day. We were on a month-long trip, as our visas stated, so naturally we wanted to explore as much of the "Land of the Southern Slavs" as best as we could. The main thoroughfare in the country translated to "Brotherhood and Unity

Motorway", ironically. The name made me smile wryly every time I saw the sign because it was so demonstratively propagandist and it also encompassed what we were up to.

Soon we were huffing and puffing excessive exhaust smoke with the foot all the way down on the accelerator pedal to the floor, chugging along the coastal route heading east-to-south crammed inside a fairly new model Yugo rent-a-car (looked similar to an older Fiat design). It was the size of a large matchbox that decelerated dramatically on inclines, slowing sufficiently enough for us to take in the surrounding 5,000-year culture dotted with 1,000-year old churches. We spent the next night in the town of ancient town of Split. Enough to enjoy a stroll through the age of the Romanesque, the Gothic, the Renaissance, the Baroque, only to return to the Byzantine. We enjoyed the local dishes of *kulen, mlinci, strukle* washed down with *travarica*, respectively paprika-flavoured salami, baked dough soaked in turkey sauce, salty pastry and herb brandy. Having survived our culinary adventure, we were up the next morning bright and early as we continued on our journey.

Yugoslavia itself is full of brown mountains but you could see the even higher alpine snow of Albania slowly looming ahead, taking up the entire windshield. As we neared those perilous peaks none of our professional English northernism of no airs and graces crept forth, as the banter deceased to the seriousness of the task ahead. Psychologically, the awesome sight of rugged Albania portrayed an emotional landscape like a volcano may erupt at any second and crack the glass canvas.

What we did next was hand over our British passports and the car keys to a hippie-looking West German couple. We had "met by design" the night before in the very large dining hall using eye contact and nods only from across the hall, and whom the next morning we had followed behind their small banged-up Opel with warped Munich plates all day long at a reasonable distance. Since I knew we were not returning the same way I presumed that three English-speaking impersonators resembling us would drive the car back and be replacing us on the flight to Britain as well. Nobody from the tour company would likely remember us at all after four weeks anyway or perhaps it was arranged that way via their people in London. A lot of people were involved in this op but due to the compartmented nature of the business we'd never meet.

At the next planned night-stop, the "married" West German "couple" exited their car in front of ours, and close-up they not surprisingly revealed dark hair and brown eyes too. By now I was sure our comrades from Israel,

Yugoslavia and the other West German duo will also be carrying the same genes. Not exactly ingenious thinking, I thought! Well done SHAPE!

If you had asked me, the matted-hair West German pair's codenames were even stranger than ours. I know they're an Aryan nation and I thought it was going a bit far to take on the darkness and image issue but they did both introduce themselves with reasonably straight faces as, "SHIGJETARI and VAJZA but you can call us 'Sierra-Two' and 'Victor-Four', even though we are now five, if you like", followed by a toothy smile and the shrugging utterance of a single word, *"Schlimmbesserung!"* He explained that it meant 'an improvement that makes things worse', a word I have since memorised, but it was a dig at the patent over-planning organised by SHAPE who must have thought it was a kind of chess game out here in the often go-with-the-flow field of action.

Later I was to learn that these two were assigned to Operation SCANDERBEG from BfV (*Bundesamt für Verfassungsschutz*, Federal Office for the Protection of the Constitution, West German counter-intelligence) to monitor the drug smuggling routes that passed through Eastern Europe on the way from Afghanistan, Iran and Turkey to West Germany and further afield thereafter. They had been in the region many times in the past doing similar work. No wonder they looked like bona fide hippies and had an air of anti-establishment mockery about them.

Still by that early evening, the five of us were now collective passengers in a beat-up older-than-old Trabant van of a dubious colour sporting East German licence plates that had emerged overnight to replace the two cars. With appropriate changes to our own presentation 'we went native' by adopting local tradition dress code appearances. The merchandise we had bought in shops along the way. Three of us then crammed in the front and my English pair on the floor rolling around in the uncomfortable back. However, the switch of vehicles told me that unknown teams of unseen others were definitely supporting us out there in the field. *A secure feeling despite knowing there were no safety nets below us out here in the deeper end. There was no turning back now as the point of no return had been crossed*

The dudes from West Germany had also duly transformed themselves at the last lodge to East Germans bohemians complete with Club cigarettes, Radeberger beer bottles and a recent copy of *Neues Deutschland*, the East German communist party daily newspaper. I noticed that the woman even applied her makeup from a Florena cosmetic case, also an East German brand. Both were a model of efficiency. But they had kept their keen sense of humour throughout, when the male half broke the ice by saying in impeccable dry English, after watching her finish fluffing her hair, "My last spouse was a great mistress but a lousy wife!" We all grinned widely at that comment.

We Englishmen now carried the ID's of Yugoslav car employees from the motor manufacturer, *Zavodi Crvena Zastava* (literally it translated to Red Flag Plant) – makers of the Yugo we had before – and we apparently lived in the city where the factory was based, in Kragujevac, which was southeast of Belgrade…though some wit thought Flagged Red Plant*s* was more apt for us!

If asked what East German tourists were doing transporting a bunch of local lads in the middle of nowhere…we were to say that we were hitchhikers and they gave us a lift. Plausible at best I thought because why weren't we driving a model of vehicle the same as the company we supposedly worked for? It didn't make sense and added to our general opinion we were forming about our game planners in corporate Brussels.

Thereon it was to become a long boring trip, mostly in silence. The only other aspect of note was a dry statement by one of my lot from England in the confines of the rear, "Ever notice that most towns around here are placed at the end of the alphabet?" To which the answer came from the German driver in English, "Actually, instead, I was thinking there was a lot of very tall people." "Yeah, I heard that the Yugoslavs are good at basketball…," came a third flat voice from the back. I sat in the front smiling at their astute observations to pass the time. Then it descended back to hush mode. I think the others, like me, were starting to fully grasp the improvised nature of the task that lay ahead of us as those mountains were now completely filling out the picturesque landscape's frame of our van's front window. This was not going to be easy the painting by numbers process but back at NATO Headquarters, SHAPE seemed to be mistakenly fashioning it as a strictly by-the-book op.

Just before crossing the Albanian border, and shortly before dusk, in the Yugoslav town of Podgorica, we were to meet the other couple of Germans near the gates to the industrial sprawl of a factory by the name of Podgorica Aluminium Kombinat. We waited only a few minutes and at the sound of a passing honk we followed a rattling Zastava lorry slowly heaving hundreds of aluminium sheets. As they had come by us, a quick glance up at the pair sitting in the vehicle's cab, plus the driver's wink and thumb up, told me these were self-evidently the absent brace from West Germany: PESHQIT ("Papa-One") and UJORI ("Uniform-Three"). The latter would be working with our "Papa-Four" (our frogman) on matters to do with waterborne operations, whenever they would meet. Their general dark complexion was now duly noted and I sighed to myself. Obviously somebody at NATO was stereotyping the Albanians somewhere. Not all of them looked like us, only most of them did.

As for the aforementioned fake East German and Yugoslav identities, they apparently were concocted in case we were stopped by the authorities after we had crossed unlawfully into Albania. There was no fall back option had we been stopped in Yugoslavia itself. Perhaps our invisible support teams would have solved that issue? Still, once at our destination, we were to say – if asked – that we were all on an "organised hunting holiday and were lost" but could duly verify who we were with our papers. The guns would be presented as proof of our leisurely intentions even if the milspecs (military specification numbers on weaponry) had been appropriately removed. At SIS this was called damage-limitation mode meaning instigating precaution. *If we were not believed, we were authorised to use them as a last resort, naturally.*

Just before nightfall, as we crossed a sturdy wooden bridge over a silent river, we did indeed spot one lone elderly man standing there with a big bore gun and a candlelit lantern on the far side of a remote wooded area who had the spooky look of a lock-keeper cum ghost at a canal. My heart squeezed then pumped again after he curtly waved us through. I had no idea what he was doing out here. I sneaked another look back at him watching us disappear: he appeared abandoned by life out here in the middle of nowhere. The sad forgotten Slav of a man faded into a static dot of light in the evening mist.

We had now entered Albania for the first time, illegally.

* * * * * * * * *

Chapter Five

Soon afterwards we began a steep steady climb through the porous unmanned border as the nocturnal heavy monsoon rain began. I was thinking it would cause the snow still visible from last winter to slush. Having switched positions, I was lying rocking gently in the back of the van and eventually fell asleep to the hammering rhythms.

I awoke slightly disorientated when both movement and downpour seemed to stop simultaneously. As we weren't moving I flung open the back door and tumbled out. In the fog the West German foursome were standing ankle-deep in the expected sludge halfway between our vehicle and another up ahead, and I instinctively thought we were stuck in the mud.

An owl hooted in the distance then, and out of the hazy greyness of the pre-dawn forest loomed eight hooded figures giving me some initial concern until I saw their smiling teeth, as we began to shake hands amicably in the eerie silence. I quickly went to wake up my snoozing duo of Brit *muzikores* (Albanian for musicians) to come and join the welcoming party.

Within a few minutes a large swarthy bulk with a salt and pepper beard made his way over to me and introduced himself in a heavy but perfectly understandable English. This was AKREPI or "Alpha-One", our small international operation's overall commander whom I knew spoke Hebrew, German, English, Serbo-Croat and Russian fluently. Unasked, maybe as a form of introduction, he told me straightaway that he was born in Germany before the last world war, had emigrated to United States and then to Israel. So the boss at P4 in London was right: it was going to be an Israeli team representing the Americans' interests. Certainly he was clearly the oldest person among the internationals and in time I couldn't help but notice that he clearly operated by what we in Britain called ORR (Ocean's Razor Rules mean that a simple explanation is preferred over a complicated one), which I liked.

All hands now present, and as the sun peeked, we were all formally introduced to each other by the towering man, everybody shaking hands 14 times. In all we were twelve men and three women.

The four Yugoslavs, whose names may or may not have been their real ones for all I knew, were initially a dour grim-faced lot. My first impression of "Bravo-One", the partisans' Team Leader, other than the fact she was obviously an attractive woman, not butch at all, somehow told me that she may have been asexual. Sexy she indeed was with her rather romantic long black mane, yet sported a visible distance in her personality. "Romeo-Three", REM, who in introduction genially said his name was "Like in Revolution-Engels-Marx" then laughed it off, was clearly the partisans' oldest individual by a couple of generations. Certainly all were Muslims from the Yugoslav province of Bosnia but could certainly pass as Albanian locals.

In conversation, "Delta-Four" turned out to be a diver from the *Shayetet 13*, which translates to Fleet 13, the élite frogmen unit of the Israeli Navy, who would be working closely with the West German Navy's "Uniform-Three" and the sole missing person at this gathering of covert specialists, "Papa-Four", from Britain's SBS. They were "The Jacques Cousteau Divers" as they soon got to be jokingly known, named after the famous French underwater TV documentary maker of that era.

To a layman the unusual order of cryptonyms in alphabetic order may seem confusing but in most non-uniform clandestine operations involving multinational military personnel code conventions follow similar patterns. Names were to be avoided in case of a situation arising of anybody being compromised, in a worst case scenario. One got used to the impersonal non-conflicting letter-number codes quite quickly. In many such ops involving a large number of covert operatives, assigned cryptonyms were changed often in the interest of security precautions. Thankfully the codes were not changed for this particular job. I, personally, was not sure I would remember mine.

With the sun now up, before we turned ourselves into the ready-made tents where the maggots (our jargon for sleeping bags) were rolled inside. I was certainly ready now for another snooze, when to my surprise, "Alpha-One" summoned the section leaders of "Delta-One" (me), "Papa-One" and

"Bravo-One" for an impromptu meeting. He announced that in the interest of neutrality among those present and due to the fact that we would soon be undertaking reconnaissance among the Albanians that communication among the four of us will be carried at all times and exclusively in Russian, a language in which all present were fluent.

On other matters we were to rotate night watch between our respective groups with everybody manning four strategic guard spots in a circumference around our camp. Day 4 in the cycle would be the Britons turn to prepare food for everybody and of our own choosing – at dinner times only. Criticism of others culinary performances, whether it be verbal or by intoning otherwise was strictly off-limits and that included how badly they cooked the meals!

And lastly hereon we were not going to use the stupid Albanian horoscope names anymore. There was a collective sigh of relief then, thank goodness, but nobody had done so thus far.

When the whiskered Israeli took off his woollen bob to enter his tent he became the first of two persons in our crew that didn't fall into my assumed now "set ethnicity" as he was shaved completely bald. I should add that all the other men had short back and sides as long hair over the collar was forbidden by the Albanian authorities (on the pretence that it was decadently Western) – a key point the SIS and SHAPE had overlooked. The only other visual exception of note was one of the Yugoslavs, "Tango-Four", who had total loss of body hair and suffered from generalised alopecia. We all knew it was this disease because he openly told us so, explaining that it was non-contagious and to not be afraid to report ailments to him in his capacity as the canvas camp's resident physician! An off-the-wall kind chap he certainly was, unconventional at all times. His first assignment was to give each of us Brits and all four of the German 'hippies' a haircut to conform to the rules of our host country, and "to make himself feel at home". One got used to this kind of deadpan stuff after a while. I even replied sarcastically, *"Falemnderit"* (thank you in Albanian) when I viewed his slash job on my head in the mirror provided.

The next day all the "Ones", me included, found ourselves heading down to a spot by Shkodër lake. By now I had already accepted that our designated leader was a ripple-effect kind of guy, even though he had the solemn preaching prose of a rabbi. On the way over he was telling us that he was a *Yehida 269* commander and explained at length what they did for a living. Unit 269 of the Israeli Army often worked behind enemy lines in Arab countries. But make things happen he certainly did and he candidly encouraged others to follow his example. I respected him enormously already. For me the proof was in how he properly used precious time in the correct military perspective by instructing a second party to come like clockwork to this exact same location at some rendezvous in time ahead to replace us. Most field CO's (commanding officers) would not have had the foresight and would have had them all come with us regardless, while tick tock and oomph was wasted. I learnt something from that guy about the management of human energy, and made a mental note of it.

It was early spring and still quite frosty that mid-morning as we danced around the sunbeams filtering through the trees as we were sliding down those slippery steep slopes. A keen observer on the lake's far banks could easily discern movement had we stepped into the many openings in the bright light. The grass scrunched its percussion to our rapid short steps, heartbeats increasing, breaths rising. The foliage wore their camouflage and the bush naturally dyed khaki, making it a perfect hiding place.

At the lakeside edge, from two different locations, we uncovered a small upside down *scafi* (Albanian for a diesel-powered inflatable raft) and a diesel outboard motor, the latter inside a heavy watertight zippered sack that was on a submerged contraption with tiny wheels and duly dragged to shore by a thin very transparent rope, almost invisible to the human eye. It was a masterful invention by "Uniform-Three" who was an NCO (non-commissioned officer) from the West German navy. How this equipment got there I could only guess but I didn't think to ask its conveyance method.

We stood there taking in the scene. The town of Shkodra could be seen on the horizon to our left, while the Drin river estuary was closer to us on our right. The others members of the group eventually made their way down to the lakeside during this time. I think he deliberately planned 10 minutes of bonding between each country's designated team leader. He was smart that guy, "Alpha-One". Maybe he wanted to quickly assess us, too, get a first impression.

On the other side of the large lake was an equally hilly and unpopulated sparse peninsula belonging to Yugoslavia but only 15 miles across on the other side of it from the designated point of access, as the crow flies, was the open Adriatic Sea that led to the Mediterranean. A very unusual sleight of topography indeed, so we were going back into Yugoslavia again, albeit temporarily. As planned, during the previous night a British submarine had dropped a team of SBS logistical specialists and in doing so had delivered my missing man "Papa-Four" and his special cargo to shore. It had sailed the previous week from the British Army's own UK supply port of Marchwood, near Southampton. Having completed its mission, the unit then headed back to ship and out to sea to await further developments. "Papa Four" was left overnight alone on the deserted shore to guard the precious cargo. This landing manoeuvre served as a "dry run" exercise for the disengagement operation as it was also going to be our way out at the end of this NOC operation.

That whole day solid was spent on ferrying the materials and provisions backward and forward utilising the miniaturised four-wheel drive tractor-cart that would eventually find itself useful up on the Albanian side of the mountains later on. And especially so on "Avenida de Porridge", which was the aptly nicknamed sticky mud stretch leading to our hilltop grey canvas garrison (so named with a smile in neutral Spanish).

Though I was seconded to the SIS I was still an officer of the Royal Navy (before joining the SIS, I had been a helicopter pilot in its Fleet Air Arm) and the reason I was part of this sea-related segment, involving our three experienced "water-based" specialists, was to be in charge of *the most fragile* of all the boxes coming ashore. This box contained two long-ish contraptions made of titanium telescopic tubing, each on a collapsible pipe-like structure and a glass-like mini-gyroscope ball atop. I was solely responsible for strategically planting one of these devices at the highest pinnacle on this very bottom of Yugoslavian land this very same day.

Upon accepting the crate made of hard waterproof plastic and carefully removing one of the units, I then prepared myself to leave the others to proceed with their mundane tasks. For my part I was going to climb and walk up to my destination with my precious contraption. There was a good reason after all for NATO/SHAPE in selecting this particular desolate landing zone. Even this chore didn't seem at all normalised – nothing on this entire trip was standard procedure – but I was following the pre-set orders (memorised during Oprep). Just as I set off somebody said to watch out for lynx and small bears that roamed the area but I didn't know if that was a joke or not. Off I went alone into the wilderness with no map but guided with directional sense in my head. And I had to come back the same way hopefully.

I spent the rest of that exhausting day just to carry out this seemingly simple installation. At the apex I could see the line of the boot of Italy south-westwards over the Strait of Otranto quite clearly with faint white specks of sails, like seagulls in the reversed sky. Standing there alone on the peak I felt like I was watching a fleet of Argonauts and Roman galleys in the distance.

I knew I would be the last to make the return zigzagging trip back over the landlocked water to Albania again. I eventually got back down and watched the sun set in silence with an equally tired Israeli "Delta-Four". Like Noah of biblical fame, he had manned the baby ark on its several returns across the lake but taking different routes each time. In the meantime, the second crew of this land-waterborne-land operation had duly shipped all the merchandise in the third leg up to home base, including my box marked "Fragile" that contained the single remaining gyroscopic apparatus.

As an aside, during that first evening's meal prepared by the Yugoslavs, after hostess "Bravo-One" had bent over to serve food into my canister, it dawned on me why I had thought about her being of a different sexual orientation. Her features were porcelain beautiful from afar but a shift of light close up to her face told me she/he was androgynous. Either that or she was a man in man's clothing complete with the ravishing feminine raven curls! I noticed too that "Lima- Three", in my team, seemed to be shyly attracted to him/her but I hadn't the heart to tell him what I thought and would let him find out on his own. But it did become something quirkily farcical to occupy my overworked mind in the plentiful down times that would come as I watched events unfold between them, as a muted pastime!

In another note of interest, whenever the Yugoslavs served the coffee on their cooking shift they unusually never failed to offer us all a Yugoslav-made brand of cigarette called Drina from a distinctive red packaging at the same time. It was always declined every time, yet they continued to still persist on every occasion. I put it down to either some custom of theirs or their growing understanding of how capitalism worked...

Consequently, the droll did arrive quite quickly when it was the British contingent's turn for night sentry work. Keeping awake naturally was always going to be a problem but the unnerving wails of nature's companions out there were memorable and served as alarm clocks. Those grey wolves' howls always jolted me upright every time I heard them because they sounded like the pack were encircling us and were only a stone's throw away. Sentry duty was also a tedious solitude staring at clouds trying not to let it blur. When the vapour finally did clear it would suddenly stop at eye level whereupon the ceiling was almost on the ground and, thus, it became easy for the imagination to get into overtime on the beautiful cinematography in front of us.

All the others also duly certified our country's reputation for blandness at the international food fare, I'm sorry to say. While they were not permitted to verbalise their opinion, the faces of our other comrades said it all. They probably did not understand that Welsh rarebit contained absolutely no rabbit meat whatsoever. Since there was plenty of evidence of rabbits living in the surrounding landscape, I determined what our next offering of food was going to be. But our dessert of powder-packet cream caramel went down much better, thank goodness. Otherwise we may have been lynched without a shot fired.

As I was tasked with placing the all-important remaining "gyro stick" I had to do it at a geographical spot of my choosing, so long as it was approximately within 20 miles radius and north or west of Tirana – several days of a trip away from where we were. So "Alpha-One" designated a team of four escorts to spend a week away from the camp on a pathfinder trip with me that would also double as a strategic limited surveillance op: Capricorn, Leo, Sagittarius and Music were thus dispatched with me. We were four men and a woman.

"Mike-Two" (Music) knew the route quite well, apparently having done it many times before, or as my "Lima-Three" jokingly put it aside to me in his cheeky monkey British humour, "I would guess he did it exactly 33 and a third Yugoslav revolutions before!" Undeniably the poor attempts at humour were weakening and would eventually dry up as concentration on the real exploits began.

I purposefully tried not to overly smile in "Mike-Two"'s company as he seemed a serious "unthoughtful" chap who spent his off hours air guitar-ing to pre-recorded heavy metal tapes on his headphones, which "Alpha-One" and he swapped almost daily. A big lad with hair fortunately left a wee bit longer than the rest of us, upon his own request at the last haircut time. On the rare occasions when he actually spoke in his own tongue, his language bordered on the deliberate and in-your-face brazen. I soon coined him "Head Banger", a music-related nickname that stuck with him. We used it when we got tired of using our codenames.

Riding in the back of a hay cart on bumpy roads towed by a sturdy donkey named Hekuran – I believe it stood locally for Hercules because of his four pillar-like legs – for the next few days was not fun at all. I had already decided that we were going to have to pinch some bicycles for the return journey. All of us suitably appeared as craggy labourers with unshaved faces, adorning *plis* (traditional white wool caps) and vests over worn torn T-shirts made of rough-like uncombed Yugoslav cotton with unkempt baggy cotton trousers of the kind Albanians preferred. Even "Sierra-Two", a masculine female and an army commando, could have been mistaken for a clean-shaven man, especially the way she naturally swaggered in her walk.

It was determined that none of us would carry arms. It was too dangerous to be caught with weaponry as it was too much to have to answer for. To compensate for this, we each had our own long knife and a box cutter – both manufactured in Eastern Europe – hidden in our wherewithal, including all manners of other usable instruments hidden in a concealed compartment such as three varieties of wooden truncheons, two good workmen's hammers and a single communist-made knuckle-duster. If only we had a construction industry air-powered nail gun I would have been satisfied but that signalled an island of wealth in the sea of poverty we sailed through, even though it was a country where it was notoriously possible to get away with anything illegal.

Coming down the hillsides we passed the military airfield that had a secret mountain cave as a hangar. Without having binoculars handy we observed a squadron of Shenyang J-6 fighters landing (about a dozen aircraft), which are Russian MiG-19's built in China. NATO codenamed them Farmers. Easy to identify even at distance as their round open noses resembled whale shark mouths' feeding on plankton. There was no way they could have flown over 5,300 miles nonstop from there to here so refuelling several times was a must. The sight of them clearly signified other intentions in the works.

Eventually on the main roads, if dirt tracks could be called that, the Chinese presence was clearly everywhere. All the freshly-installed clocks in the ancient village squares as well as on, what could be best described as local town halls with their doors always shuttered, featured Chinese characters and showed a time that *wasn't what it was where we were.* I was to later learn that it was the actual time in Beijing – 17 hours difference. So as a result of this edict government offices opened in early morning darkness and closed when daylight arrived, in accordance with this amazing shake-your-head bureaucratic stupidity. Though the times on them were always deemed correct, the seconds' hands never functioned at all as if they malfunctioned on purpose in some attempt to make local life move even slower than it was.

Of the few factories we passed it seemed that wire making was the main choice of manufacture. Chimney-smoking plants where old imported piles of automobile batteries were recycled into gunpowder seemed the next popular choice of production.

As we slowly clipped-clopped by I had enough time to translate some of the official slogans painted red on banners in pictograms (drawn Chinese characters). *"Rely on the working class wholeheartedly!"* stated one loudly. Screamed another, *"Long live Mao Zedong thought!"* Plenty of portraits of the recently deceased chairman were hanging from walls, many already torn from weather-related wear. I noticed too that the prominent wart on his chin had mysteriously and artistically disappeared on all of them, airbrushed out like it seemed Albania was planned to be. No images of his replacement Hua were spotted anywhere. We doubted the locals could understand the many adages because few could read in their own language, never mind speak in a foreign one. Granted, imagining what the depictions meant was well within the realm of possibilities for the average Albanian. Neither did we detect any resentment of anything Chinese by Albanians, nor welcoming for that matter. It just seemed a disconcerting docility towards indoctrination, a zombie-like acceptance. At least out here in the countryside.

Lorry loads of troops of disinterested yellow men rumbled by us now at regular dusty intervals, announcing their increased presence in this country and confirming the reason why we were there in the first place. *It was quite a back-tingling surreal sight to witness with the submissiveness being a backdrop.* Thankfully they had no reason to set up roadblocks yet and didn't as they probably thought they already had the Albanian people safely locked inside a psychological bubble of sorts within their own land.

As our first night's stop was right out in the big sky off the main north to south thoroughfare, we took great pains to have Hek protected, as hauntingly harmonic howls could again be heard close by at dusk. We naturally didn't want the animal to fall prey or even ourselves for that matter, so each one of us spent a couple of hours awake and sitting next to the poor scared fellow, who could probably smell the gnashing hungriness downwind. It's an especially weird feeling knowing killer eyes are watching your every move as potential food as you sit wrapped in a blanket stoking the fire, so you could understand how he felt as a potential next meal too. Whenever I shone the torch behind me into the darkness some dozen beady "glistening marbles" rotated positions less than 50 yards away. I wished then we had dog urine available to smear on ourselves as it would have removed the human scent to those peckish wolves. When dawn came the wild chorus had faded but the cacophony of sounds remains vivid in the memory's audio track. I had spent most of my designated awake time assigned to that poor creature with my back to the aforementioned emaciated others, as I knew any lead attacker would come hushed and stealthily quick from upwind where our collective smells weren't betrayed as its next meal.

Nevertheless, in the daylight hours we continued on our slow crawl to the capital – Hek had his animal blinkers on so I'm sure he must've slept as he walked. We took turns sleeping each night in the open air on our travelling haystack and washing in the mornings in the many streams cascading down from the surrounding hills. When going to the john for a big one we took care to hide our inexpensive Yugoslav toilet paper roll as that would signal another oddity among the peasants, who were presumably used to a more manual means of cleanliness, like large leafs and clumps of grass.

Right after cleaning our teeth, "Bravo-Three" daily circulated a small can courtesy of the Israeli Army and inscribed in Arabic print, it contained an orangey paste with no flavour, which we would smear on our teeth to cover the western whiteness to make us out to be the dentist-attending we were and tobacco smokers we weren't. But we each kept a dark green packet of cheap but considered exclusive Drava cigarettes, made by Albanians in the Yugoslav province of Kosovo (where Albanians were in the majority), ready to offer others, if need be. Additionally, all present knew better than to walk like we were once in the military and we had to make do with no deodorant, allowing ourselves to display our sweaty armpits just like other Albanian workers did…and, boy, did some of them have BO big time that the eyes watered!

For our breakfast, barley and chicory mixed passed for coffee though closer to the instant kind rather than the percolated variety. One evening, within full view of camped gypsy caravans, just to really integrate ourselves and show that we were poor simple folk not worth robbing, we took the trouble of preparing grass boiled in stream water that tasted like weak green tea. To onlookers that outnumbered us out there it rendered the impression that while we had something to drink we weren't worthy of the free other helpings they may have craved from us, so they left us alone.

In a country that had no birth registers and never kept a record of anything, we had to have an oral history ready and not a written one. If anybody was to speak to us we were to let "Mike-Two" respond first as he spoke the local lingo. If that did not suffice, it was acceptable to launch into pidgin Russian as it was most educated Albanians second language, even though we were not supposed to be that schooled ourselves being Yugoslav workers. Failing that, as mentioned earlier, if the speaker intuitively appeared to be not satisfied and if the situation allowed for it, we were to manually eliminate that person or persons. Fortunately, on this journey it never even came remotely close to that.

We were getting closer to Tirana now. The numbers on the road had visibly multiplied. We passed a dilapidated sign to the international commercial airport. The junction was heavily guarded by both a Chinese and an Albanian Army unit on a joint exercise – it looked shambolic with the little Chinese well turned out and the goliath Albanians sloppy at best and smoking on the job. What that sign didn't say that conjoined to it was Rinas, the country's largest air station, the main centre of Chinese military operations presumably in conjunction with the armed forces of Albania, which were puny by comparison. We naturally made a note of the logistics there and ways to bypass it.

In doing this kind of work you have to see what the eyes don't see, I suppose a genus of premonition. Once we were on the fringe of Tirana it was as if I was staring through spyglasses that I focused on an object that became overly magnified. All of a sudden I saw exactly where I wanted to position the gyroscopic stand even though I wasn't in the mode yet to search for it, it presented itself to me.

The first one that I had positioned at the pinnacle in the very last mile inside Yugoslavia under a week ago and this very last stick of magnet were the sole two guidance devices used for the whole op. *In the event our Chinese "invaders" were not persuaded to leave our continent by the means we were going to present to them soon, then the "markers" would lead twin untraceable American rockets fired thousands of miles away from the eastern shores of the Atlantic to Albania. Upon homing on the guidance device, the rockets would then obliterate the secret covered airport and its main centre of military communications and operations.* This was at a time when satellites could not yet properly gauge an exact grid zone and guided missiles were still at an early stage of computerisation.

The ubiquitous grey bunker was right there silently staring at me near the top of the surrounding brown elevation. In truth I was aiming a little higher up the political ladder. It was a decrepit mansion on the edge of a tired town set on an incline of a hill.

The designated spot to place the device was the top floor of the dilapidated presidential palace of Albania's dictator Enver Hoxha. I noticed that the flagless flagpole was broken and in dire need of fixing. I had found the downwards extension and perfect hiding place for my guiding instrument. *What better place to symbolically locate a replacement Albanian pennon on top of it?* I beamed for the first time in a long time.

* * * * * * * * * *

The most extraordinary coincidences work out for us when we dare to delve deeper into the unknown. It gives us each access to an understanding that previously was not thinkable. Footholds start to appear where there were none. This story of ours continued unfolding…

Throughout the slow four-heel ride on our donkey-pulled cart, as we hoofed it to the capital of Albania in order to undertake this forward reconnaissance, I had plenty of time to ponder our conundrum. We were a FHT (field humint team) of 16 albeit with abundant resources facing a force of 2,000 troops, an estimated 500 "specialists" (business development advisors) in-country from China and a modest contingent of Albanian forces however small they were. On top of that, troops numbering 20,000 were reportedly on their way. By any measure it was a formidable task to get the Chinese out of Europe, and quickly. We were tasked with the role of being magicians.

We had been away nearly a fortnight already and the first Chinese ships would be here in approximately two months. It took roughly 10 weeks to sail the 13,800-odd miles from any of the major terminals in China to Albania via the Cape of Good Hope, South Africa. It was possible that the earliest arrivals could come in half that time via Egypt's Suez Canal. In the open sea it was harder to prevent but the downside for the Chinese, if they used the latter way through, was that the policing authorities could spot a vessel with a red flag with five golden stars easily enough and apprehend them for any reasons they chose. It was also possible a percentage of the cargo was shipped under some other flags of convenience from ports elsewhere that weren't monitored by SHAPE. We had to be prepared for anything.

Being privy to the various game plans made me prioritise each task into a logical order of sub-tasks. Due to the semi-compartmented nature of our work I wasn't completely conversant with the details of what exactly the navy boys were doing as I was so busy on my own land-based strategies.

Placement of the rocket guidance devices was really intended to serve as a fall-back option in the event all else had failed. It was the worst case scenario with the resulting collateral damage unimaginable and the prospect of untold innocent casualties too awful to contemplate.

The various sizes of aluminium sheets we had were for the least life-threatening concept and involved reflection of light for maximum exposure. It was wacky enough to work. If a bouncing bomb could reach an impregnable dam then so could this right out-of-leftfield idea. We were still developing the concept.

In precise military intelligence terms I personally preferred not to prosecute an assault (attack) during this exploitation (searched for objective) while debottlenecking (solving a problem). We were racing against time and instead of persisting with the drip-feed of paralysis by analysis there was no better way than this feet on the ground exercise to get a feel for things.

We three men ventured into the centre of Tirana soon after dusk to check out the minefield – do some surveillance – leaving a woman and the donkey to keep each other company at a safe well-populated camp site on the edge of town. Hungry four-legged predators from the mountains didn't hang around near big towns but those like us with two legs did.

Strangely otherworldly at the coalface itself the city was void of inhabitants as if a blackout had been enforced ahead of schedule. However, plenty of starving dogs and cats could be seen noisily scavenging the waste. We finally saw a semblance of humankind riding a pair of bicycles hastening across the main square, their shadows swallowed into the dark tunnel of the street at the far side.

Albanians didn't have the luxury of lights and red flashing brakes on their bikes, never mind donning useless safety items such as coloured helmets and fluorescent jackets. Hand signals didn't occur much in acknowledgement or gratitude, they just pedalled wherever they wished with no bells and whistles operating in a basic outdoors survival mode, occasionally cursing at whoever crossed their path. No right of way existed, it was every one-track mind for himself, no courtesies evident whatsoever while living completely in the moment. The same rules applied to carts and the few vehicles on the road; head-on, sideways, across you, on top of you, a weaving slow motion snarling mess when en masse during the day. The rule of law in any form did not exist. Yet despite the antagonism perplexingly it was the opposite of a revolution in progress, all done in an unsmiling depressed-style, to a dejecting soundtrack – no glittery-adorned heavy metal Western city high street this. Did they not care that another alien nation was taking over theirs? You had to be blind not to notice. Albania was functioning in a desensitised-mode.

What also probably dampened enthusiasm on the surface was that the Chinese civilian authorities had implemented *waiwen* (stability maintenance) by giving mindless unemployed youths with large builds an officious armband to wear in order to enforce long held Oriental superstitions and taboos. The task of patrolling the streets of Tirana during curfew hours from midnight to dawn fell on this giant riff-raff who then had the power to accuse innocents of any real or imagined transgression, and they did. Tobacco was the currency among the Chinese so that's what they paid the Albanian big boys with. They were all too happy to accept the cigarettes so they could trade them later for cash.

History had so much proof where that led to eventually. It was anarchy implemented from the bottom up. The briefing document I'd perused on the waiwen stated that the puzzling edict had been initially issued to enforce a ban on outdoor drying of laundry during nocturnal hours. The Chinese felt the wandering spirits would soak negative yin energy into the wet clothes at night. The waiwen were duly tasked to destroy any damp clothes left out hanging at nightfall. The thugs went to extraordinary measures to carry out the order. They even broke down doors and rampaged over fences to pour paraffin over the offending garments and set them on fire, even while still on clotheslines.

In another grotesque example of lawlessness older inebriates making their way home in the afterhours were forced by these bullying goons to urinate on the spot where they were cornered. In sniggering fashion, they first made them seek permission from the land gods by extending their palms aimlessly to the sky and praying futilely to these deities. The poor souls were only allowed to take a piss when the hoodlums decided that permission was duly granted. For good measure the thugs gave drunkards that didn't obey a beating and sometimes would pee on the prone bodies afterwards.

And matters got worse as one can imagine when they got drunk with their own power. The prohibition of sex by Albanians on the 1st and 15th days of the lunar Chinese calendar (to coincide with the new and full moon) was another madly senseless perversion. These dates were intended to be practiced as days of sacrifice but instead resulted in some rumoured rape and sodomy by a few of the waiwen as their enforcing of the dates got mixed up with the European calendar and what sexual preference entailed, likely also fuelled by alcohol.

Once out and about stealthily after midnight you got a clear sense that these incredibly stupid diktats actually provoked individual locals to respond in anger but they collectively managed to keep it in check. You'd think there's only so much pushing anyone around that one can take. To the outsider it was a self-inflicted destructive programme of control to get the populace of Tirana to simmer and boil beneath the surface. We would try to exploit that, no doubt. A tinderbox ready to light its fuse when it was time but a lot depended on the Albanian mind set. What the Chinese had psychologically already put into motion was a move towards dependency on the invader that would spiral into total control. Once blind obedience was established domination would follow, a process never to be reversed. Coupled with relentless propaganda the Albanian people would struggle to read the tea leaves and would eventually become powerless. The last nail in the coffin would be the introduction of the Chinese class structure system for life, *hukou* (forced household registration). It tied the person to where they were born forever. True communism, no freedom of movement, exploitation at its worst and in Albania's case while also being hungry a lot.

The last line of George Orwell's "Animal Farm" said it best about this situation, "The farm is taken over by the pigs as a one-species dictatorship"…

Keeping a purposeful low profile, we eventually roamed in the direction of the twin disappearing act on bikes at that large deserted square. As we neared the corner we heard the unmistakable echo of a cinema soundtrack filtering down the alley way. Walking towards the din the spoken words interspersed with much laughter slowly invaded the consciousness. They were not in Albanian, Yugoslavian, Russian, Greek or Chinese – but in London-English! Then loud laughter followed. We all glanced at each other quizzically at the bizarre atmosphere. Coming down the short stone-paved corridor towards the flickering magnet that lured us, a large park with an outdoor full wide screen came into view.

On the huge screen a British comedian called Norman Wisdom was appearing in a black and white film and doing his version of Charlie Chaplin and Benny Hill. He was being watched by teeming thousands in the cavernous free open air theatre! A single light bulb of a man with a sideways cloth cap on was radiating sunshine onto the grinning faces of a people who had nothing to smile about in real life. The grainy and obviously bootlegged picture was coming to an end soon and the audience roared roundly not for the first time at his slapstick humour all the way to the end. Then the credits began while everybody piled out happily, the young and old, men and women together, while I stood there reading the credits: Produced by the UK's Rank Organisation in 1953, the bootlegged movie was *Trouble In Store*.

In all my stories I have to say this little crazy episode took the Oscar. It was totally unexpected and beyond unreal. I even saw a young man exiting wearing a Brighton & Hove Albion blue and white scarf with "Seagulls" on it, which I was to learn upon return to Britain was Norman Wisdom's favourite football club in England! It turned out that the comic was Albania's most famous celebrity and I wondered why that startling fact was not mentioned in our SIS pre-brief during Oprep.

A good link came out being there though. The projectionist struck up a conversation with "Mike-Two". While he was momentarily distracted with some chore to do with his ancient machinery I instructed my man to get his contact details. He duly obliged and gave us all we needed to find him. And with that information in hand off we went.

If you are a quasi-Buddhist atheist floating around in an obscure agnostic land with Muslim roots, amid Christian-dominated Europe with Orthodoxy as neighbours, with the godless enemy being who they were, you paid attention to stupid little thing like what the name of a British movie is to help give you a sense of cogency. Because there was very little else to go on. Not a lot made sense out here so one instinctively listened to the nonsensical message sometimes.

And so I did...and ironically I had already set in motion a scheme that fitted this local scenario.

* * * * * * * * *

The leader of Albania, Enver Hoxha – whose pink skin in some ways resembled that of a pig's – liked to hand out free copies of his thick autobiographical books to his people who had an illiteracy rate of 85%. It explained to me the situation on the ground here: useless promotion while he served his darling citizen lambs with triviality who when accepting it thought it would be great to use in the fire stoves when the wood got too damp. He often went on self-idolising local jaunts with his small entourage in tow in a high profile procession consisting of three recently gifted brand new motorised rickshaws (tuk-tuks) from China. There was something chilling about this clown that reminded me of both the fable of the Emperor's new clothes and George Orwell's fairy tale – *"In January food fell short... ...Starvation seemed to stare them in the face"* – and he's parading around like *he's a bestselling author without a care in the world about where his next meal is coming from.*

That was when we took the opportunity to fix that flag pole. At the gate of the rose-coloured granite baroque-style palace Chinese soldiers were standing on guard instead of Albanian nationals. There was an expression at SIS called "Mandarinese" loosely meaning meandering words spoken by the UK's ruling class mandarins that don't arrive at the point. On that day it came in handy when speaking to real men from China. By a combination of deliberate confusion and our purity of conviction, the Chinese guards let us in rather than question us further. Our work activities were in full view of them throughout our stay on the grounds. I thought it was going to be difficult but it became the easiest task of the entire operation – to plant the last guidance stick in place of a broken flag pole with no flag on the roof. The Chinese seemed entirely uninterested in what we were doing. It took us 20 minutes from start to finish. On the way out down the gravel driveway we even offered them some of our home-made spicy nettle chowder made from the land that we'd brought to snack on but they politely declined.

* * * * * * * * *

We went back to our burlap palace mountain hideout the same way we came. We'd grown fond of Hek and didn't want to leave him there even though bicycles aplenty were there for the taking. The approximately 150 kilometres return trip was a week away altogether and lots of what *not* to do was learned, and then some. Instead of riding the bikes we stole, we shipped them home in our wooden cart on wheels for future use. They were all basic models made in China no less. When I said straight-faced that we needed to look for a tandem bicycle for Hek's use "Mike-Two" responded, "Why? He's an animal!" Still it made everybody else laugh. So different are cultures and our ironies and puns.

In my absence a courier had delivered the bulky goods from London's West End that included a modern mini-projector that ran on batteries plus a rolled mini-screen. Whether it came by road or dropped from the sky or via submarine or slingshot I would never know. As I was preparing to view the contents and integrate all the brainstorming parts into an actionable functioning tactical framework (or "mapping the heat" somebody once quipped), I was looking into my cup of tea when I saw the whirlpool ripple effect in it. It was an aftershock of an earthquake that we must have been on the fringes of because nobody actually felt it. Ten days later we felt a more powerful tremor as the ground below shook. Of course, seismic activity can never be predicted precisely but requests for more information showed that Albania had its fair share of quakes and solar eclipses over the years. We decided then to manufacture a synthetic "natural planetary cause" of our own combining the use of the recently delivered animation on celluloid and reflecting it off the aluminium sheets placed strategically where the Chinese troops could see it.

London and Manchester in the UK at the time had a powerful children's animation industry. When I'd gone to see them before leaving Britain I'd asked for archived material that could be edited quickly into various programmable lengths. Using China specific bad luck symbols I asked for a pair of talking crows in a tree or rooftop dubbed into Mandarin and Cantonese to squawk "to not meet anyone that day" and "to cancel all appointments immediately" and "to go home now". *Crows were the ultimate bringers of bad news to the Chinese.*

I also wanted them to create a short silent scene using Chinese actors based in the west. Whereupon they would be dressed in Chinese military uniforms, napping on beds with a mirror facing it with the science fiction image of their sleeping selves then drifting into the mirror itself and remaining trapped screaming and unheard in the in-between world between unconsciousness and wakefulness. It would be interspersed with dreamlike scenes of Albanians loading bodies that were still alive onto ox-drawn carts by the hundreds. Actually one was used in a studio that was replicated from different angles – for unknown disposal with Caucasian women throwing red flowers on the bodies and hologram ghosts spiriting away their souls. *To have a mirror facing the bed while one slept was taboo in China.*

I stressed the importance of repeating the number four as much as possible and in quadruple image form as well. It sounds like death in the Chinese language (both pronounced "si"). It's like our 13, unlucky for some of us; *but four was bad for all of them.*

Last but not least to find a male Oriental actor made-up to look like Hua Guofeng. They cleverly superimposed his face in the end but I needed the filmmakers to especially pan slowly down to his legs under the table where he was sitting that showed them shaking them in an irritating way. As there was no word in English for this annoying table-vibrating habit I coined it "gnitatirri", which was irritating backwards. *The Chinese believed it was kicking away all their hard-gained prosperity.*

When the noise around the footage reached a crescendo the gods would be heard but not seen screeching "annihilate" repeatedly – *"Jian! Jian! Jian!"*

I saw their filmed presentations alone before inviting others in to view it. We were all satisfied with the short production of durations varying from two minutes minimum to a maximum five minutes on a loop. It could work and we'd give it a go.

Through teamwork we'd implemented an extremely effective phantom deception and disinformation programme about the Chinese doomsday on the very same day of them learning about it. By screening bad luck as a strategy of propaganda, knowing that the majority of the troops were simple peasant men from the countryside, the message was: It was preferable for them to depart Albania immediately. We'd tie it in with a fake earthquake using pyrotechnics and earth shattering explosions. Army Day, Tuesday, 1 August 1978 (on the Gregorian calendar) was the day of release. Chinese servicemen would be allowed half a day off that day. We would undermine their morale by organising a farewell party thrown by the spirits who were angry at their imposition in a continent far away from their own.

Vigilia Pretium Liberatis
The Price of Freedom Is Vigilance

From that point onwards the "firework plan" involved not only pyro technicians and lighting experts faraway in Britain but German chemists, American computer scientists, electric engineers, parapsychologists and physicists from everywhere but without them knowing what was actually doing down and where and when. Its organisation was major pre-production that had to work.

* * * * * * * * *

"Alpha-One" informed me that an unspecified fleet of navies were doing their utmost to delay the advancement by sea of the large convoy of Chinese troop carriers and merchant vessels. It ranged from faking pirate raids to fishing trawlers accidentally on purpose being broadsided to false bad weather transmission and intercepting radio programmes with gloomy disinformation about their final destination in Eastern Europe. The main fleet was sailing around South Africa at the time apparently. The passage through the Straits of Gibraltar from the Atlantic Ocean into the Mediterranean Sea would face an embargo of "select" ships and would be boarded by armed customs officers assisted by special forces from unknown nations not wearing identifiable uniforms linking them to any particular country. They would seek illegal contraband as well as plant evidence of drugs that the sniffer dogs would "find". Everything within their power was being put into motion to deter the Chinese reaching Albania.

Our trio of water-based lads already in-country were apparently busy checking out the two deep water ports: Durrës on the mainland that was close to Tirana and the southern isle of Sazanit, which was near Vlorë, with the view to mining the deeper channels to the harbour, if the situation required so. Shallower channels are already getting blocked by sunken old boats, which would funnel all vessels into fewer choices. Apparently some seagoing passers-by enquired what was going on and they were told that they were under government orders to create coral reefs…without saying which government.

Any merchant ships making it through the net or through the Red Sea-Egyptian route would likely dock at the northern location. While the troop carrying vessels and their armed escorts would probably moor off the island in the south, which was strategic to halting any traffic entering the Adriatic Sea through the narrow Straits of Otranto that separated Italy and Albania.

Some communications had been intercepted that there would be an increase in alternative air transport because of the unsurmountable problems being faced at sea. *They had to know it wasn't a coincidence surely?* We didn't know what that would entail but it would not be beyond SHAPE to resolve to shooting them out of the sky by scrambled fighters on the pretext it was an invasion of European airspace. There was some truth to that irony based on the Chinese actions already in place on the ground and at sea. Some sovereign law was interpreted to mean a country's territory extended as far up over it as possible. It was getting serious with the world community none the wiser to the threat Europe was facing from Asia.

The last two pole-looking identical instruments made of a special all-weather enduring alloy that I had set up both contained a unique compass navigation system. Dual SLBMs (submarine launched ballistic missiles) simultaneously fired from separate nuclear submarines' orbital flight path could be accurately guided from the deep north of the Madeira Islands over the Mediterranean Sea in order to avoid Europe's densely populated areas, steering them towards its land based Albanian twin central military targets. Arcing downwards at a speed of Mach 23 the guidance markers' gyroscopic sensor served as a final direction finder and would trigger the rockets' own internal automatic warning to unleash its deadly payload within a fraction of a second of swooshing over them at 15,000 miles an hour (24,100 km/h). The warheads denotation mechanisms would be primed to explode in air burst form, which would cause wide maximum damage. The first would be aimed at the air station that had a mammoth cave – actually fixed to enter it and impact inside the cavern – while the second was pointed at the conning tower at the main military airport that housed the majority of Chinese troops. God only knows what the outcome would be…this commented by an atheist but the death toll would be uncountable while not accountable. We would try our damnable best to convince them to leave before resorting to annihilating them altogether along with untold civilian casualties. All this destruction achieved in the blink of an eye.

Despite my supreme fitness level whenever I thought about it I had heart palpitations. What a huge responsibility it was.

And when would we know if we had failed? It was when the electricity and water supply was cut. We'd know it was the pre-attack warning signal and we had 24 hours from then to get out of Albania by our own submarine waiting for us. Where we were we had no running water, only natural water from the springs, but looking down from our vantage point over the town and the airport if all the lights went out…I was determined, like all the others, to not allow that to happen.

* * * * * * * * *

The devil remained in the details now, we'd puzzled it out, the "what if" sorted. Normally it was the other way on but the trick with this op was we had to "see" how it would unfold in 3D and not in normal sight mode. Two identical film reels were placed on order for immediate delivery.

Both airport locations were inaccessible so we'd organise it to bring them outside their camps. Plenty of 150-proof *maotai* (a street slang word), also known as *baijui* meaning "white liquor" distilled from fermented sorghum, a type of grass related to sugar cane, was being imported by air from Hong Kong into Greece and would be driven across the border in crates mislabelled on the boxes as ouzo. Visually it looked the same.

The aluminium sheets plan was falling into place now. Of course its execution only applied to the northern cave airport as its grid zone was almost below our mountain camp as the crow flies. It was a case now of where to set it up where it could be seen, from where the Army Day celebration would be staged.

The projectionist was hired for our free party scheduled on the day in the capital that was a free bus ride from the military airport. That open air cinema location in Tirana we'd seen before was chosen as the southern venue.

Small unmarked propeller planes from the boot of Italy would fly in low when the parties got underway and drop strips of light metal reflectors to both block Chinese radar functioning temporarily plus it would be a visual feast of glitter.

Some of those technical experts came up with interesting submissions: The best being the use of 12-gauge specialised shotgun shells that fired M-80 firecrackers some 50 yards before causing a special effect noise. It was the equivalent of a quarter stick of dynamite. They suggested to place both the satchel and fireworks at strategic locations not with time delay fuses but radio controlled. The intention was to create the impression of the gods' displeasure with the Chinese and could be activated around a captive audience just at the point where the voices from nowhere were yelling *"Jian! Jian! Jian!"* The combination of hearing "annihilate" repeatedly and the sound of bomb sounds were designed to unnerve the Chinese soldiers on a half-day break that would hopefully cause mutiny back at their camp. Those in charge would be outnumbered, unable to stop the stampede of its panicked warriors.

The Albanian Army were almost a non-entity in all our planning. It helped us that they were still using hand-me-down American-made time-consuming RS-1 radios and medium speed MSRS-48 tape-transmission radio systems from the sixties. Weaponry was more antiquated than that; World War II Red Army discards. For a small mountainous land, they had a lot of monster hairy men with trim haircuts and blue beards. They either didn't know how to smile and when they did they had longish molars as fangs for teeth, kind of the nearest thing to a human werewolf. A bit spooky, to witness the sight of it made one shiver. This might be the beginning of a telling of a joke but the punch line was that we pondered at length what we should do about them, concluding that the answer was: *Nothing.* We didn't feel they had the wherewithal and impetus to fight us or join the cause, in either direction. They operated aimlessly in the in-between space of peacefulness and aliveness so we decided to leave them be. On the face of it their predilection for regularly keeping short back and sides was where their mind set really lay. Maybe they knew it made them less scary. And, of course, it was standard that they had the cigarette in their mouths, unbuttoned tunics, et al. A fine fighting force they were not.

With three weeks to go it was a just a question of ironing out the kinks, getting the logistics into place, while hoping that elsewhere the other aspects were progressing according to plan and on schedule. It would build to a crescendo and go bang in one form or another. Then we could pack up and go home ourselves.

* * * * * * * * *

Then a few days later an absolutely funny thing happened. I was informed that convoys of Chinese troops in large numbers were driving north at speed from southern Albania. We had to see why and three of us jumped on the rickety-old bicycles that we'd stolen. Coming down the hill at speed was easy enough and we'd have to walk back up the slopes 10 miles. Even before reaching the plateau we could see the rolling cloud dust of the stream of lorries in the distance. What was going on?

Pedalling through Shkodra one could see the few Chinese businesses boarded up. My brows furrowed but we kept heading towards the airport further south of the urban centre. The fields there had a clear view of the airport in the distance and an amazing sight appeared as we approached it: Dozens upon dozens of Chinese transport planes had their engines running and people were boarding them in droves. At the back the crews were throwing on mounds of bags. It didn't make sense what we were seeing. Once given the "thumbs up" the pilots taxied to the long single runway and without waiting took off into the sky, one after the other until there was silence. It would seem that the fighter jets had already departed. The air station was a ghost town.

It was getting dark now so we elected to head back to camp to report our findings. Halfway up the steep incline our single truck we had originally come into the country behind came rolling down the hill with a couple of vans and car in tow. "Alpha-One" smiled and told us to get in, to abandon the bikes there. We did as we were told. He said that he received word that the vast seaborne shipment of food and armaments had turned around and gone back to China. He had no explanation why but could confirm that our operation had been completed three weeks ahead of schedule. We told him what we'd already witnessed. He said we'd all likely know precisely what happened when we returned to our respective homelands.

At the bottom by the lake we four British lads jumped out, took our bags (someone had packed what little I'd brought with me), bade bye to everybody en masse, and we watched them disappear off into the darkness. We duly found the small raft hidden there, the motor started at the fourth attempt – unlucky for some, I thought – and we chugged across the eerie flatness without talking. Speech carries even further on water than engine noise does. Dismounting at the other side's shore we fastened it securely – it would be anybody's to claim now – and trekked a breathless three hours over the hill in pitch blackness down to the Adriatic-Mediterranean.

On the first hour hand of the clock that came by a hand-held torch beamed into the sky once in circular form in the pitch blackness. It came from a spot some hundreds of yards to our right so we trundled over to there over slippery rocks. Upon arrival two fellows in civilian clothes and caps on asked our individual names in English, nodded confirmation, made a short radio call then stood facing silently out to sea. We followed suit in our tiredness. It was quite amazing really, after all that we'd been through in the past few strenuous seven weeks, to see that submarine break the surface like a huge whale. I got goose-bumps. I was going home, I deserved it, even if all that humongous effort came to nothing. I was more than curious what had transpired.

Within 20 minutes we were aboard that sub and bathed in its bright interior light. The food that they served us was brilliant given that we hadn't really eaten that well living in the mountains off the land. I weighed myself on a scale in the officers' shower room and I'd lost 14 pounds (6.35 kilograms). The hot water shave was heaven beneath the waves. I slept like a log.

I woke up to a change in engine hum. We were about to dock in Malta at dawn. Then a specially arranged RAF flight delivered us four hours later into Northolt, a suburb of northwest London. The waiting car had us at Century House, SIS' HQ, in a traffic-free 45 minutes where we were informed over late-morning coffee that our work had not been in vain.

With the twin attacks planned on Albania in stages 1 and 2 (if 1 failed) and the countdown clock for military action ticking, the Chinese ambassadors to London, Washington DC and Bonn were summoned urgently on 4 July 1978 to see the British Prime Minister, the American President and the German Chancellor's office respectively. They were told in no uncertain terms what would happen if they didn't leave Albania immediately. It took Beijing 48-72 hours to conclude that we weren't joking and they started the process of pulling out at once.

We fellows were each told we had ably accomplished what was needed of us and to enjoy a week off at home. The same car took us to Victoria mainline railway station where kerbside I bade goodbyes to my three comrades. I presumed from there they either caught the tube to St Pancras-Kings Cross railway station or took a train down to Gatwick for flights to their nearest home airports in northern England.

As for me, I took the underground to Hounslow West then the bus to Heathrow airport and boarded the first flight heading to Zürich. Upon landing I took a bus ride to Berne. I knew the route well. After buying my Swissair airline ticket I headed to the newsagent inside terminal two. I scanned all the international press headlines. There was absolutely no mention of a Sino-Albania problem rearing its ugly dragon-like head. Not even in any of the middle pages I flipped through, not a pipsqueak word mentioned anywhere.

Many of the articles were about the Swedish tennis player Bjorn Borg who was predicted to win his third Wimbledon in succession that weekend. The dates on all the newspapers was Saturday, 8 July 1978.

At least, I thought, the Albanians kids won't be learning to read and speak Mandarin and Cantonese at school anymore than I'll be conversing in Swiss any time soon. Both improbable.

* * * * * * * * *

Chapter Six

*W*hen I was last in the West Bank in 2002 I visited the ramshackle office of the Palestine Liberation Organisation in Ramallah. From their records I confirmed the official date of death of the person mentioned in my story as well as the correct Anglicised spelling of his name. For certain, he was born in Tulkarm, Palestine, in 1936. In 2007 I also perused the archives of Nice-Matin, a widely circulated and respected daily newspaper in the south of France. My painstaking search of the manual records (pre-1996 computerised times) did not uncover a single citation of the event I am about to recount nor any mention of the person's name (in any variation of spelling).

Assisting me in my endeavours was a French citizen of good standing who corroborated my findings or lack thereof. In addition, the staff in attendance conducted further checking in the paper's research department. Not a single reference whatsoever was unearthed as a result of these combined efforts. Yet I know the incident had occurred simply because I was present on the scene at the time and I witnessed the events as they unfolded first hand. I can only surmise that there was a powerful political reason for suppressing the reporting of the incident in the general press. One day the cream will float to the surface and I will discover the answer. This is my version of what happened:

Quis custodiet ipsos custodies?
Who watches the watchmen?
If no question mark is inserted
then no answer is given.
The devil plays games with my soul.

Saturday, 14 July 1979, Berne, Switzerland:

With Vibeke away on a trip, I was enjoying a relaxing day in my flat at 43 Dufourstrasse when towards late-afternoon the telephone rang. "Anderson? London calling. We've got a state red, immediate action. Get your arse down to Marseille at once. Tomorrow morning between 07:00 and 09:00 hours you should be on-site in the vicinity of the Consulate of Panama, which is located right on the waterfront of the old harbour. You'll see a familiar face there. He is your POC (point of contact) for as long as you are required. Over and out."

The few charter and cargo flights out of Berne were memorised and none of them went directly to Marignane, Marseille's airport. So I quickly dug out my summer schedule guide for Basle, Geneva and Zürich airports, all an hour and half fast drives away from the Swiss watch-like centre spoke of Berne. The twice-weekly Caravelles to the Mediterranean city weren't operating on the weekend from either Geneva or Zürich, and Basle had no outbound flights either. Travel by train wasn't an option since there were too many changes and connections to make, and it would have taken way too long. I decided to drive in my faithful Audi instead. It was owned by the Firm after all. I scribbled a note to Vibeke then grabbed my always readily packed overnight bag in case of emergencies like this one and took off.

The drive west alongside Lake Geneva was always pleasing on the eye. Plenty of water activities were in progress as it was summer party time for the Swiss and tourists alike. It had been a beautiful day and this early evening wasn't going to disappoint either. The magnificent Alps rose above us all. The Swiss-French border crossing had gone smoothly, too. After winding down the mountain slopes to the fringes of a pleasant Lyon, I was soon on the A6 dual carriageway, the French main north-south artery bombing along.

Sunday, 15 July 1979, Marseille, France:

After one pit stop in early morning at an all-night motorway petrol station, I took a fifteen-minute nap to recharge my own batteries. I then grabbed some refreshments and I arrived on the outskirts of northern Marseille – then France's third most populated metropolis – just as dawn broke.

The deeper into the heart of this still awakening dark city I ventured the more I became aware of the surly stares of its inhabitants. North African Arab types, for the most part unsmiling, were hanging out in small groups on street corners. Their disposition was one that suggested I was being checked to see if I was mugging material, even as I sat in the Audi at red traffic lights. I decided with my day-old stubble of beard, that when I stepped out of my tin can I was to appear rough-hewn myself, chew gum and walk straight-up aggressively while flexing my muscles. I might be able to handle three of them well, I thought to myself, but more than that number would be a lost cause. And there were many groups of more than a trio to be seen.

After stopping at a well-lit roundabout to check the local Métro map and since I had plenty of time, I decided to park the car and take the underground train to the *Vieux Port* (Old Port) stop. I'd never been here before but logic dictated that parking becomes more difficult to find as one ventures closer into any city centre. Plus, I didn't know yet the nature and duration of the mission I was being summoned for. So better be safe than sorry and leave it in the suburbs, I thought, and less chance the rollers would be missing when I got back. This place was like the East New York of Europe.

I ended up parking the Audi in a secluded street at the junction of Rond-Point du Prado and Parc Amable Chanot. I wrote down the location to remind myself where I left it. The subway station bearing the name Rond-Point du Prado was at the nearby corner, only a few minutes' walk away. I took notice of the subway stop to remind me of the station to come back to.

Just over a quarter of an hour later I found myself strolling down the almost deserted La Canibiere, one of the city's main boulevards. The area decidedly had the Sunday morning-look; the shops hadn't opened yet (if they were going to open at all) on this holiest of Catholic days. Below me, some half a mile down the slope, the white blobs of boats and vessels could be seen bobbing in the romantic old harbour. The closer I got to the harbour the more Muslim men I saw, which was not a comfortable feeling, even to black belt me. Fortunately, I noticed mobile security men with dogs patrolling the street even at this still early time of day. I wondered what the night-time traffic would look like. It seemed to me very much a war zone in peacetime. Something was going on.

I made a wrong turn at the bottom there – it was either left or right at the waterfront – but I quickly got my bearings back when I spotted the Panamanian flag drooped further back along the waterfront in the opposite direction. You'd think they'd hang a good clean one out of national pride but this one was threadbare and soiled, which fitted the sleaziness of the whole neighbourhood. As I looked around, the *Notre Dame de la Garde* (Our Lady of the Guard) cathedral on a hilltop overlooking the area was a sight to behold as the early morning sun reflected its rays off the magnificent dome. As I was standing there and marvelling at it, the first toll of the bells for the day was underway announcing the time with the first of the eight rings. I still had an hour to make contact.

Standing there I saw no one I was supposed to know. In fact, no one was there at all on that corner. It was now precisely a minute past 8:00 AM. I strolled a few yards across the triangle towards another corner like a hesitant tourist, away from the moored trawlers and Moors hanging out across the street. I was starting to think it was payday for their fishing jobs or a strike was being organised.

Simultaneously I saw both Forsyth and James at each end of the short cobblestone street noticing, too, that the sign above me read *rue Reine des Belges* (Queen of the Belgians Street). As I stood there motionless, neither one betrayed any signs of recognition. So I sat and ordered a coffee at the café that was conveniently located there. I was its first customer of the day, a lone individual sitting outside. With my back against the wall I glanced to my left at James again, who was some 75 yards at the end of the street on a junction, where he was intently reading a thick Sunday newspaper while at the same time smoking a cigarette. Frankly he looked to me like he was on a stakeout: no dog-walking exercise, no having a break from a workout, not even acting like he was waiting for somebody to pick him up from that spot. The location itself wasn't where you'd normally choose to read a paper; too obvious to the trained eye, I thought, but maybe he had no other choice but to park himself there. Sitting on the corner wall 25 yards to my right of the *Bourse et Chambre de Commerce* (Exchange and Chamber of Commerce) fortress of a building that lay in front of me, was Forsyth. With his back toward me, he was idly gazing in the other direction. Due to his seniority, I presumed he was the appointed POC. He was an older man, who *did* look like he was mostly wondering why his collecting party was late. He constantly looked both ways up and down the length of La Canibiere, and occasionally lazily behind himself in James' direction at the far end of the 100 yards length of rue Reine des Belges. He projected mild exasperation as he periodically checked his watch and ran his hand slowly once through his greying hair. He never looked once in my direction and for a moment I thought that he was actually expecting me to arrive by car. But then maybe not.

I ordered a second cup and a croissant. No signal was received so I stayed put. I was quite confident by now that they knew I was present. The third time I looked to my right, a dark blue four-door Peugeot had stopped by Forsyth as he jumped down off his perch and got in the front passenger door kerb side. As the car slowly moved off towards the nearby corner where the harbour was I observed him roll down the window as he pointed a finger in front of himself curving it around animatedly to the right, his head turned towards the driver. I took that as the deliberate signal intended for me. I had already paid my bill so I got up and strolled back in the opposite direction to that designated Panama consulate meeting point just around the corner. Sure enough the Peugeot had come around the block and was already there rolling along with Forsyth urgently beckoning me. I quickly climbed into the back seat.

We all shook hands. "Anderson, this is Latham. He's driving for now but eventually if and when this show gets on the road we'll all be taking turns at the wheel. Likewise, if it doesn't involve the use of a vehicle then we'll have to resort to waterfall effects. I take it you already saw where James was – right? – plus you brought a change of clothes?" (Waterfall surveillance requires the observation team to pass in front of the subject then circle around again in a different disguise.)

I nodded in response, allowing him to keep talking. "OK, listen up," he continued, as we cruised at a snail's pace past an old church on our side of the pavement in dire need of a paint job, "for now we are all going to rotate every 30 minutes to each other's general surveillance points. Whoever is in the place where James is now is to take the steering wheel and keep going around the block clockwise. The hotel we just passed behind, near where you jumped in, is called the Grand Hotel de Genève. The only door in and out of the place is almost where James can currently be seen. The subject or subjects in question are staying there. Checked in yesterday and that's when we requested another fourth person to better handle the logistical nightmare of monitoring the multiple escape routes thereafter – four bloody ways to turn and we don't know which one it can or will be…or even if they'll split from each other there. Plus, also we don't know how many he will be with, whomever he met in there, if at all. We don't want to lose track of any of them, naturally."

"The main rabbit (target of surveillance) is a nasty little chap called Zuheir Muhsin, or Zuhayr Muhsin, depending how you'd pronounce and spell it. Age 43, he's the ex-head of Syrian-funded *Al-Saiqa* – The Thunderbolt to you – the murder squad of the PLO (Palestine Liberation Organisation). Also likes to be known as the 'Butcher of Damour'. The guy's responsible for quite a large number of hits, but chiefly the massacre of hundreds of Lebanese Christians in January 1976. If you must know how despicable this cunt is, he likes to slice his victims' penises off and shove them in their mouths – dead or alive."

Forsyth must have seen my wince in the rear view mirror, "Not to worry, we are to just follow him or them when they come out. We haven't got any equipment (guns), as it is. Some other party who has that will be in communication with us shortly." He waved his two-way radio off his lap for me to see.

"By the way, as no operational name has been designated to the main rabbit – just in case it's required – I've decided we are going to code him 'The Queen Mum' and the others will duly be 'Corgi-1', 'Corgi-2' and 'Corgi-3'. If they split up, you'll be designated to follow one of them." Latham and I both glanced at each other with smiling eyes through the rear mirror.

We were there hanging around for another couple of hours, following the prescribed routine. Around then I began to feel drowsy, as I'd basically been up all night. I knew Forsyth was from SIS headquarters in London. He had been stationed all over the Middle East and he spoke Arabic fluently. He had returned home to England recently in the run up to his retirement. James was my age, was in my training class, who came out with high passes and was a former SBS (Special Boat Service) lad. He was based around the curve of the Mediterranean in the capital of the Spanish Costa Brava and was in charge of the quiet Barcelona SIS sub-station. Apparently, Latham too was from London, but he was a non-entity to me. All of us were Englishmen who were supposed to be behaving like innocuous Frenchmen. The car was a local rental as the window sticker told me.

During one of the switches, as I moved to a new surveillance location, I noted an emblem – an eagle and a full key next to each other – far above the five-storied hotel's main doors that itself stood up a few steps from the street. Perhaps it was indeed the Belgian royal family's crest. Okay, whatever, I thought, as I connected the dots imaginatively, the rabbit correctly needed a code name and that's where Forsyth must have got his cue from. He made up The Queen Mum from ours, the mother of our queen. It was a bit insulting to the jackpots (targeted bad guys) to be known as an old woman and her three dogs. I shook my head. He must've had his reasons.

Of course it had to happen when it was my turn steering the Peugeot. Latham was not standing where he was the last time I came around. There was no sight of anybody walking up and down the short street now and I couldn't see if anybody was at the far end either. I speeded up and turned right off at the end of La Canibiere, where the signs pointed towards the airport and Aix de Provence. There right under that Panama flag stood all three of them, looking anxious to get going.

When they all piled in, Forsyth rasped, "Four of the buggers came out. The Queen Mum and three BGs (bodyguards), sorry Corgis – clearly Pallies, all of them, Palestinians – trying to look like they're part of the local crowd. Quickly turn around and head in the opposite direction. Follow the signs to Toulon and Cannes. Try not to go too fast but you need to get in sight of a particularly common Citroen saloon. There's plenty of the same make on the road but I'll point it out when I see it ahead."

It wasn't easy turning around. I had to do it at a no left sign. Explaining that the urgent mood of my passengers forced me to do the illegal turn, would not have sounded a good excuse to the local gendarmerie had they forced us to stop. I looked before I did it to make sure that there were no police cars in sight or foot patrols around. Churlish characters were floating around and the wolf packs were increasing in number as if the presumed strike was to begin soon. It obviously gave the four baddies a cover of sorts. I was glad to be getting out of there. A crowded Marseille is definitely not my kind of town.

In light traffic we climbed up and drove away from the old port with the cathedral on our right. All the roads were funnelling towards the A8 ahead. A few minutes passed and Forsyth was duly pointing at a dark blue car, which was the same exact colour as ours.

Seconds later we had passed through the *autoroute's* toll booth and handed a docket from the attendant. The driver of the Citroen really put his foot down then. He went at a speed that would attract the unwelcome attention of the cops, eventually. Cussing to myself I had to follow suit and that meant that we'd be noticed by them too, eventually. *Maybe that was exactly the point of their exercise, to see who was following them.* The azure sea on our right was rocketing past, another nice day was in the making despite the foreboding in the air.

Forsyth was making some calls now in French, speaking rapidly. After receiving one, he smiled at me, "The fucking Frogs intel fellows are going to start a fire soon, get the traffic off the motorway down to the slower moving RD 6098 coastal route. Bloody cheek of it!" James and Latham had already dozed off in the back seat. I cursed at my overly tired predicament.

Sure enough within half an hour we had grinded to a halt and I got myself on the inside lane. The object of our attention was some 10 cars in front, and the space between us would remain so for some time. We were now east of Toulon, the French Navy ships clearly visible at sea in the distance.

After a picturesque Saint-Tropez, the road signs started to read Corniche d'Azur and we entered the sleepy Var provincial town of Saint-Aygulf. I had permitted the gap between us and the Citroen we were following to increase to some two dozen vehicles. I couldn't help but notice being the driver that the numerous traffic lights all went in our favour and the railway level crossing gates were always up – at least 25 cars filing through in one go, a record! Once an ambulance with its blue lights spinning, was literally crawling in the opposite direction – they usually are speeding! At another time, even a speck of a helicopter passed over far, far up above, and circled around a few times – over what could it be! Was I imagining we were being monitored, filmed even? The improbable possibility that the half a dozen or so uniformed gendarmerie cops standing roadside all seemed to have their backs to the Citroen and our car at the exact moment we passed, *all must have been an amazing coincidence.*

Suddenly Forsyth's radio began to crackle loudly. He snapped it up and listened intently. The static woke up the sleeping pair in the back, who had apparently been up all night like I had, as they sat upright quickly.

We could hear them on the commo chatter. It was the guttural sound of Hebrew, without a doubt. "Our contacts, the Israeli *Shayetet 13*, which translates to Fleet 13, the élite frogmen unit of the Israeli Navy," uttered Forsyth to nobody in particular. In the rear mirror I could see James and Latham's twin focus bore holes in the back of Forsyth's head, as I did likewise from the driver's seat. For helpful added measure he uttered, "We are only the surveillance team. They are going to FPA those bastards ahead." (FPA stands for focused preventative actions, code for assassinate.)

When he announced that my exhaustion evaporated and I was suddenly wide-awake with all the senses coming alive. The pair behind me looked wired now as well.

Somebody was about to say something from the back when Forsyth abruptly raised his hand, adjusting the intercom volume position. The Israelis voices jacked up, like they were having some problem with what sounded like a SURC (small unit river craft). The angry mix of roaring water and humming engine echoed around the car's interior. Was it a run aground or low water problem? Then we heard splashing-like wading followed by grunts.

A low but confident voice was heard saying in accented English, "Our Bombard is taking in water. Delay indefinite. Keep tracking HVT (high value target). I am sorry. We will catch up with you."

I got the impression from the exchange that we were ahead of their landing area. We were in Saint-Raphaël now, crossing a small bridge over a canal or river from a similar looking beachfront area called Fréjus. Or so the signs read.

I wasn't wrong on my surmising. Forsyth had his map on his lap and his thumb jerked backwards from where we'd passed. The backseat pair were leaning forward now. I was the only one keeping the consigned in my sights. Everyone else was glued now on the map, while an electric fizz engulfed us all.

"They were supposed to come in at the river mouth at L'Argens." I had no idea where Forsyth meant. For clarification he added, "Pretending to be members of CIECA. The French have a training camp back there somewhere, divers looking like divers returning to home base. Fits."

The SBS lad, James, enlightened Latham and me at that point, thankfully. "It stands for *Centre d'Instruction et d'Entraînment au Combat Amphile*, the amphibious military school we passed way back. Fuck."

I kept doing my job. The Citroen was moving along smoothly like we were. The traffic was getting into a steady flow now, no one bothering to pass anyone as we were all well behaved and each car on the road was observing a constant speed. *There was a perceptive 'lull before the storm feel' to it.* The suburban township of Boulouris came and went. The name of Agay was next.

The Citroen pulled up into a small metered car area just after the long white sanded beach of Agay ended. We motored on past them, the back pair crouching down out of sight. I observed four dark men in western holiday attire starting to exit the vehicle. Two of them had the familiar appearance of the Muslims of Marseille while the other two had a distinctly different appearance. "Ladies and gentlemen may I present to you Her Royal Highness The Queen Mother along with her doggies going for walkies," said a sarcastic voice from the backseat, looking behind as we passed them.

The radio was alive again. A vehicle engine was heard firing up. The same calm voice said, "We are on our way finally. What is your position please?" Forsyth told them.

After a minute the voice rasped, "OK, we are taking the A8 to Cannes and will rendezvous with you there in…on the hour, over and out." Forsyth switched off as we all glanced at our watches. It was 45 minutes to go. I pulled in at a lip of a hill that gave us a view of Agay. I was thinking that the major motorway was supposed to be closed due to a fire…better not let resourcefulness conquer reality.

Latham was already strolling back down the road for a look-see. Forsyth beckoned him back. "They'll pass by us here eventually." I hoped he was right, I was thinking that they could easily turn around and go back in the opposite direction. I wasn't going to argue, he was in charge, not me. Maybe there was a covert French team out here with us as well. But I didn't think to ask and certainly there was no indication of others present.

There was no instruction for a change of driver either so I reversed the Peugeot into a hidden lane and parked it behind the shade of a huge tree. There was no way they'd know we were there. After a taut long-ish 25 minutes the Citroen finally came by us. I let seven or eight cars pass before coming out slowly to join in the stream of diverted traffic again.

The lovely coastal village of Théoule-sur-Mer came and went. *The tension was discernible now.* Nobody spoke. No intercom on. A hamlet called La Napoule was gone before I noticed we were in it. A small propeller plane came in low from over the sea, crossed the road ahead of us, landing on some unseen runway to our left.

It was a long flat stretch now. An endless beach starboard, some low buildings of holiday flats to port. One minute to the hour on my watch. Right on time the incoming message crackled. "We are in Cannes. What is your and the HVT's position please? Forsyth duly responded, "Entering Cannes west side, coastal route."

"You are to follow our instructions now, when given." Forsyth confirmed abeyance.

It was ages before there was any further commo. Instinctively without comment from anybody I narrowed the gap to the Citroen to about half or maybe four vehicles – discreetly overtaking mostly at pedestrian crossings on the inside lane by moving off before them. We came around the old harbour near Cannes town centre. The Ile de Lérins ferry entrance on the right was clearly marked. Tourist types milling around everywhere. However, the Palestinians' car didn't follow the road into the famous La Croisette as expected. Instead it began to pick up speed, disappeared quickly down some narrow streets towards the signs to the A8 again, up a long straight incline, approaching suburban Mougins. I got the impression the driver knew the way. The incoming sudden click made me jump.

"You are in a dark blue Peugeot, yes? And the HVT is in a dark blue

Citroen approximately one hundred metres apart, yes?" Forsyth affirmed so. Head-banging heavy rock sounds filled my head now.

"Please, we need to create a stop. Immediately pass HVT and effect a stop. You are in full view of us." There was a sudden urgency to the command. Forsyth nodded but I'd already passed the few cars in front but on the outside. Then the high value target came by and one other before it in succession. Someone honked his horn at length for my infringement of his space. Going to another overtake now, I had made an oncoming car swerve to avoid us, its full beam headlights flashing on and off angrily at me. Certainly those in the Citroen had noticed my actions, too, no doubt.

There was a roundabout coming up, about a half-mile at the top of the hill. Forsyth hand went on my shoulder; I effected a purposeful 'out-of-control' slide in perfectly good road conditions, coming to a skidding halt and blocking one lane of the northbound two. James and Latham slid as fast as they could out of the back rear side door, the far side, unseen by any following vehicle passengers, backsides disappearing down the bank. Forsyth immediately jumped out and opened the bonnet, throwing the lid up and looking inside the hood. I sat there doing nothing, my driver's side door open, not sure what to expect or do next – a surreal feeling, kind of looking at yourself from afar.

Two drivers, who had witnessed the car skid, drove by warily with windows wound down, mouths moving and angrily gesticulating at me for my apparent recklessness. But neither stopped to check if everybody was OK though. Then a few spooky seconds passed and the Citroen came up slowly, all the Arab men's faces staring at me with disdain as I sat motionless. To all the rebel "queen's men" I looked like I was a total imbecile but I also detected a taut concern mixed with a dose of suspicion, too. I could see the expressions of the two nearest to me quite clearly as their windows were also down. Their hands noticeably out of sight and I envisioned they had concealed weapons under there. Our eyes locked.

Right at that moment two men wearing dark balaclavas riding an almost silent motorcycle heading in the same direction approached the Citroen from its blind side. The one on the back let loose a loud barrage of fast short-nuzzle machine gun fire. Maybe only 20 seconds but that was a long while in Uzi time. Shattered pane and shrieking bullets cannoning heavily into metal in rapid succession raged, the thunder with the lightning. I hit the ground outside the car, crouching, simultaneously holding my ears and covering my head. The booming racket of breaking glass and metallic thudding stopped abruptly, the air thick with smoke and burnt rubber. My hair was covered in sharp splinters. Only yards away from me the Citroen's front two tyres had burst and one of the bodies from the rear was sprawled half in and half out of the car in front of me, blood gushing from his neck. A blackened severed hand lay feet away from my face where I laid on the road. Steam was shooting up into the blue from the immobilised engine that was still running. Spent shell casings littered the area with some continuing to roll about at my prone eye level. In the seconds of shrill silence occasional broken bits spiralled down like drops of hard rain.

Forsyth was screaming now at me from the passenger seat of the car to get in. The car lid was already slammed down as he had probably dived away like I had. Adrenaline pumping, ears ringing, I scrambled up and jumped into the seat as I was told. We then took off like a hound's hare. I never saw James and Latham again. Lord knows where they went to? I never found out, nor did I care. I just wanted to get the hell out of there.

I burned rubber of a different kind up the track to that roundabout, then my professional training kicked in and I *reduced* speed to encircle it. Forsyth was pointing in certain lefts and rights to overtake, and I obeyed him without thinking. It was a fog for me as I scraped particles of debris out of my scalp, forcibly popping my hearing back to normal, blowing hard holding my nose. Then the stench of sulphur penetrated the growing trepidation as I drove in the same direction east as the killers turned in…as we went down the wee dip towards the entrance to the A8 again, you could see a motorbike weaving in and out of the traffic less than a mile ahead, then it soared away up and to the left. When we reached that bend it was just straight slope of motorway ahead, they'd throttled it and had roared from sight.

As we passed the road signs for Antibes there were a series of blips like Morse code coming from the radio that had fallen under the seat on his side. As he retrieved it the corkscrew feeling was already uncurling discernibly in Forsyth's voice and all he said into it calmly in confirmation was, "We cannot contact the subject at this time." Then he clicked off. I never said anything being junior to his senior.

Subsequently I stopped at a major railway station that I cannot remember; perhaps it was Nice-Ville Thiers. Outside that *gare* there Forsyth finally took the wheel himself saying he was "returning the vehicle". I am also surmising today that it was at Aéroport Nice Côte d'Azur, which is situated only a half an hour leisurely drive from that station, though I can't swear he departed from there. As he drove off I noticed the licence plate had an "06" on the end, the same prefix as a lot of vehicles I was driving behind when I arrived into that city. This numbering system tells the average driver in France which region the location the car is registered in. (Later I did speak to him at his home, relayed through from his office number, immediately upon my arrival back in Switzerland 12 hours later. He sounded reasonably relaxed, so in this respect I assume now that he flew directly to London Heathrow or Gatwick from the nearby Nice airport. Or there was a private plane at his disposal, perhaps. In any case he did say in semi code-speak "that the dogs never finished their walk due to the hard rain".)

In any case, back to the day of the incident, I next purchased a one-way railway ticket in French francs. I headed back to Marseille Saint-Charles station – I remember I spent the time wincingly removing two slivers of razor-sharp glass that were embedded into my fingers. I arrived there three hours later, whereupon I took a taxi and located my Audi all wheels still intact, thank goodness. Then I proceeded home without stopping even once, the need to sleep never returned any time on the trip north. I kept reliving the moment of the attack time and time again, a stuck action replay on a loop. Like the shards, it is seared deep into my memory as I was at the scene and closer than most witnesses would ever want to be. I didn't worry about the dark young fit bloke I noticed that sat further down from me across the aisle on that train trip, but only as far as the Saint-Raphaël stop, and he never looked up once. The magazine he was brazenly reading in public was *Ba-Machaneh* (In-Camp), the official Israeli Army magazine. To me he was clearly acting on "commercial cover" (posing as a businessman) but likely returning to his point of entry into France. I'm pretty sure he didn't know who I was.

Years later, and as I've already written, I discovered that this incident was never reported in the local newspaper? Why? In today's day and age what are the political reasons for the continuing suppression of this event? Why, too, would the experienced Forsyth from the SIS ID two guys as Palestinians when I could clearly see that they were not, and I could easily compare their images to the others congregated there? There's a big visual difference between the two Arab cultures – the gap is like black and white – like say a Finn and a Portuguese. The French were involved too by temporarily closing down a section of a major national motorway. On hindsight I realise that the Israelis did use a flash suppressor on that unmistakable Uzi, which is exactly what it means – no bright light of shots emitting from the machine gun – that tells me too that they were prepared to use it at night time, if need be, or it was originally planned for the night before but was vetoed or delayed. What also particularly galls me is that I was exposed for possible identification. Worse is that I easily could have been hit by a stray bullet. Luckily it was only sharp glass instead for my troubles plus decades of cross-examination.

The way my soul is, it implores an answer.

Since writing this account I was told by telephone in 2007 by a US-based retired Israeli Mossad intelligence officer whom I knew way back when, who wished to remain anonymous and would not or could not confirm the actual date, but after my request he made discreet inquiries himself and that this secret covert wet affair (elimination) job was most likely the one they had called Operation ROEH HAZIRIM (literally Swineherd but in Hebrew it translates to Shepherd of Pigs…understand that due to Kashrut laws there's not many pigs in Israel as they don't slaughter them to eat) with local signals coordination undertaken by their Unit 8200. The latter's participation explains to me that the dedicated wavebands on the day were specially encrypted, which in turn also tells me why the commo was so open and largely lacking in pre-designated coded military jargon – only them and us could hear each other though. The opportunity to act as they did clearly was of primary essence – so no time to plan an attack in meticulous detail – and that's why it occurred in broad daylight and was moved up the schedule in the impromptu manner that it suddenly was. Perhaps the car was presumed to be on its way to Italy, less than 40 minutes fast drive away on that motorway, and political jurisdiction of the green-lighted involved parties would likely have ended there? So the job on the jackpots was completed and canned in Cannes, France, instead.

Addendum: It appears that since I wrote this account and uploaded a rough copy to my website that several copycat entries on this incident can now be found on Wikipedia. Now that it has I can confirm that it was what is known at SIS as TWEP (termination with extreme prejudice) because the next time I was in London headquarters my file entry stated that I had been on a job dated the date of when I received the call. The entry read simply RDS. So I went to someone I knew in operations and asked him what it stood for and his answer was, "Revolutionary Development Support". I then checked with another individual I knew about it who replied that no such unit officially exists and winked at me. So the way it works is this: It always is made to legally look like circumstantial evidence and that those persons in the know could prove that they were not present when the TIO (tactical intelligence op) took place. It was a PK (political killing).

Note: Assassination or liquidation is not a legal term in international law but interestingly it is lawful under the United Nations' charter. At SIS it was understood that we were entitled to act on what was known verbally as "anticipatory self-defence". I was disappointingly beginning to see I worked for a criminal organisation in the name of democracy. I was doing the opposite of what I thought I was supposed to be doing...

* * * * * * * * *

Chapter Seven

I knew exactly why I was being sent to the Soviet Caucasus on an NOC job for a fortnight. The Secret Intelligence Service is after all a unit of the bigger picture called P-R-O-F-I-T in capitals and in bold. We were often enrolled when it suited our masters and mandarins in the hallways of British commerce to be the reconnoitre riding ahead of the business game plans that were to follow. Still not quite pre-industrial espionage but somebody had to go in and tender a lay of the land report covering specifics required in the future such as rating the possibilities, gauging the local attitude, the political players and their enemies. A key element of the task ahead was to surmise what could go wrong, or right and spot anything else that pertained to the matter at hand. In short I was to proffer an opinion on whether it could be done or not. Thus from the findings the authorities and corporations could devise an action plan to fit the equation.

Why I knew upfront but for *who* exactly I would never know. I could only surmise that the likely beneficiary was a UK-based multinational consortium that earned for its shareholders more from its global operations than the British government did from its domestic revenues. So it was a case of doing as you were told for a piece of the tax pile to come.

My usual box of tricks that I had learned years ago became useful for this operation. I was going on-stage under a bona fide cover while waving a magic wand elsewhere. I must admit my knowledge of running the college gigs had helped when I was a teenager. I had been on the arts & entertainment committee that booked the bands for performances and I often went to Newcastle Airport to welcome the group members, shepherd them to their hotel while honouring their riders (hospitality requests) in the dressing rooms, while their roadies set up their drum kits and gear on the stage. In doing so I had met some very famous artists before I turned 18.

Then my life took on the path it did but some past experiences come in handy sometimes like they did on this one. Over 10 years later I re-enacted almost the same role as a hired management consultant for one of the groups from Moscow at what was to be known as the "Soviet Woodstock" in Tbilisi, the Soviet Socialist Republic of Georgia. The original American milestone had lasted three days and was held a decade earlier. Russian propaganda wanted to outdo the west by planning their festival to be three times longer. The nine-day music event was held during 8-16 March 1980 and was called the Spring Rhythms Festival-Tbilisi-80 (*Festivalya Vesennye Ritmy-Tbilisi-80*). *It was the first ever official rock music festival in the Soviet Union.*

The state sanctioned historic occasion was intended to pacify the Soviet youth's increasing love of the western-based sound that later spawned many imitators across and behind the Iron Curtain. It was ground-breaking in that it was permitted to even happen at all after so many years of being labelled by the communist rulers as a capitalist tool to corrupt the minds of the young. Though to call it like it is the occasion did not just offer rock music as folk, choral, chamber, blues, jazz and funk did the rounds. Though most certainly no heavy metal or punk was allowed. Some 20 groups from 17 cities across the Soviet Union partook in the festival and the unreported attendance – I'd estimate it was 100,000 – was large enough for an operator like myself to disappear for several days to perform other primary objectives. What I saw and thought was retained in my head for a detailed future commentary that would be furnished without photographs but with plenty of expertly-drawn diagrams.

Note: My undertakings during this episode are still apparently not declassified so I cannot disclose what precisely I was doing when I buggered off on recce trips. But what I have included herein relate to the escapades I had during that time that are a story in itself, which also took me into neighbouring Armenia.

* * * * * * * * *

It had been a long 24 hours' mini-bus drive nonstop with a change of drivers from the snowy wet slush of Moscow. Our travel papers were in order and didn't attract any unwanted scrutiny from the uniforms along the way despite the long hair.

We were now on the much warmer Russian Riviera at the end of its winter high season, of which its epicentre was Sochi. On the slow drive through the town by the Black Sea we passed by the two-year old pearl-coloured skyscraper Zhemchuzhina Hotel on the beachfront. The four-man rock group, their four Muscovite roadies and my eyes popped out at the wiggling sexy bodies in swimsuits. Bikinis weren't permitted but the next best thing was amply on display.

We had arrived in *Soci* in time for dinner and checked in further up the hill at the specially built spa for the original staff members of the KGB. Our cheap rooms paid for by the concert organiser faced away from the sea. After their live performance was over on the second day of the festival in Tbilisi they would be heading home again. I was going to stay on and make my own way back to Moscow later.

Behind us and beyond were steep mountains, which on the other side was the land of the Cossacks. The edge of the known world. We were one more day's drive away from the very bottom of ethnic Russia, also known as the Caucasus.

Having travelled to so many underdeveloped countries,
all of them want democracy deep-down,
but it has to be their own model
and not the one the west wants them to have.

If you go into the central Asian republics, it is almost like stepping back to a medieval century. Learning about cultural differences takes a high level of patience. In a sea of cruel faces often the locals usually don't understand what they've done that's different to you – and vice versa, us to them – plus there's a class of people that isn't recognised, or doesn't recognise itself. It was a cloak-and-dagger world where any tiny aberration can spin a life into varied patterns no one dreamed of...

The next day after a half-hour steady climb straight up into the 3,500-foot rocky peaks, it was noticeably cooler by the time we reached the top. There was no indication of the end of the road being in sight, but the obviously rebellious Georgians had the impudent presence of mind to put up a large sign stating *Gruzinskaya* – both in Cyrillic and Roman with a bold dark red line through it – it was Russian for Georgia, with brighter red *SAKARTVELO* in capitals gingerly over it, the name of their own country in their Georgian language.

By night we were hibernating in a hostel, 20 miles west of the Georgian capital of Tbilisi. It was a very cold night and we were all slightly beat for the worse that evening, so we turned in early. I had a small pocket world atlas in my case. As I flipped through to see where I was parking myself for the night, I came to realise that I was a quarter of an inch in Georgia right on the junction of the borders of three historically fiercely warring neighbours: Armenia, Turkey and Azerbaijan. Iran was an inch further south.

In the morning I went outside for some air. The view was breath-taking. The feeling of knowing the imagined fault lines of four countries on the canvas of the world were out there in touching distance near the horizon, giving the aura an exciting potency. The centuries old Byzantine system of the region had a new double enemy – satellites which brought freedom of rights ultimately with it. It was no longer just an excusable secessionist fight between Christianity, Islam and Orthodoxy. Instead there was a growing validity in both technological advancement and sustaining tradition. The problem with everybody here was it was either all or nothing, no compromise in the middle. And that was the problem: *No give.* Each person played their cards close to their chest and everything became an effrontery to their psyche in some form.

From what little I knew from my geography lessons at school, reading the news throughout the years and my SIS Oprep report, Georgia had been politically gang-banged by its three cousins next door and its step-uncle, Russia. It had been in this mental condition since the days of the Romans and the Parthians, BC.

From what I'd seen of the people in the rural areas so far, they were still primitive Homo sapiens. Their determining ambience was thinly disguised under the shabby cloak of threadbare communism. It was as if our presence here among them had insulted them as a people. A weird unspoken message of perceived hatred was transmitted as they smiled at you while exposing their crookedly stained teeth. A couple of peasants had the temerity to insinuate we must be homosexual for having long hair. We perceived ethnic Russians were clearly not made to feel at home.

And soon there was going to a mind-blowing rock concert in their near midst. Still the populace of cosmopolitan Tbilisi communist-style were discernibly far more open-minded than their cousins from the countryside.

The last leg to the outskirts of the Georgian capital where the event was being held, setting up the gig, doing the sound check and assimilating ourselves with others in the VIP section went as smoothly as could be expected. Not exactly like I remember the beery mess backstage at our college concerts way back when in my teens. It seemed the polite communist version was far more disciplined and less likely to cause a rumpus even though they sucked down distilled vodka like it was water.

The first day of live performances duly ironed out any kinks by the time my clients took the stage. They were received well by the large crowd who demanded an encore, which they got, and all in all everybody seemed happy with how everything turned out. *Interestingly the goal wasn't to become world famous and sell gazillion records but to genuinely spread peace across the globe.* Needless to state but the event received no media coverage outside the Soviet Union at the time. They did manage though to make the event into a competition with votes and every artist that had a song rated also featured on a vinyl album distributed worldwide by the state-run record label Melodiya in 1981.

(This last fact I only discovered years later when I was browsing through the compilation LP music racks in HMV's main record store on London's Oxford Street when searching for a Christmas gift for a favourite aunt of mine.)

The following morning the band's vehicle was loaded again, some sexy groupies invited themselves to hitch a lift back to Moscow and we all bade farewell to each other. I told them I had eight days of concert time left "to attend to" plus had scheduled one extra day for myself "to enjoy the local sights". None of this being true, of course.

As luck would have it I had befriended two off-duty Red Army beefcakes in their early twenties from Leningrad (St Petersburg) that only had enough money to obtain tickets for two days of music. In the darkness of the night and flashing stage lights I didn't previously notice that they had donned dark nylon long-haired wigs! Underneath the mops were blonde crew cuts. I hired them to drive me around in their jalopy on the pretence that I hadn't been to Armenia before. And nor had they. Plus, they had to be back in Tbilisi around the same time. So it was a good deal for all of us. They even had the candid temerity to show me the two stolen service pistols from their army unit in the car compartment.

We set off for the Armenian border and reached there in 90 minutes. The nondescript border posts, much like entering Georgia before, also had the country written in two languages, one in upper and lower case and the other in bold: *Armanskaja* (Russian for Armenia) and *HAYASTAN* (Armenian for Armenia). "Welcome to Armenia regardless," I said to Misha and Oleg in Russian from the back seat, "Armenia is what other countries call it." They were not particularly the worldly types and were enjoying being educated about travel. They apparently had no qualms about being called up for national service as conscripts years earlier and had willingly joined the armed forces with the goal of getting to see more of the world.

At no time did they suspect me of being other than Russian as my accent was still perfect. I'd stuck to my previous ID from the last time I was in the Soviet Union, in that I was born and raised in Rostov-na-Donu and had served as an officer in the air force. They weren't a duo that asked a lot of questions as their own current armed forces time had drummed into them not to. On this particular occasion I'd unusually been issued a British corp diplomatique passport under an assumed name and the visa was granted for two weeks. If there were any discrepancies that cropped up later I would have already departed. Upon arrival in Moscow by air the SIS head of station had swopped my British papers and replaced it with the documents in the Russian name I had operated under before. Along with plenty of clothes that suited what I was about to do, including shoe and boot sizes that were a perfect fit. I had to admit the Moscow-based fellows had done a good job of it. The roubles in cash I was given was more than enough.

A long day later, as we still motored along in the car, finding the mountainous scenery rather monotonous by now. Misha, who I had begun to notice was quite far-sighted and was driving at the time, broke the silence and boredom by swiftly and plausibly intoning, "I hope you're up to this." Oleg and I looked quizzically at him.

A little tingle on my neck always told me to be ready for a good one. And he pointed ahead at two figures walking along the road incline in the distance that disappeared around a corner.

We continued to ascend a few hundred more feet into the rocky terrain. Suddenly coming around an outcrop of boulders we passed two giant men strolling along the side of the road, or should I say, doing a kind of gangling slow motion lop-sided walk. We all twisted to glance again at them again. Misha was tittering like an idiot at our fast reflex reactions in unison.

"Those men were huge!" Oleg exclaimed. "Small little Armenia has big people."

I knew what it was though. "People with acromegaly, unfortunately, a disease that is a form of gigantism."

We passed a woman and three men, the ugliest, freakish, most surreal deformed group I'd ever seen standing huddled together in my life – like small trees with moving branches as arms with peeking eyes through holes in the bark. They all returned our looks out the back of the car going past them. One of them waved in a slow retarded manner, slightly off the usual enthusiastic way of showing greetings. Oleg and Misha waved back hesitantly.

Ahead was a pack of houses around a tiny square, where a couple of other sizeable individuals were sitting outside at a table. We pulled up in front of the largest house. A miniature plump but standard-sized middle-aged woman with a colourful apron appeared, happy to see us, and beaming ever so brightly. She was clearly an extrovert and obviously the communal leader. She was beckoning us to come in.

Her name was Svetlana, and she was very Russian with her Tartar-like red oval exultant face and roundly distributed weight. She served us tea and as it was starting to get dark she was quite adamant that we stayed the night there. We agreed. There was no malice in the air, only friendship.

We were cordially shown to separate rooms at the back of the house and given a few minutes to refresh ourselves. Absolutely every conceivable thing was extra large! The king-size wooden bed was average in width but peculiarly elongated to eight feet. I shook my head at the strange scene and wished for once I'd carried a camera to record the phenomenon.

At the long timbered table in the spacious kitchen area, I joined the slightly pantomimic Svetlana and a now decidedly pacific Oleg and Misha for dinner, which was being rustled up. She was already jabbering away in medical terms. Like the two young Russians I sat patiently and listened. The many facts I picked up were quite fascinating.

It seems that Svetlana here was the main proponent of caring for acromegalic young people from all over the former Soviet Union, not the dwarfs but their bigger cousins. Families in under populated regions abandoned their grossly over-sized children for fear of being ostracised in the peasant community, and the Soviet state sent them to her here in Armanskaja.

The average measurements of the 30 "children" she had responsibility for was 7'0" for the girls and 7'2" for the boys. I glanced through at the kitchen and saw two massively overweight exceptionally hairy girls preparing food in the same slow motion I'd witnessed so far. I felt as if I was in a weird reverie; a dream-like Beanstalk-land and my name was Jack. It was hard not to stare in fascination at them and their uncontrollable growing bodies.

Her "happy family"'s average shoe size was 18+, weighed 22-stone

(308 pounds or 140 kilograms), chests for men at 53" and the women 7-8" more, with all waists around 44". These extraordinary figures applied only to the younger generation. That was because nobody was over 40 years old – because they were dead. "My dears are always excessively tired, extremely thirsty and have very poor concentration." Svetlana had stopped her almost full-time smiling momentarily to wipe a tear.

Acromegaly was a disorder marked by progressive enlargement of the head, face, hands and feet. A result of inordinate secretion of somatotropin, a protein hormone that promotes body growth, fat mobilisation and inhibits glucose utilisation. Diabetes mellitus was common among her "babies" causing intolerance to carbohydrates. Heart problems were expected in all of them. None of us thought it was funny when she exclaimed that she even had one young fellow who also suffered from acrophobia, a fear of heights. Though I internally shook my head at the amazing contradiction of word similarity and condition.

Her statistics varied, from six out of a 100,000 people suffering from acromegaly in the old Russia, to around six per three million today. If that was true it was *The* Real *Land of the Jolly Green Giant*s! "It's so rare really. To get a better perspective, take the diameter of a small coin as representing one person and measure against the length of seven trips across the Volga River."

When I enquired with Svetlana how all of them ended up in this precise spot, she seemed perplexed for an answer. Her only somewhat apologetic comment was, "A few years ago, we were category seven. That meant we were earmarked for depopulation and our few houses were to be demolished. Plus, the authorities told me there would be no investment in this village of only 50 inhabitants – 30 patients and 20 staff. We were so small that it wasn't even marked on the map, and still isn't. But when they sent a crew of workers up the mountain to prepare dismantling, they took one look at the 'boys' and ran back down screaming in fright."

I had to suppress a chuckle at that "horror story". I could just picture their surprised faces, if the reaction by the two Russian fellas and I were anybody to go by, based on our earlier jump around when we were arriving.

Some normal looking people served food called *basturma*, a spicy cured-beef speciality. Apparently half the staff was ethnic Russians still, a quarter were nationals from other former Soviet states, and five were Armenian. All of them were women and all were or had been mothers of children who had suffered from this remarkable disease of the gigantic.

One of them, a rather thin lady, was constantly playing an instrument that looked like an oboe called a *duduk*, which emanated a melodic but eerie harrowing sound. While sometimes standing to listen to her playing, more than a few times we were told by shy smiling faces without an ounce of sexual innuendo or sounding insulting, "How nice it is to have a man with an ordinary appearance to look at for a few days."

The three normal men that came in the car spent four uncommon days at that remarkable camp for big people. Well we went off for the day every day but returned to spend the nights there, all happily free on the house. They wouldn't accept any money from us but I did leave some inside Svetlana's apron pocket for her to find on the last hour of the last day.

At one time we played an insane game of five-a-side football in the dusky square at the top of a mountain against a team of five of these almost immobile monstrous humans. We had two of the normal women playing for us. Needless we say we won by a big score. *They would have killed us at basketball though.* But it seemed they did enjoy the 10-minute exercise that verged on the caricature coming to life, almost. After the game, one of the giants spoke haltingly to me, his face all darkly puffy, "I'm so uncomfortable in my own skin with this rash."

As much as I tried I couldn't think of a single word to say back to him. Instead I just gave him a hug while wiping a discreet tear.

"Unlike Gulliver in Lilliput, here we are not trussed by restrictive bonds that prevent you from reaching your maximum," was the theatrical Svetlana's unforgettable statement at the short sporting spectacle she'd just witnessed by her charges. When she said that, I'm sure I must have stopped in my tracks and gawked at her for a profound long minute as well. It was like participating on a stage in a melodrama. I refuse to call the episode a pantomime because there was nothing jocular about it, sadly.

When we left for good, a couple of dozen extraordinary over-sized human beings had stood there waving at us as we drove off. They dwarfed the tiny ruddy-faced Svetlana as she stood in the middle of the pack. Even Oleg and Misha had their hands flapping out of the windows.

I don't know about the other two but that last sight of the big people is firmly entrenched in my memory. A team photograph with the impish impresario present. It was a dramatic setting beyond any reasonable admissible credence.

* * * * * * * * *

Of course their car was never in perfect working order to start with but fortunately one of them, Oleg, was very mechanically-minded. We were forced to stop to fix engine problems a couple of times.

On that short one-hour drive down the hillsides, along the road running parallel to the Kasan River to the Armenian capital of Yerevan, both Oleg and Misha were severely knifed by bandits. I saw the whole thing. Looking at what little I could see through the windscreen from the rear seat of the car on the far side from them, where I sat with my back door open. On their near side the back door closed. I don't think the two Armenians knew I was there as I had sat in silence (memorising my findings for my impending intel report). They'd thought it was two against two. Fortunately, the tinted windows had contributed to this notion.

Though it may come across as premonition, seconds prior to the ambush, I had been scrutinising what was left of a wall just a few feet across from me. It had reminded me of charred blue cheese with varying sizes of holes and jagged burns around them. I was just through thinking that wall had seen a hell of a lot of gunpowder action.

It had happened when the car had rolled to a stop down a bank when the battery had gone dead. We were on the outskirts of a small village. On hindsight, perhaps the two Soviet Army boys should not have been saying somewhat pompously in Russian to the passing natives, *"Dat prikurit."* It meant literally, "Give me a light." Not as in smoking a cigarette but in boosting the flat battery with jumper cables. It didn't come across as if they were asking for help, more like a demand to the peasants. I'd heard the overdone widely grinning helpful young villager with nicotinic-stained teeth in his mid-twenties loudly say *"Yakshi, yakshi,"* in acknowledging help as he bowed twice subserviently, and he had walked fast a quarter of an hour enthusiastically towards the nearby houses.

Within another five he had returned with an elderly driver in a rundown colourless van from another era in dire need of a spray job. It had pulled up facing opposite but across from us with a gap of a few feet. I was flipping through a pocket-size language translation mini-computer that our Russian drivers had in their possession and had loaned to me, and was still pondering why would the young Armenian respond with the words "no problem" twice seemingly so sarcastically, apparently in Azeri and not Armenian. It didn't fit the equation.

The answer came as the younger man had rushed out of the van's nearside door. As Oleg and Misha had bent under the open bonnet together he had suddenly sliced the two Russians from behind with several swings of a homemade machete. The blonde crew-cut Misha in a reflex action shot him twice in the head at close range with his other good arm, while his main right hand dangled by a tendon. The older Armenian sat frozen in the driver's seat on the far side – surprised by Misha's fast reaction – stared across with his hands aloft while the Russian, in extreme pain, trained his pistol steadily on him. After a quick scan around the surroundings, slowly Misha sank on to one knee, while refusing to lower his sight through the van's nearside open passenger door, targeting at the only man he could see in his near vicinity.

One could see immediately Oleg was in danger of dying. He'd instinctively jumped sideways as the blow had come, but the blade had caught him on the side of the head between the lower jaw and his neck. Had he been wearing a metal helmet it still would not have saved him. White bone jutted out with spots of sprouting red and he was lying there on his back between the dead engines of the two vehicles, spitting blood. He could have been decapitated. If I wasn't there, I don't think he would have survived.

I'd been on my feet at once, yelling to Misha, instructing him to connect the cables and to get in the front seat of our car. I leaped over the dead man, with half of his head obliterated, and ran around the outside of both motors to the live Armenian sitting there blubbering loudly. I yanked him unceremoniously out of the car seat, as a knife clattered to the floor from his lap, shoving him hard into the deck of dust by the side of the road. By now, Misha had limped half way around the back of the van and had his handgun trained on the facedown prone man. Glancing in the van's reverse mirror, I could see a few dozen villagers were scrambling out, en masse, in the four hundred yards distance toward where the clash had taken place, after hearing the sound of a double spat echo of Misha's pistol. One could see some of the men were armed with hammers and sickles.

Misha had done the job I'd told him to do. I turned the van's ignition and pumped the pedal a few times, as Misha did likewise in our car. Eventually our old banger rumbled into life. I shot out past the two men and unplugged the two red and black cables, and slammed *both lids down*. Why I did the van's bonnet as well, I'll never know, strangely perhaps out of habit. As I came around and passed him, Oleg actually had the presence of mind to prime his pistol and hand it up blindly to me where he laid, then he'd crawled by himself into the back of our car, unable to stand up himself upright and get in the door. I had grabbed the gun from him and motioned

Misha to get into the car. For good measure Misha cracked the man lying in front of him viciously on the back of the head. Meanwhile I was getting a profusely bleeding Oleg on both his unsteady feet and the two of them piled into the backseat as the two rear doors banged shut simultaneously. The doors' automatic locks clicking action sounded very much like another clip of shots fired, making me suddenly duck my head unnecessarily in panic.

I dived into the driver's seat, hit the accelerator and bumpily overran the dead man. There's not much you can do for them if they are already dead. The car sped right at the advancing crowd of angry villagers blocking the road ahead. I didn't care if I hit any of them; I just wanted to get the hell out of there. What was left of three of us versus 24 with a wolf-pack mentality was no match, and I didn't know if they were armed with guns or not. I wasn't going to stick around to find out either!

I ploughed through them at easily 100 miles an hour. I know I sideswiped at least one of them as there was a heavy thud on my side of the car. The other side's back window sustained a crack but its non-bullet-proof glass became an instant white cobweb at the point of impact before disintegrating rapidly onto the road. My driver mirror showed no sign of the two in the back as they cowered down. But the wild group we'd passed were still throwing rocks at us. You could hear a couple bouncing off the boot. If anybody had a gun, they missed the target.

Our military training had saved our lives.

For the life of me I don't know how I found it, as I'd never been to Yerevan before. As I sped like a madman careening along the road toward the capital, I read the road signs in slow motion like an intelligent driver is supposed to. Fortunately, they had them up in Russian, unlike out in boondocks, otherwise I would have got lost in translation alone. Twenty minutes later I screeched to a halt outside a hospital complex, honking like a maniac.

When the back door flew open, a river of red spilled out on to my feet. Oleg looked dead already to me, but the medics had quickly appeared and he was administered emergency treatment immediately.

The doctors' training had saved their lives.

The now topless well-muscled Misha amazed me. His hand had been wrapped in his shirt, as he resolutely followed the crowd congregating around Oleg on a stretcher into the inviting jaws of the ashen building.

I was only thinking of our belongings in the boot of the car and, to my own amazement in the pandemonium, I went and calmly parked the banged-up car in the car park 50 yards away – a bloody single tyre trail in crimson dashes followed the vehicle. I locked the vehicle normally, with a squishing feeling in my shoes, and strolled alongside the newly laden reddish path back to where the others had noisily disappeared down the hallway. I was soaked from top to bottom in nervous sweat.

It was an uproar in that hospital! People were shouting wildly back-and-forth at each other for what seemed like hours. But by that evening, it was clear that both the Russian pair were out of danger with limbs remaining intact. I went in to see them but they were both still under anaesthetics.

My own time was running out so I elected then to catch the last train of the day to go back to Tbilisi. Amid all this insanity I had ended up returning to the car to retrieve my own bag. While there I wrote a short note of thanks to the two young Russians, placed it in an envelope the receptionist had given me, then stuffed another kind of notes inside it, sealed it and left it inside one wig stuffed inside the other one in the sole suitcase they shared. I was sure they'd notice that oddity immediately upon opening it. Returning to the ward I left the car key back with the head nurse to give it to them, telling her where they could find their car.

A kindly real ambulance driver gave me lift to Yerevan's main railway station. Sitting in the front cab with him I reflected soberly that in a hospital's emergency waiting room every emotion is witnessed: birth, happiness, the unknown, pain and death. It was interspersed with the scent of freshly cut flowers and the sweet sickly stench of fresh blood, along with various medications that wafted in the air.

* * * * * * * * *

At the station, despite language difficulties, I'd verified that this was going to be a slow train ride and it was going to be an all-nighter, arriving in the Georgian capital of Tbilisi at 7:00 AM the next morning. I noticed they had combined a row of passenger carriages behind a goods train laden with farm animals, which transformed it into a red eye into the blackness of hell with a smell. As the ancient steam engine chugged out of downtown Yerevan just before midnight in the darkness, one could see from the dim lights that the city was expanding outward, leaving an almost blank black centre, a bullet hole kind of effect on the psyche.

It was only then when I lifted my tired feet to rest them up on the top of my bag in front of me that the wet stickiness of still-to-dry blood oozed out of my shoes with a sucking plop on to the clean compartment floor. The smell was sickly and it became a slipshod berth indeed, with me trying not to make too much of a mess while both my feet were still lifted in the air. The man further down and across from me in the carriage never seemed to notice my frequent facial grimaces or the insistent dripping. For a few minutes the clumpy drops spookily fell in unison with the clicking of the railway tracks beneath me. Still the civilian man ignored me as he continued to read his newspaper, while I went on my merry way past him to-and-from the antiquated washroom down the rattling corridor.

The fact that my fellow passenger indicated normalcy about my odd predicament told me something about this remote area of the world. It became an object lesson in the merits of elsewhere, a sad comedy born out of disaster. *When I look back on some of the crazy times in my life, it has at times been a high-wire act without a safety net – but I always landed upright.*

The control at the border back into Georgia seemed tense on both sides. The fact that it was three in the morning may have had something to do with it. In the grey gloom of the mountains on the dimly-lit platform I got a sense that after the train was on its way, everybody working there would be on their way home, and a new platoon would take over duties. Everyone and everything looked worn and tired. It's quite spooky up there alone in the dark in an outlandish country. *I expected the unexpected to be the norm.*

I'd fortunately spruced up considerably well before arrival, albeit sockless, though my Moscow-issued Soviet passport seemed a bit of a novelty to the departure desk in Armenia and at the Georgian arrival desk a few yards over, despite both countries being a part of the Union. Both tired bleary men took it to their respective commanding officer's to flip through for approval. I guess it wasn't an everyday occurrence up in these somehow touchingly romantic sparse peaks. Who really knows where their heads were at up here? Still that "you are not welcome here" feeling continued to hang in the air, an invisible noose around the neck.

An hour or so later the show was on the road again. I stayed awake to enjoy the dawn as we weaved through the rocky terrain but I missed the grand entrance crawling into Tbilisi, sitting upright only as the train grounded to a vibrant stuttered shudder. Out of the window, it was an old world station, a relic from the previous century. I was one of the last passengers to disembark and strolled quite slowly along the platform pulling my case. The crowd ahead were being bottle-necked by an authoritative uniformed ticket collector at the gate.

As is customary with me, I could see two spook types monitoring me from 50 yards away at the end of the line. They knew I'd seen them and they began their twin zeroing at me as they shoved against the tide of commonalty pushing to exit. I got a mild spine creep up my back and started to walk slower to force the drumbeat in my ears to obey. I desperately needed to regulate my breathing right then. A few minutes later the biggest guy strode up to me and said my passport's name in perfect Russian. "Lieutenant-General Gioradze of the KGB is waiting to have breakfast with you at the airport. We are to escort you there during your brief stay in our country. Welcome to Tbilisi, Georgia." The other man discreetly took my suitcase. There was nothing I could do but remain calm and do as they said. How they knew it was me and that I was going to the airport was bewildering. As the heat crawls slowly across your soul I willed it to not to let my imagination take over.

But strangely they weren't threatening or obnoxious in their demeanour. Sitting in the back of an Iranian-made Peyhan, the interior was not entirely dissimilar to a larger model Yugo. These two Georgians were pretty genial, pointing out places of interest on the fast ride out of the capital. As usual I knew a thing or two about the international game of football so I had mentioned the only Georgian player I knew. As soon I brought up Slava Metreveli's name everything had become different. Now I was their instant pal simply because I, a Russian to them, knew the national idol by name. They told me he played 48 times for the Soviet Union and were very proud of his achievements. *Every little bit helps in a dire situation.* My two escorts also broke with security protocol and introduced themselves as Kakha and Avtandtil. Next it was my cue to ask them what their boss' first name was and the answer was Igor. To know that helped calmed my singed nerves I thought.

The airport was across the other side of metropolis from the main railway station so we traversed through the city centre. The upside was that I was saving a lot in taxi fare; I was going to find out the downside soon enough.

Tbilisi was almost as big as Moscow, it seemed. Thousands of inhabitants were on their way to work at this early hour. We sat at a traffic light for 10 minutes at one time, which was on "green" but the cross street's transport had blocked the flow. While there was gridlock in progress, it was a chance to take in the feel of the streets and I wound down my back seat car window.

Lots of young people were milling around with children of their own already. Tbilisi, too, like Yerevan, had its fallout's from society panhandling from those with nothing to spare for themselves. One old badgered woman begged me through the open car window. She was pretty once, and she struck me that she was a former prostitute and there was a whiff of cheap fragrance. Shopkeepers were shooing her away, some even throwing small stones at her hard. Now she was battered between anxiety and anger after a life of casual brutality and moral assassination. Strained parents were also screaming and hitting their screaming children violently in full view of bored onlookers. Paying the price later of a tidal pull few moments of pleasure years ago. All the while every driver around us was pushing on his droned horns incessantly. It added to a haunted emotionalism, which continued to hold my attention like a metal clamp. Yet this was early morning, what would it be like later in the long day? I yearned for the good old days of just over a week ago in Western Europe, among cultures not on the brink where we barely think to blast noise at nothing.

The check-in at Aeroflot had also gone smoothly. Once the security boys had flashed their identity badges at the airline staff, we'd gate crashed to the front of the queue. I'd expected that, after seeing the way they'd previously brushed aside the angrily whistling traffic policeman outside the terminal. He was mad at them for leaving the car in the no parking zone. The over-zealous cop walked away with his tail between his legs, whimpering.

And so into the vacuum I stepped head-up with a brave face waiting for the blue touch paper to be lit. The burly head honcho was having his breakfast and reading the morning paper when we arrived. He brusquely waved the smaller, or perhaps less senior of the two escorts away. Avtandtil had winked at me briefly as he took off back to the car. Igor, the fussy boss-type, wasn't particularly in a good mood this morning, most probably hung over from the night before, and his miserable disposition shone through. The bigger man, Kakha, who spoke perfect Russian, remained standing by Gioradze's table half to attention, as I found a nearby wooden chair and carried it up to the table. I hid my nervousness well and waited patiently for him to invite me to be seated, including gesturing if I may sit. As no motion was forthcoming, I stood there out of deference to him. Who knows what the local custom was and I wished not to infringe upon it.

Finally, he'd finished his chewing but not the article he was digesting. Without looking up from his newspaper, his voice had that morning deep roughness. I thought he was going to use a translator but he didn't, he thanked me for finding the time to see him in Russian and that he only wanted to thank me personally. That puzzled the heck out of me. I still had no clue yet as to why I was standing sockless in front of him.

"Well I have two hours before my flight to Moscow is called so you can thank me as often as you would like to," I responded calmly in my best aristocratic Russian.

My statement was designed to make him look up at me, which he then did. He then slowly took me in, a full top to bottom and back up observance, including the oddity of nudity below the trousers. I'd put him at my own age. I must have ticked some boxes in his head and a strange transference happened then, as if he had categorised me as an apparatchik and *shikarnyy* (posh) at that. He stood up, waved his hand and invited me to sit down in the best kiss-my-arse fashion given his slight bow. It seemed to me I was suddenly a person worth cultivating.

After the niceties were out of the way and a breakfast ordered for me, he fixed his stare on me again. It made me shiver internally then but my face remained cool.

Even though I had explored all the possibilities his comment wasn't what I expected. "I understand two of my detachment will not be travelling on their tour of duty to Afghanistan due to injuries sustained in your presence while in Armenia. They called in late last night as they were expected to do under such circumstances." He stopped to sip his tea before continuing, "Do you mind telling me what you were all doing there?"

I stuck to my game plan and replied that I was interested to see the countryside and paid them for their services. For reasons that went beyond normalcy I added that I "wanted to see if there was any business to be done" in the region. I don't think he wholly believed me, not from the way he kept looking into me.

"May I ask you a question?" I asked, doing my best to side-track his attention elsewhere. I understood men of his mentality a bit. He invited me to proceed.

"The men who picked me up at the station and brought me here said you were a Lieutenant-General in the KGB and you've just told me you are going to Afghanistan. What is your regiment, that is if you can tell me?"

He looked proud then, puffed his chest a bit and announced grandly, "We are *osobogo naznacheniya* (special purpose) troop *Kaskad* (Cascade) in the 8th Guards Directorate. We have been posted to Kandahar, leaving next week."

I played dumb, "Special purpose is the same as special forces?"

"That is correct."

"Well I can assure you can be proud of the two young chaps I hired to have a driving holiday around Armenia. In all the time we were together they didn't once mention they were so highly trained, only that they hailed from Leningrad."

That seemed to bring a smile of pride to his face just as my breakfast arrived. "One was my best sniper and the other, his best mate, could fix anything that was broken."

I related to him about the attack the day before. Perhaps he could shed some light on the incident. I was more than curious, given that I could have died.

He folded his newspaper carefully and fixed his steely eyes on me. "There are many assaults daily on strangers in this very dangerous part of the world. You are in the cauldron of a dramatically changing society. The peoples of the Trans-Caucasus region are angry at anything, anybody. I can tell you tourism will not be a growth industry for my country or for any of our neighbours for many years to come while we try to reduce the flames beneath the boiling mood of our respective societies."

I raised my eyebrows as if this was news to me. He pulled out a neatly folded piece of notepaper from his inside pocket of his jacket. "I had my contact in Yerevan specifically investigate your particular incident. I don't like learning surprises the way I did. He concluded that three local men were killed. One instantly from multiple gunshot wounds in the head; one battered to death from a blow or blows to the head; and one died hours later after being run over by a car speeding through a crowd." So Misha murdered the old man I thought; and I'm the hit-and-run driver.

"All par for the course. One verbal report I received stated that the village had been known to harbour rebels sympathetic to the ethnic Armenian problems in Azerbaijan, and that they were allied to the opposition nationalist Dashnak party. Another indicates that the Iranian intelligence unit, SAVAMA, *Sazamaneh Etela'at va Amniateh Mihan*, are behind it all. Either way, to me, that's an excuse to rob and loot. They are nothing but pirates and thieves hiding behind a cause, even if they only earn wages in roubles of the equivalent of US$10 a month, if at all. They must have liked the watches and clothes you wore."

I learned that the Georgians and Armenians were predominantly Christian while the Azeris and the rest of the region were Muslim. There was a bitter war going on over Nagorno-Karabakh, a disputed enclave where Armenians separatist fighters were trapped in the wrong country. There were a lot of rumours of planned harvesting of the vast natural reserves in the Caspian Sea by an international consortium. Whatever the logistics were, the longer-term political goal by the parties was to deprive Iran of an opportunity to extend its economic influence in the region. Because with Iran came their most fundamental militant brand of Shi'a Islam, a body of teaching generally known also as *sharia*, and not even the Azeris and Turks – both Muslims – wanted it. It had many splintering divisions within its secular religion and its implementation varied from one Islamic land to another. They also had their own strong traditions and national identities to consider in the volatile flammable fermentation.

Plus, to add fuel to the fire, while this pot was fuming, the non-Muslims who were stuck in the centre of this hot oven – the Armenians – had their own hatred erupting at all things related to Russians, who they blamed for abandoning them to their fate against the marauding Islamic faith. It was a barbecue roasted half way down the fuse, ready to be burnt to a crisp at any given time. "The guns will talk again and again," was his conclusion on the whole quasi politics-religion-communism-capitalism issue.

At that point the morose boss dismissed Kakha suddenly and continued in his heavily accented Russian. "They lie like rugs too," suggested Gioradze not too subtly. "Which doesn't help my investigations. It's so bad, I'm inclined to take one of the sweeter bribes and stop this ridiculous practical joke, you understand? The normal life here is about embezzlement, bribes and kickbacks – corruption is king! But the good side of me says that I'll only do it if my country benefits from the exercise." He smiled dully at his own hint of an ambition with absolutely no enthusiasm.

By way of pacifying him I volunteered to him that while I was based in Moscow I too had heard the talk about Big Crude Oil and Big Natural Gas coming to these lands.

It was as if I had hit him over the head with a sickle and hammer as his hard, but cool, demeanour visibly went taut before my eyes. *Balancing on the tightrope of highly-strung emotion and trying to avoid the precipices of the jagged rocks inside his wired mental landscape.*

The man had simply stopped talking and just sat there going through the motions of paying for his food. A thin film of perspiration shined as he turned his head to the waitress. I got the impression he was close to the end of his rope *before* going into a war zone. His resonance of stress was pulsating low but measurable shock waves were directed at me. His knees were oscillating that annoyingly sifted nervous energy I've always found distracting and his facial movements betrayed tension. He'd already subconsciously given me a clue – the part about the backhanders. It *had* been tendered to him heretofore. I was convinced of that, and he was just pondering it over about when and where it suited him. To me he was conducting his life like he was covering his tracks, so that when he does piss off, nothing could be found on him, as if it mattered by then. I took out some money to pay for my part of our breakfast together.

With my action, it inadvertently gave him the opportunity to switch the subject. Individuals in his current mode usually do when they had other things on their mind, so when they talk to others they think one has nothing to do with the other. I, after all, had the same to him earlier. Sometimes it was totally related; sometimes not at all. A bit like going fishing without having bait handy. "Parts of Georgia are in for another year without summer," he snorted suddenly. I begged for an explanation with my expression but his headlights shone past me at something just off to my left ear.

The heavily accented voice continued, "The land-based oil wells are on fire in Azerbaijan and the smoke drifts this way, creating a permanent cloud over our country. We know for a fact the Iranians dynamited the rigs and wish to keep them alight. By doing so they keep pressure on our region to succumb to their financial aid, while at the same time the Azeris will lose substantial revenues. We all know what comes with that Iranian money. Their assassination agents from the Iranian Ministry of Intelligence & Security are always training the *Dushman* (enemy). They're always up to no good in the name of Allah.

"If that wasn't bad enough, Moscow Centre is continually on my case to send spy teams to their barely remaining satellite nations in the nearby Autonomous Republic of North Ossertia and in Dagestan. The Chechens are also giving everybody problems trying to achieve independence. How do you turn off a whistling kettle if you have no hands." It was a statement, not a question. He trailed off in thought.

He drank the last of his lukewarm tea with a final gulp and looked at his wristwatch. "I've had enough. It's never ending. Did I answer your question?" He beckoned over the nearby Kakha and instructed him in Russian to take him home to his "Krtsanisi city residence." Abruptly he was gone with his shadow in tow. Oddly, he never shook my hand in greetings or in departure. There went a rude man with a lot on his mind. The excess weight on his brain needed to be burned off. Still to give him the benefit of the doubt, it sounded like he was on his way home after working all night, and not on the way to the office this morning.

He never mentioned that his monetary interests were probably allied with the Russians' *novaya politika* (new policy). Russia never really married Georgia; it was more a common law arrangement following a sexual proposal delivered on its knees, following her being forcibly widowed by the Soviet Union. Their oil companies, Lukoil, Yukos and Sibneft, already had billions of barrels in reserve. Any one of them was bigger than Amoco, Royal Dutch/Shell and British Petroleum. A little known fact in the west. Georgia was only subservient to her masters in the grand scheme of things because she allowed them to be and to so participate in the profits.

I went and purchased some clean socks in a shop in the airport. The flight north from Tbilisi to the Russian capital was uneventful. Within hours I was already outbound home to London with a switch of passports, luggage and pocket money. No receipts were asked for. It would be entered in accounting as a stipend anyway.

I tendered my detailed dossier to the SIS for likely re-editing and embellishments for eyes further up the steps of the temple of money via the Cabinet Office's new projects considerations team. There was, however, no mention in my report of a rock festival, young men from Russian special forces on holiday with bad fake wigs who nearly died, nor of giants and a dwarf, and killers with knives. I also omitted an exclusive two hours chatting about current affairs with a junior KGB general going to fight a war with the *mujahideen* (struggling people doing jihad, in Arabic) in Afghanistan who were funded by the west. Clearly the lesson learned from the brief encounter was that the Soviet Union intended to stay on longer than everybody thought at the time.

What was neatly typed there was everything else that I'm not allowed to divulge.

My immediate boss did say to me that I had garnered a helluva lot of information in so short a time span. If only he knew what else happened… It really is a wonderful fascinating world out there, if only one is ready to face it full on into its fury.

On hindsight this is the real mean world of real intelligence gathering, being on the real mean streets where the real mean information is, and learning it from real mean people the real mean way. It's not about having to kill anybody; it's about paying honest attention to what's happening in front of you (and looking behind oneself, too). Everybody's got to share in the spoils, not just the few.

* * * * * * * * *

Chapter Eight

*If you knew the precise time of your death
what would you do to prepare for it?*

For a moment I was speechless, as if a cricketer had bowled a sly grass cutter underarm along the ground with the slithering ball getting through my defences to hit the stumps and a bail slowly dropping off. I just couldn't believe I was being reassigned back to Bulgaria. The last time I had been there, some five years earlier, I served 11 weeks of brutal and solitary confinement in a prison monstrosity after being accused of espionage. I'd suffered regular beatings and torture that I was still coming to terms with their after-effects. I thought back then I was going to burn in hell but mercifully I didn't fry. After the ordeal I had no desire to ever see that place again for as long as I lived. Yet now The Firm were sending me back for a special op job! *They were making me climb back on the horse that I had fallen off from.* The news I'd just read had me gawking like an idiot.

Actually the Oprep's (Operational Report) language had specifically stated that the term "run interference" was being applied. That meant the mission would be conducted without the knowledge or hindrance of certain departments at SIS as well as within the British government. Ostensibly it was taken to avoid bureaucratic delays and paperwork that would be generated between the parties, so that expediency would not be lost. It was a fast track forward move that was illegal, according to the letter of the law, while at the same time it was orally endorsed by ministers. As a younger man I followed orders but experience educated me to tread carefully in slippery environs that started with red flags.

"So it's a hush job," I said matter-of-factly, finally looking up, into the patriarchal face of the elderly line officer in whose office I'd been ushered into. The plastic plate on the glass-pane door had stated H/BUL/OPS (the London-based Head of SIS' operations in Bulgaria). The man had held his position for decades but it was the first time I'd met him. "Has a codename been designated for the operation yet or is that to be kept quiet too?"

"Yes, it's Operation X," he replied pan-faced in his rather posh accent, then he quasi-smirked as he glanced at his watch. I got the distinct impression he was waiting for someone else and was being inconsiderate by unnecessarily playing with my emotions just in the name of killing time. I was very junior to him, so perhaps he felt he was permitted to boot me around at will. That was the reason I despised coming to London at all as it was dysfunctional at the best of times.

"Bugger you too, sir," I replied politely to his evidently dry tone, "that's not very funny considering my particular circumstances the last time I was there." He was taken aback by my brazen but calm facial response to an SBO (senior British officer) and expressed his displeasure by pointedly raising his eyebrows. With my own sarcasm and my poor choice of words I'd allowed my fear to creep through to the surface, and I was kicking myself under the table for that because that last one pricked under his skin. Besides I really didn't at all like his taunting and lack of deference. After all it was under his watch back in 1976 that I was enslaved while he was country head of SIS operations inside Bulgaria. So he must have known of my human inner pain. Had he no perception of the consequences? "Poor form, old boy," he replied flatly.

Maybe he was another desensitised arsehole. There were quite a few 'to the manor born' types in this building, where social standing in his generation was of utmost importance. For me coming to SIS HQ always seemed like I was entering a secret world of winks and nods along the corridor. It never failed to give me a creepy alien feeling that I was just a dispensable passer-by and the puking outsider of a P (production) officer. Identifying a problem was not the same as curing it but to most of these in-house R (requirement) officers, it was. To me the world interacted in a different way but I still had to endure this form of in-office hazing, simply just to prove that I wasn't a pushover. You could never in a million years disprove the mandarins' in charge one-size fits-all policy that was in keeping with all the diktats passed down. Britain's Foreign & Commonwealth Office, Ministry of Defence, Secret Intelligence Service (MI6) and Security

Service (MI5) all fell into line obediently.

In the end it was frequently the wee tweaks and snap decisions of covert field operators like me who saved the day. By expertly hiding these actions from the bosses we avoided the tremendous costs of sending thousands of troops to risk their lives, not to mention the machinery required on-site to perform the job. But some of these bureaucrats didn't comprehend what went on out there in the field; a bit of winging it by the seat of your pants was needed sometimes. *Smart people can play dumb but dumb people can't play smart*, often came to mind when I was there. The solution would be to let sleeping dogs lie and move on. I shrugged off the bait to bite and let him chew on it.

I had arrived home only that morning from the Berne station in Switzerland. So the strange and strained mating dance and pushing of psychological buttons at SIS' Century House had started already. It always did and I never got used to the intellectual bullying that went on, and it was all executed in the name of the ruling class' consciousness that was rather peculiarly exclusive to England, and still is.

My superior and I didn't seem much to like each other as it was, right off the back, but my blood was pumping loudly still. He was a smart, older Englishmen of a certain standing that believed in exercising his power by naturally mocking everyone with a haughty studious silence. After an eternity he eventually half-smiled, unapologetically and looked away briefly. He then drilled back into my eyes before his pale face hardened, as if resuming the war of no words. It was then that I thought the bastard's skin hadn't seen daylight for ages and he could have been constipated. Finally, to relieve the perceived tension I half-threw him back the file I was still holding. To my mind, I had just psychologically scored two goals against him: His look-away and my chucking move. I begrudged unnecessary attacks on my dignity or anyone else's as it was a higher form of character assassination. I deserved better treatment. But he wasn't going to afford me such satisfaction.

"Anderson, was that really meant to be a statement of record followed by a supposed declaration of intent? You know full well I could write you up on the SAF (Staff Appraisal Form) for using a swear word towards a senior officer then belligerently tossing a report back at me." It was an attempt at intimidation but the light film of perspiration in an air conditioned room betrayed his toothless nip. I already had a track record for being a maverick, so I performed a devil may dare fake grin all for him by letting him see all my gnashing teeth then slowly putting my feet up on a chair for good measure. I wasn't the type that played the victim but trying to be dignified about it wasn't easy.

So I just sat there defiantly with my eyelids flickering in controlled anger and feeling the cold sweat leaking from my internal defrosting fridge. It felt much like the way insomnia stretches the already tense gut as a long minute ticked by. I conceded a late goal back to him, *a 2-1 away win to me then*. I detested having to deal with these officious types with a holier-than-thou attitude that treated the whole stupid stratagem as a political-sports contest of sorts while they waited for retirement, the gold watch, gold pen and gold cufflinks...

Suddenly the door flung open just behind me, startling us both. Another aged man's voice sang, "Now, now, you two, that's enough palaver." He must have been listening in somehow, perhaps by holding an ear against the door's mottled glass window? I smiled weakly, *mentally* I hadn't allowed the other fellow to score one back on me but I allowed one anyway...to my reasoning. I stood my ground to him. I got up to greet the entrant.

I didn't know who this new bloke was but I had no choice but to take his outstretched hand that was already introducing itself in mine. The snot, the first fellow I'd met, had stood up stiffly for him too, which told me the visitor was senior in more ways than one.

"I'm H/SOF (Head of SIS' Sofia station, an undeclared intelligence officer)," he smiled coldly on cue, bending to sit down as I observed his bald patch at 45 degrees. "Just arrived here from Bulgaria yesterday, especially to help you prepare for this important op. I've got tons of stuff for you to digest."

He popped on his wire spectacles and immediately fished out two colour photographs, holding them up for me to see. One was of an obviously deceased man with racoon eyes complemented by a fountain of red across his shirt to confirm so. The other was a mug shot of a different person who was very much alive but striking an unsmiling pose at something beyond and below the unusual camera angle. Both subjects clearly didn't know they were photographed at the time. "This was my local administrative staff manager six months ago. A mild-mannered Bulgarian national with a low-level security clearance who was good at his job, a family man. He was shot dead on his way home in Sofia by an assassin who I have painstakingly finally identified." Putting down the left picture he tapped the second one right on the unhappy individual's crooked nose. "He did it evidently. Or ordered it anyway."

I moved around the table and slowly sat down next to him in the place where the intimidating now mum line officer was previously sitting, requiring him to re-seat a position elsewhere in his own office. I smiled at my subtle substitution move. "And who is he, may I ask?"

"I don't have a proper name yet and not even sure I'll obtain one. In any case this thug goes by the nickname of '60' – six-oh – ...supposedly, and I'm serious, because I understand he gives his victims sixty seconds to live after he has trained his gun on their faces. That's an awful long time to know that you are going to die. Not that anybody I know has confirmed it but apparently he derives pleasure from watching them squirm. More times than not they have to kneel before him before he fires at point blank range behind their ear."

"But how would you know that?" I asked, "Have you spoken to somebody that survived death by him or are you talking from the standpoint of fantasy?"

The plonker whose London office we were occupying found his fingernails of sudden interest while the man from Sofia office stared inside me for quiet long seconds, hesitated, shook his head and stuttered, "No, no, of course not. I'm repeating an actual rumour that one of our... – so far a very dependable Bulgarian source, a third-hand witness, as it were – has passed on to us. I do find you a rather sharp chappie, I must say Anderson. A bit contemptuous."

Chappie? As in a schoolboy? I didn't say anything. I could have mentioned that I was treated exactly the same way a short while ago. I picked up the photo to study it. You couldn't mistake this fellow. He had a huge completely bald head that was much larger in proportion to the body, the camera's downwards angle notwithstanding. His jaw jutted out almost as much as his cold but contradictory pig pink innocent eyes did. Kind of like a largely expressionless big baby wrestler. "Not the kind that would cry at pictures of cute wee animals. But if I were casting for a movie, he would be perfect for the role of the killer who lived next door," I gibed, trying to release my still knotted nervousness. The subject's manner exuded all things to do with corruption, underhandedness and a perceived bad rotten persona to the core. "What do you know about our lovey-dovey Mr '60' then, obviously by word-of-mouth?"

He hesitated then cleared his throat for emphasis. "Well, as you can see, he suffers from cherubim, a condition that can't be treated, which is to say he's naturally chubby with a rosy complexion. But he is in actual fact a long-time chum of the President of Bulgaria, Todor Zhivkov, and he also happens to be the personal BG (bodyguard) of the head honcho's daughter."

Three more pix were then pulled out of his file and placed neatly in front of me, in specific order from left to right: A PR glossy shot of a petite dark-haired woman in her late-30's, a very official photograph of an old man, and a third pic of both of them posing together with a party of others at some state-like function. "Liudmila Zhivkova. Aged 39. A current photo. Nothing more than a glorified fishwife-cum-daughter really. Her father, same period. Plus, all the others in the clan, taken fairly recently, at a banquet."

She had an elegant yet ordinary beauty about her and at the same time she projected the face of a victim wounded under circumstances unknown to me. Her father on the other hand looked like he was on display at a Soviet wax museum, with his arms glued alongside his torso, or maybe he was listening to the national anthem at the time. I observed a collection of dark and intensely cruel faces that gave me good reasons to have extreme prejudice against.

The Sofia station head cleared his throat again and sat back to read a document in his choice plum-under-the-tongue awfully-awfully posh accent, pointing at the middle snap of the elderly chap. "Todor Zhivkov, communist ruler of Bulgaria since 1954 to this day, 1981. While his physical health appears okay, his political health is in decline due to the effects of his mental health, which are caused by being occupied with everyday problems that were not every day. Goes by the nickname Tato."

I could not contain a glimmer of a smile at the oddly comical phrasing in the report and mildly shook my head in wonder. I thought to myself that an entry level staff member just out of kindergarten must have written it in a hurry. But the reader didn't seem to notice the absurdity of the language. "Any spelling mistakes there?" I said with a straight face.

Ignoring my prompt and with his eyes down he kept perusing the document for content, perhaps searching for more pertinence than the previous verbiage. He then continued: "As you know all the Eastern bloc countries are not free and their own governments are stitched by the hand of Moscow in a kind of *dvoyevlastiye*, which means their societies are designed in such a way that it is knitted as a dual lining into the overall fabric of Communism. However, Bulgaria goes one better. It likes to remove its internal and external enemies but doesn't bother to tell Mother Russia what it does. Like an unruly son, if you get my gist."

I kind of did but there was nothing I didn't know so far. He may as well have described our own in-house UK relationships and the people within its sphere, so I just nodded cautiously. I knew he was leading up to something though. He looked up momentarily, removed his glasses and fixed his look on mine as if sizing me up. "Tsk-tsk. Don't fool yourself, old chap. Don't allow my words to create their own reality. *Risks cannot be completely eliminated but they can be minimised.*" That told me he wasn't always a desk-bound fellow. Had maybe done something out in the field himself. He was based in Sofia after all. Not an easy place to be in the cold war.

Yet I knew that, too, but still didn't know what he really meant so played safe by maintaining my best goose egg face. I think my quips were getting to him but I did like his last volley back at me: there was some backbone spunk there at least. He commanded my attention commendably.

Specs back on, he was focused on the paper again. "When there is no reaction from the Bulgarian public to anything he does, bad boys like him think what they did wrong is acceptable. It's what I would have called 'naïve enthusiasm' because he's really like a wild animal searching for prey to kill needlessly all the time. A blood-lust legal Bulgarian Jack the Ripper with a gun and then some. It won't be swept under the carpet as they hope it will." How on earth would he know that last bit I thought, tight-lipped? There's something he's not saying and besides who is 'they'?

"Basically the people in-the-know there don't talk because nobody wants to rock the boat…," the London-based officer volunteered brightly, looking smug with his marvellous insightful non-contribution. They both gave each other their best old boys' network glances, making me feel more like the trespasser that I was. I was a servant with two masters, there at their beck and call.

"…Yes, exactly," our man in Sofia agreed. "So my point is: We can pull off this job with less exposure than normal and any witnesses to the event won't say boo anyway. That is the psychological portrait of the straightjacketed Bulgar public right now, hey what."

"So," I said, sounding my best to be perplexed, which I was, "what *exactly* is the precise game plan here then…?"

…Thus, it is a typical example of how tasks were verbally developed at Century House, SIS' London headquarters at the time. Complex life and death missions were flippantly treated as a board game of some kind. In my humble opinion, it was akin to a fast race circuit plans designed by amateurish racing drivers sitting on swivel chairs with wheels in their office suites in high-rises. They are far removed from the cambered street below and yet they take the credit by claiming success when the problem was barely solved by the man actually out there in the open. And if this is not enough these same managers

then later get the credit for having prevented any further problems. There is also a lot of back patting among them, all performed in their distinctive private club-member accents. There was no comfortable slot whatsoever for their comportment in the real world of life and death, an environment where I sometimes visited for a living. The generalised sweeping statements of their opaque world were in sharp contrast to the finer-tuned scrutiny of mine.

Intelligence officers of this category from the office who had never set foot in a combat zone, albeit, were jolly good at making very elegant phone calls though that were interpreted by the listener as exercising a certain delicate deep political pressure to achieve the desired ends. That part was definitely something mostly blunt me couldn't do so well, I admitted so to myself.

Like most field operators, I had started my career at SIS headquarters on the analytical side but was transferred rather swiftly to the operational side once some of the head honchos figured out I had a knack of making the worm turn somehow, some way, and reasonably quickly. To me HQ was an air-locked time capsule, not really on top of the situation but in charge of it nevertheless. I would come when summoned, listen to the controllers, get my orders and if working by myself I would then pretty much improvise as I went along the path thereon. The projected end result on paper almost never reflected the actual events and what found its way into the eventual official documents wasn't true most of the time, either. I'd only been in the service a fortnight when I first learnt the fact that any file "not processed" had no number designated to it so therefore officially did not exist, and won't ever…

Well, as it was eventually explained to me over the course of HQ's usual pantomimic word quiz game, "60" was a certified psychopath who murdered people at will and often, without any command from those above him. He was able to abuse his own position frequently because he enjoyed the luxury of being next to the kid of the number one man, so he was both the protector and the protected. The fact that I could die by his hand was somehow missing in the play of directives being delivered to me, and that had bothered me. And never once did they bring up the fact that I'd nearly expired there before in this exact same country I was being sent to. I came to realise that these twin twats couldn't have cared less about such frivolities. It was a personal psychological barrier if there was ever one to hurdle over in one's life: And in truth *I was scared shitless.*

But, apparently, "60" had indeed made one big fatal mistake. Knowingly or unknowingly, he had bumped off one of our key men and he was going to pay for it, as deemed by Her Majesty's Secret Intelligence Service's inner circle that was unofficially sanctioning a bloodletting reprisal. The holiest of the holy had decided so, and I had to obey their verdict.

While I wasn't going to be cast as the one doing the actual bad deed, I was nevertheless going to have a supporting role in the preparation and execution of the operation. That meant I would be an actor on the black fringe of the bright spotlight and would be a witness to it on centre stage. I was going to do the ground work and await further orders in-country.

So he was slated for elimination and I was unwillingly chosen to participate in the compartmented pre-production. Somewhere, somebody on the top floor must have presumed I wanted to exact some revenge of my own for what they did to me previously. What else could it be? Of that I was sold on but it was far from the complete story. Five years later I had no anger left, only apprehension. Otherwise why pick me? Were they trying to drain any raw emotions I had left? I was never a cold-blooded non-judicial executioner though in my time I had indeed slain in defence of my life, which in turn was conducted in the name of my blameless country.

Likewise, I was instinctively convinced there was more to the op than met the eye but I would probably never ever learn the central logistics of the four W's though I did know one of them already: *Who.* My job then was to obediently follow the script and that's *What* they thought I did well. Being an occasional institutional killer on behalf of one's country, *When* the need arose, it was assumed to be an acceptable part of advancing one's career at SIS. It was therefore simply assumed by the higher-ups to be nothing but a one-week non-official cover task in the plot to kill a killer. The *Why* I was to learn as events unfolded.

But I had my own points of contention. First, nothing can be planned on paper in the real changing-by-the-minute astute world of covert international espionage – *nothing at all.* Secondly, there was a clearly discernible climate at HQ in those days from the top down from those old farts to us lower gits following orders to constantly remind us of this pecking order and to make us well aware that we were considered expendable...if it ever came down to it. Finally, if anybody irrespective of their rank that tried to control the operational risks but went about it in an over-zealous manner, he or she was unintentionally assumed to be attracting undue attention to themselves in the protection of their own 'hidden agendas'. In my case they were clearly wrong to assume this. Not everybody sought promotion. I was happy doing what I was doing having just turned 30. My Danish girlfriend was ill and I wanted to nurse her back to health. That's where my head was. It was as simple as that.

Objectivity is understood very differently in each culture. In my own Anglo-Saxon nation, it was in many cases compromised because of the deeply-seated class system. It was also blinkered enough to ensure failure from the onset. But Britain is not entirely alone in its elitist thinking either. Every nation has its one thousand or so who feel they are above everything and not answerable to the millions of people they hold power over. This fact had dawned on me some time ago.

With all that in mind, I shall herein try my best to explain this highly complex and explosive mission that I found myself in. To use a metaphor, it was a potent mix of ingredients added into someone else's pot of boiling minestrone soup and it had a mass of long threads of pasta boiling simultaneously. The taste, or rather what transpired next, was the weirdest experience in my life up to that time but the sepia tint did eventually seep over the top in juicy colour, and fantastically so. *And what you think you are doing isn't so, not by a thousand miles.*

* * * * * * * * *

(Long dull hours under slow harsh lights,
steel doors clanging through endless dim nights,
concrete floors with silhouette scars,
stark flat shadows and cold iron bars.)

'15 July 1981 – *Narodna Republika Bălgariya'* had just been stamped in my authentic Romanian passport at the frontier kiosk between the People's Republic of Bulgaria and Romania…I was fighting an attack of bad memories of the time my real Englishman self was last here that momentarily unhinged me. I stood in the sluggish queue leading towards that single bored green uniformed passport official, who had momentarily stifled a yawn of the disinterested…it was suddenly an encouraging sign as he was starting to be less attentive to people like me! *In a sense I was fighting my inner fear. I was on the verge of getting back on that wild bucking bronco again, the same one I fell off badly once before…but my adrenaline started to kick in to conquer it.* He never even gave me a second glance. The double bang of his metal stamper made me blink twice, as I confidently crossed the point of no return…the trembling me was left on the other side of the line while a newly bolstered and calmer persona crossed over with me to this side… I felt the pinpricks in my heart and heard the sound of booming receding as I walked on back into the world of NOC.

Once in-country I began to assess how I looked through the eyes of others. It alternated between the non-natural movement of slow motion and then reverted back in my mind's eye to speed the tape into normal sight mode again. Functioning parts were clicking back into focus frame-by frame in camera-controlled order. The butterflies were thankfully now resting kindly on the helipad of safety. The drabness of the previously tunnel-like corridor widened to welcome the sunlight ahead, while the echo of my footsteps weakened on the linoleum behind.

Exiting that terminal and across the dusty walkway was a border town's usual tired-looking bus station scenery in front of me. In the glass I saw my mirror image walking along with my small battered suitcase past the spanking huge red and white billboard at street level. Its reflection extolled backwards in Cyrillic the virtues of the *Bǎlgarska Komunisticheska Partiya*, or BKP in short. As I looked away to read it forward it deciphered from *Bǎlgarski* (Bulgarian) to read: Communist Party of Bulgaria.

Columns of obedient and unsmiling people, stood with their backs to the giant sign patiently waiting in orderly lines. Many were sucking stinking second-grade imported Turkish cigarettes or fart-smell Dukats (a popular cheap Russian brand), while the belching buses were blowing dark fumes into our lungs as they sat stationary with doors closed till way past the scheduled departure time. All the while they had their engines running in typical communist economical mode. I filed in at the longest queue marked *Sofiya*. There were several faces I'd recognised that were also on the same hour and a half-long non-stop bus ride with me from Bucharest to Ruse, this nondescript town where we were all parked in now. A ruse for what I wondered imaginatively – even its name meant wily subterfuge – as it's mostly all the same deceptively boring square concrete blocks of the same colour.

The man standing in front of me was reading that day's foreign news section of the Romanian morning paper that, ironically, showed a group photo featuring Liudmila Zhivkova in the centre. She'd just been appointed to the powerful position of chair of the Bulgarian Commission of Science, Culture and Art and had been responsible for the successful national celebration of the country's 1,300[th] anniversary several years earlier. I knew that info from a week ago at SIS but it was today's news behind the Iron Curtain when reporting about itself. I didn't spot "60" there among the sea of grainy black and white faces on the page. 'Wherever you are lad, your accidental assistant to an assassin is coming to get you,' I thought grimly.

My own real country's "culture department" had given me a crash course in basic Romanian that lasted just a few days. It was needed to provide me with the cover of a Romanian man who had lived in Moscow for 20 years and who was just a year younger than the real me. The poor bloke had died a week ago in a car crash but thank goodness such record-keeping was slow in the overly centralised communist cosmos. In any event I would have left here by the time the data had been recorded in the land of his birth, if it was at all. And so it was the same with their media reporting, as I'd just evidenced.

Fortunately, though my Russian was flawless, and I could fall back on it more convincingly once in Bulgaria, but still I understood enough of that Romanian newspaper article and its cynical promotion of propaganda. Russian, Bulgarian and Romanian are Slavonic languages but they are spoken with very different accents. Bit like listening to Brits, Aussies and South Africans.

Standing there like a mannequin I observed all manner of Iron Curtain-manufactured transport parade through the square where the bus station stood: I saw clanking Cspel lorries, a Romanian Aro jeep, mini Balaton cars from Hungary, a Czech three-wheeler Velorex and even a Smyk micro car from Poland. I was again reminded that it's a different planet here inside the Marxist biosphere. A wholly different mind set stares out of the shop window at you.

Finally aboard that Hungarian-made packed clunky Ikarus bus – it was another 186 miles (300 km) to the capital – an uncomfortable all-seater especially designed for the workforce class, I went through a brief chronicle of Zhivkova again in my head: She was born in Bulgaria this same summer month in 1942; spoke perfect English; graduated from Sofia University, then studied history and art at Moscow State University Lomonossov, before finishing her education of history in Britain's Oxford University; she was also a vegetarian and openly practised Buddhism and Hinduism in a land of old Orthodoxy and new atheists. Nevertheless, from all accounts she was depicted as a decent caring person in the local public eye, who devoted time to mental health issues. Married to the head of Bulgarian state TV, she had two small children, but she was so outlandishly reform-minded in a most decadent style that staid, conservative communists evidently found her actions offensive, if not obscene by their standards. In her bulky SIS file somebody had unnecessarily hand-written and underlined a summary of words in pencil, *'Crosses the divide from the overly enthusiastic to the ill-advised'*…and, for some strange reason, I now remembered that striking leaden sentence more than all the neatly typed stuff. *Was that our opinion or theirs or both?*

"60" on the other hand was heavily involved in a Bulgarian

international trading company named Kintex, which was part of a paper mill (SIS jargon for a spy network). It smuggled arms into the east and drugs into the west, and shared its profits with senior intelligence officers at *Darjavna Sugarnost*, the Bulgarian state security service. That piece of information had been furnished by Georgi Markov, an exiled Bulgarian dissident writer who worked as a translator for the *BBC* and in return for his tip-off to SIS a few years earlier, as widely reported at the time in the media, was then murdered for being a traitor. The Bulgarian hit man or woman delivered the poison from the tip of an umbrella being pricked on the back of his heel as he stood waiting on the platform in the London Underground in September 1978. Paradoxically the SIS file I'd read recently had remarkably stated otherwise: 'A single iridium pellet laced with rycin was shot from an air pistol into victim's thigh and entered blood stream quickly causing expiration.'

As a measure of "60"'s thinking, it was surmised that the specific day of Markov's death was chosen to celebrate President Zhivkov's birthday, which made him out to be a nationalist. But it was yet another murky statistic of the Bulgarian Mafioso government's "dirty" operations of not advising their socialist Soviet masters of their real capitalistic intent. *How on earth did SIS know that Markov was suddenly a traitor and that was what "60" thought?* This question remained unanswered because I didn't think of asking it but the story certainly didn't add up. And while I usually asked a lot of questions…within myself some were unthinkable to actually espouse, so this one stayed inside me.

"60" was believed, without a reasonable doubt, to be in charge of the wet affairs team that carried that particular job out, meaning that he headed the murder squad. From all accounts he was still also addicted to killing for pleasure, even in his presumed retirement. It was a morbid open secret hobby of his, with more than a dozen notches accredited to his numbered name. And nothing was being done about it until now. *Or so I was told.*

My bosses didn't know I'd spent time in the SIS' library to swot up further information. I'd perused the equally thick general file exclusively on the Kintex concern that "60" was associated with and it had revealed whole bottom-line scenarios of ugly answers. It was a huge profit-making export arm of the aforementioned Bulgarian communist party's secret service, flagrantly operating as a conduit and trading post for all things illegal between the west and east, and in both directions. *Most outrageously those links thrived even between perceived political enemy nation-states that were still fighting bitter wars against each other.* Many of the British firms involved were owned by

Czech-born Robert Maxwell, a well-known UK media baron and a former
Member of Parliament of the British government. What had shocked me
that day was the transportation of weapons being classified as "secret
transit" in my country yet contradictorily lumped into the same product
category as items like liquor and tobacco when it changed hands in Bulgaria.
Shipments were all done openly, like normal business transactions: *A glass
ceiling that existed above the customary configuration of the society the average citizen
lived in and thought we knew*

*There were some eye-watering pointers in that folder that would make anybody lose
faith in humanity. It stank like a septic tank's fumes to the high heavens. What were we
all fighting for then? Were we the people being masturbated on by a smiling string-pulling
and profit-making political class? That naturalised British billionaire's newspaper empire
preached us disinformation daily while the owner and his affiliates operated in the spirit of
the exact opposite…*

This most secret of secret intelligence officers, who rode and died with
state secrets, exhaled slowly and gazed across the aisle out of the left-sided
stained unclean window of the bus at the unseen hills ahead. I could speak
of Bulgaria's stark inconsistencies from experience having been here once
before, yet I am still following orders blindly though with much more
foresight. I was beginning to rumble against the machinated lies and I could
feel my bile rise at the injustices. Thoughts of the prison again flashed
intermittently in my mind on this trip. I still had not found out whether I
was rotting in the jail in Lovech or the one in Skravena, and I really didn't
want to find out either. *You are only as clever as your last mistake Anderson.*
Going deeper into the skin-crawling fear zone of this shithole country again
was akin to Sisyphus constantly peeling a mouldy onion; underneath each
layer is another layer of something else rotting that would make anyone
want to shed even more tears. I inhaled deeply when I glimpsed my likeness
against the glass on my right and quickly looked away as the first seeds of
sheer shame were planted in my head. *It was a watershed moment in my career, at
that precise moment.*

Up came the first manned roadblock. I was told to expect at least one
on this route. Conscripts from the *Armiya* (Army) stood around outside the
bus talking among themselves. Others were leaning on the wall further away
smoking and looking bored with matted hair, their caps off. Their officer,
an older man, his brown uniform appearing too tight on him, stood at the
foot of the bus door barking orders. Two teenaged soldiers in fresh
uniforms holding switched off pistols lamely in their hands clambered
aboard. They looked slightly skittish and wandered up the aisle slowly, to

make it look like they were doing their job. Fortunately, they had no air of intimidation about them but still it was wise not to have strong eye contact, thereby drawing attention to oneself. I was seated in the middle section of the bus curb side, parked on their left as they advanced, and I tried to look wearied and faked a tired long yawn just as they came level with me. They reached the back, obviously found nothing of great interest or anybody to question, then turned and headed back down the way they came a little faster. The head honcho curtly waved the bus driver to proceed, the door clanged shut and we chugged off again. It seemed a normal daily occurrence judging from everybody's low-key reaction to the five-minute delay. This troop of boys would repeat the chores probably dozens of times more throughout their trying training day.

Normally in such instances I would place anything I was transporting elsewhere in the rack, where I could see it above and in front of me, but on this occasion I didn't as I wasn't carrying anything that could incriminate me. Still it's an odd feeling when you experience that "stuck still zone", when you know there's no space to escape to in front, and nor can you turn back...just sitting there like a lame duck slowly squeezing in your already tense guts trying to project normalcy, while hoping that nobody will ask you why as a Romanian I couldn't speak it that well...

Next, as a part of my own training, I consciously tried to appear relaxed while keeping my mind razor sharp so anything that was even of minor interest to occupy the mind was purposely noted:

...There are lots of raspberries in the fields in Bulgaria so it's no wonder they have a reputation for drinking lots of *rakia*, a very potent fruit brandy. I'd been forewarned about going lightly on the stuff, if presented with the opportunity ...

...The bus shunted to a halt twice more, not for any military reason, but to avoid the odd lost goatherd roaming across the country roads. It's a wonder we didn't hit one of them. I got to thinking perhaps there's some local medieval rituals attached to the animals, like the cows in India...

...At every little village we slowed to pass through I noticed too that many small homes displayed a Three-Handed Virgin on the windows sills... (I later learnt that it was a healing icon that kept bad spirits away. A strange belief that is openly played considering religion was officially banned.)

...Exhausted, eyelids drooping, I eventually did fall asleep, fortunately, and no more checkpoints popped up in the mystical homeland of the mortal Orpheus that I drifted off into... I was the fictional Argonaut sailing into the maelstrom to avoid a tragedy...

* * * * * * * * * *

That late afternoon, as we were entering Sofia city centre, I was awakened by the passenger next to me who had turned on tinny music from a portable transistor radio. As I stretched the bus hit some potholes and my first glimpse out was of a cemetery of cement angels dancing stiffly to their tunes. Then the Tsum department store rode by. Next was the mausoleum of Georgi Dimitrov, a Stalinist prime minister from the end of World War II. Apart from those landmarks the place remained the same one-colour off-grey as I had remembered it. You have to understand that the city was so frayed into my personal portfolio that I didn't wish to take any more unnecessary mental photographs for long-term storage in my memory bank, so I willingly blocked them out. I knew I was doing it.

Soon we were all piling out at the crowded bus station. So far so good, nobody had paid any particular attention to me and I in turn ignored everyone else with one single exception. In the mass of milling humanity, a little old gypsy woman had asked me the way to the tomb of Dimitrov in Russian and I actually knew the answer! She kindly blessed me, too, when we departed. I have long realised that I must look like I know my way around because The Lost approach me everywhere in the world! A good sign as it looked like I belonged plus I needed to have some faith in what I was doing.

I had been instructed to walk like a local, not be in a hurry even if late, to the designated POC (point of contact) at nearby St Nedelya Square but I found myself there sooner than I thought. Standing around, the sign on the small green-domed Orthodox church stated in three languages, including Russian: "Services to deflect the eye of evil is held only on Thursdays". I shook my head at that but at this exact spot I was to rendezvous in 30 minutes time with my POC.

A low voice next to me intoned in English, "Ah, I see you're making yourself feel good right now – sensing the obvious – the correct strategy of early surveillance, well done." I ignored it and didn't even glance over, as there was nobody I knew there anyway even though dozens were walking past. I knew it was my intuition speaking to me. It always did in such instances of acclimatising to a new domain, especially in enemy territory.

I picked up my tatty case and slowly started to wander away, looking at some imaginary thing in the distance as if I intended to head over there. *It's an inside out way of making a living really, a bit like performing on an empty stage. I'm looking at myself in the scenes from the first row now. Often craziness is accepted as normal but shit happens in this business. Almost art on film. If I ever hear a tape whirring in my head one day, I will know then that I have gone too far and slowly turned mad from the sustained stress. That would be the final signal telling me to stop this act, pull the curtain and exit the big game in one piece to live the rest of my life sanely.*

Upon reaching my destination across the plaza I casually gazed back at the church I'd just passed. There was no sign of anything of note here at ground level, nobody paying undue attention to me and no face or style of walk that looked like I'd seen it before. People were beginning to head home and calling it a day, so food time was soon to follow.

I decided to strategically situate myself on a bench there and keep an eye out so I ordered a *shopska salata*, a chilled medley of chopped cucumbers and tomatoes topped with spicy white goat cheese, at the food stand next to me. It was delicious and I munched it quickly, lubricating it down with bottled mineral water. Upon finishing my meal, I put my head back in relaxation mode. Once again, now taking a different fixed position, I checked for any mounted stags (surveillance lookouts) from windows or the top of parked larger vehicles within the few hundred yards radius around me. But nothing of note reared its ugly head. *Momentum can be killed in a moment if not anticipated.* A part of my training was to think of alternate scenarios and what to do and not do beyond the predictable responses – the safety valve as it were. But the way ahead looked crystal clear and felt so in my gut.

Right on time my access agent (go between) strolled up, lit a cigarette and stood there taking in the sights, and looking tired. He was a moustachioed man in his early 40's. He was darker skinned than most and had a much slimmer build than the average Joe in the city. His main feature was his gaunt cheerless and characterless face. Bulgarians are generally swarthy and stocky but this fellow was even more so in pigmentation and less so in proportions. He hadn't seen me but wasn't expected to, as he had no idea what I looked like. The Oprep unit in London could describe a flea to a "T" and everything about him was exactly as the picture I had drawn in my head, including the giveaway CEB* in large Russian-style capitals in

---

* The Anglicised Soviet Ekonomicheskoi Vzaimopomoshchi reads CEB in Cyrillic (or Council for Mutual Economic Assistance). COMECON was the Moscow-based trading organisation that linked the communist countries. A fairly commonly seen logo and name in those days.

white on the small worn dark blue hold-all on his left shoulder that clinched it. The lighting of his fag on-site was an eminent warning of his departure in one minute. It also meant that if we don't do it today then I'll be here again tomorrow, same time, same place.

I had already paid my bill, checked my cheap Russian-made watch and calmly strolled over towards him carrying my own bag. I was one of some three dozen others doing the same exact thing at that precise moment, just walking across a square. The church bell tolled just once as I was half way across and the man over there with the fragile frame started to walk away on that pre-determined audio signal, much at the same speed as he'd arrived. He didn't even look at the time like most unfamiliar people would have. He was clearly used to hearing the chimes, a confirmed local.

So far, so good. It wasn't going to be a long stroll, not more than twenty minutes at a medium pace. As we walked away the tolling bells receded behind. "The Stick" lived in the area, apparently, appeared like he'd recently completed a chore. It was definitely the demeanour of heading back to somewhere else he'd just left, rather than the hurried action of someone going to fresh pastures. But he still had *one more important task to do for the day – the delivery of me. I can't explain my train of thoughts but they led me to think he was good at this, very good in fact. Meanwhile I crossed the street twice and went through one shop's door and out quite quickly through another for good measure to avoid detection. This was not a 'follow the leader routine'. No step to his step for me. It would have been a dead giveaway to anybody doing any shadowing.*

He was also the golden key holder to the safe house I was to stay in and he was leading me to it. He casually did everything he was supposed to do but in a deliberate manner of not trying, kind of winding down his long day. He stopped eventually, threw away his next cigarette – another sign to me that we had arrived – into the gutter, gazed in a shop window momentarily instead of looking around himself, staying remote and focused in a lazy way, passing time, allowing whoever to catch up with him. He'd done this before, no doubt about it.

We were already in the oldest part of town and buildings were tightly spaced now and in a state of disrepair giving the area a slightly ghetto-like feel. There were more non-Bulgarians it seemed, and poorer in the pocket, judging by their dress codes. The streets were cobblestoned here and the lampposts likewise appeared more than a hundred years old. Now it came his turn to cross the road over on to my side and he did so unhurriedly going down the first alley not far in front of me. No shifty looks from this one as he disappeared. An experienced professional operator, I had concluded.

I passed the unlit backstreet that he had turned into without looking down it, and then I continued for other 20 yards or so. Then I hesitantly stopped and checked my visibly-displayed bus ticket I had kept in my jacket as if there was a note scribbled on it, and retraced my steps holding the paper note in front of me. Coming back now the other way nothing seemed out of place and no one was paying any particular attention to me. At the same time, no one was deliberately ignoring me either – also a giveaway clue. Plenty of folks were doing their own thing at the end of another tiring day at work.

Then I headed into the narrow alleyway and down the dark space beckoning me. It was only when I entered it that I ominously saw the ageing face of Janus, the Roman god of doorways and passageways, etched into the stone wall. *It was supposed to have two masks – the front and back looking in opposite directions – yet this creation had only one?* My mind was starting to play momentary symbolism tricks again but my legs kept on moving, the sound of my shoes on the stone beneath me not overly betraying my presence.

In my temporary sightlessness the passage wafted of wet wool, tea brewing and aged urine. A few steps in, I stood prone for ten seconds while my eyes adjusted. There was only one door at the end. No puffed glow in the corner followed by karate ninjas screaming and rushing at me, thankfully. The only sounds were my slightly echoing footsteps towards that looming framework ahead and a single nasal rush as I exhaled my strain that had built up.

Just as I was going to knock on the door the same bloke opened it and I quickly entered as it clicked shut behind me. We were inside a thin corridor. I was inches away from his melancholic face now and literally breathing this man. I was close enough to see the few white hairs in his whiskers, bloodspots, stained teeth and smelling his clothes stinking like an ashtray. He had a weak smile that stretched the skin over his skull, as he introduced himself by shaking mine limply with his hand then placing it on his heart, saying softly, "Pouladvand." His slow-ish animation struck me as the exact opposite of one being affected in the extreme, a calming effect. Thereon, I never got to know him by any other name, just Pouladvand. He'd pronounced it softly in three distinct syllables. I would never know if it was his real name. I doubted if it was. He never asked me mine, wasn't supposed to either.

Within that day I had guessed that he was an Iranian exile, if not then Lebanese or Syrian at worse, possibly Turk – on that same page of the atlas anyhow. I presumed he was a Muslim based on his hand on heart greetings. But maybe he was even a fundamentalist, as his one foot to the other deportment from close up suggested he wasn't tremendously comfortable with our proximity and bodies touching. For some strange reason he preferred to initially speak to me in a mixture of poor limited French and heavily accented English. I got an odd sense it was so that the neighbours wouldn't be able to figure what we were saying. This is why I thought he was likely an Iranian. Generally, the Lebs speak both languages much better and shake hands more assertively, a bit more pizzazz about them. Questioning him about his credentials wasn't part of the equation though as he must have undergone a POA (provisional operational approval, basic background check) before being assigned this role by the same elderly boss I had met in London, H/SOF.

"The walls *vieux et* (old and) thin. Many non-Bulgarians live here," was his reasoning for keeping his voice low. His lazy hand movements but expressive eyes helped me understand him better. He motioned at the peeling dry plaster wall and beyond. I nodded in comprehension. It made sense. There was a murmur of a radio voice filtering through from somewhere beyond, outside the parapet.

"*Je reviens*. I come back in *une heure avec* some hot food for you. *Aussi* mandates I have received. Please rest." His hands indicated I lie down for a while. Then he was off back out. All I could do was nod once mutely at the wall.

I was only to stay and eat here for up to five nights. According to Oprep he would bring the food every morning and evening along with one or two envelopes containing instructions for me. I assumed that even if he managed to peek at the note, he would not have time to fathom the code…however, if he copied the note then it was only a matter of time for others to figure out the gist of the message. But I'd be off out of this safe house by then hopefully.

It seemed that he lived quite close by, as the dishes were always oven hot, as close as perhaps next door. If H/SOF had a number two it would be SOF/1, so I figured he would be organising everything else. My hands were already perusing through the contents of a sack that had been left in the corner, presumably courtesy of them, delivered by the courier Pouladvand. I would never get to meet whoever that number two man was and he would never know what I looked like either, at least not in the flesh. It was safer that way and the rules of our game. But I didn't really know, I was just temporarily filling in the blanks in my head. It was an ever-changing thought process for anyone in my position and situation.

Pouladvand was the designated go-between delivering messages back and forth, and carrying out any wish within reason that I may ask of him while I did some groundwork. Not only was he the holder of the brass key but also he was the golden link. We were putting a lot of trust in him. Still I felt comfortable with him straightaway, though I was quite sure he didn't know the specific nature of what was going down here either. The material knowledge was way too confidential for a conduit and a foreigner, at that, to be privy to.

Contrary to common belief real espionage is often passive work with no glamour whatsoever. I was reminded so as I walked into and around the main barren single room for the first time, duly noting the one fairly new mattress on the floor, some folded blankets on the end of it, two wooden chairs and a wooden table. A Soviet-brand Yunost portable TV was there, if it worked. That was it. It must have rained hard recently as the top corners were damp and the tired remaining hours of daylight shone through the solitary small window. The cracked paint gave the wall a master's timeworn oil canvas look about it with its choice of almost colourless blended hues. There was an open space in the other wall with rows of hanging plastic beads, but no door, to what was presumably the loo and washroom behind it.

En suite Bulgarian category with room service, homemade meals included for the guest. I'd always tried to make myself as comfortable as possible in such situations but that was the best description I could give this minimalist cube. No other devices either, no cameras, no bugs that I could trace. At least it was clean and not emitting that dank odour of chemical or the smell of years of cooked food ingrained into the partitions that some antiquated rooms can give off. I welcomed all that, and thankfully there were no unwelcome cockroaches roaming the prairie.

I unpacked what cheap little belongings I'd purchased in Bucharest the day before for my scheduled short stay. I'd already napped on the bus, thanks. I sat on the rickety wooden chair, took my shoes off and put my feet up on the only other one that also creaked. My time of being had arrived. Then I forced myself to concentrate for the hour.

I am a student of the atmosphere now.
I am inhaling it
Before surrendering to it.
And I am to be learned soonest.

* * * * * * * * *

Listen to the room it always speaks to you.

The busy cellar tavern at the bottom of the ancient, cool, winding stone steps could be heard resonating nearer. The quadruple blast of warm air, tobacco, music and din of people thumped me as I rounded the last downward spiral.

To my amazement there must have been at least sixty people crammed in this tight space of an underground bunker that was designed for half the number. A comity of communists, many still in their work clothes, some attractive girls at the bar. The mostly 2 to 1 male clientele consisted of distinctly mid-level managers in cheap poorly-cut polyester suits and loosened nylon ties with their assumed other halves or want-to-be paramours in tow. A straight bar it would be called back home, no gays, no cross-dressers, as if they were permitted behind the Iron Curtain.

I got myself a frothing lager. I was thinking if I came here again I should come with a companion, preferably a woman, so I wouldn't look too obviously alone. The overwhelming numbers of flirting pairs made me feel naked. This location was identified as the after work daily watering hole of "60". I was sure I would be able to recognise him, if and when I saw him. He was what we internally at SIS called a "cremation job" where he'd kill the subject efficiently and quietly, after his customary little teasing and that the thrill of the end of their life is nigh, had worn off. Because he operated in that fixed creepy mode, I wholly expected him to keep his style low, like mine was.

I was dead wrong. The boisterous racket knocking above the human hum was around the nook at the far end, turned out to be him, all by himself, like a big flashing light bulb due to his drunken bobbing bald head with the wee spotlight shining on it. He was the only person wearing sunglasses, too, and sat right in a dark corner at that, bar the beam on him. He was pouring so much pepper on his meat right then that I morbidly drew an imaginary parallel between deceased ashes and the dried herb. The busy "wenchy" barmaid who had just arrived at his timbered table with a large pitcher of pilsner was taking away the empty one he'd already downed. He had been banging obnoxiously on the table top to announce himself to me, as well as all and sundry. I noted he didn't thank her or anything. She seemed used to his loud conduct and neglected him in return. They must know each other by now, I thought. If this tavern is indeed his daily local hangout, then a pattern of silently ignoring each other must have long been established. Based on her demeanour I got a sense from that brief encounter that she didn't like him much.

He wolfed his food down like a rushed-for-time workingman does. No etiquette whatsoever, even tucked the white napkin into his collar that lay over a stomach bloated on brewed hops. Somehow it made him look like a spoilt grown up child playing the bratty rock star. The fork served really as a pitchfork repeatedly stabbing the steak, mouth going down halfway to meet the approaching food. Now seeing him in person and not just peering into the un-curtained frame of a photograph, I put his age at the same as the operational nickname we'd given him. When he finished his unceremonious dinner in record time he sat back and burped loudly without covering his mouth, then began taking in the occupants of the room. I turned away slowly at that moment in time, my back facing him.

It gave me a break to think about my first impression of him: A pig he certainly was despite the beef. One tended to assume that the larger the forehead, the higher the intelligence of the person. Why I entertained that thought must be borne out of dogma since it certainly couldn't apply to "60" in any shape or form. An empty stomach is deaf to reason but his was probably the same when full, I also rationalised. A quick peek witnessed the black pudding dessert was next sucked into his bottomless maw. His ugly mannerisms revealed to me that he was incapable of any reasonable introspection. An arsehole, a first class dick he was, yob even.

I instinctively knew right then – when the photographed subject is finally seen live and the environment sampled – that he knew he was above-the-law. He was involved in a racket so far above most people's thinking that he could stoop as far below it as well and at will. There was something else niggling me but I couldn't figure what it was at the time. He somehow appeared to be floating above the ground, here but not here.

When I next glanced back at him through the crowd, a thick probably Cuban cigar was now sticking out rudely from his mouth like a second tongue, which the real classless one was licking the outer leaves for perceived aroma. He took his time repeatedly lighting it and blowing out the first primary suck directly at the next diner and his female companion. He offered no apology, and ignored their glares revealing that they found his smoke offensive to the taste on their palates. Man's a jerk, I thought. What a frigging wally.

I was certainly willing myself to despise him, too, to justify my future actions and he helped me inch towards that goal admirably. Obviously for him a compromise was required on only one side – not his – and it was clear to me that he was used to getting his way, much like the school bully's lofty mien that needed someone to straighten him out, *somebody like me*. I, the willing point man from the executioner's party, was going to do that for him without regret.

Some bloke came and sat down right next to that bald fat bastard now on the bench. He was not his friend but belonged to the table on the other side of "60". I noticed that the heavy didn't make the usual polite gestured movement, like most decent people would do to squeeze in a new presence in their near vicinity. He just sat there like an obnoxious lump refusing to move the few inches needed to accommodate the new arrival. Everybody else budged but not him. That suggested to me that he felt overly secure where he was, while continuing to be inconsiderate.

I scanned everybody else in there for a while and eventually noticed one fellow surf in "60"'s direction every 30 seconds or so. Not in the same way perhaps I was doing but in a closer and more protective way. 'BG,' I thought. 'Probably PBG (personal bodyguard).' I made a mental note of him. Right handed, 40's, stylish dark straight hair, nice complexion, possible fast beard growth, seemed like he could run with pace, good looking lad who had a face that could change his appearance convincingly, no visible scars, unusually large gold wedding ring, no sucking down alcohol while on duty either. Street fighter, hard boy though as his knobbly knuckles told me. For a fraction of a second I thought I'd seen him before someplace then I glanced away to avoid staring.

I looked at "60" again. I turned away quickly as he appeared to be in scrutinising mode again. It was hard to know when a blind-looking man was looking at you or not. Most people in a crowd spend 85% of their time unconsciously returning their focus as a point of reference to one person whether it is of sexual attraction or simply that they are wearing odd clothes or doing something unusual. Bearing this in mind, I didn't want to appear to be rubber-necking at him too long either.

He stood up now, clumsily, not to depart but to go to the loo, leaving his cigar burning in the ashtray. Until he did that it never occurred to me that the alluring sexy lone woman that I could have fancied and still wearing her coat near the door, wasn't some kind of hostess just arriving at work but in fact also another PBG. I just happened to be looking at her at the time wondering why she hadn't taken her coat off yet, to see that her eyes never left his back until it disappeared behind the men's room door. Her practiced eye and body movement explained her job: a military girl at one point in her life. I concluded then that the male was responsible for the inside while she was the outside cover, the backup by design. It was the close protection and the even closer protection, the watcher of the watchman. *Silly me, our designated triggerman could have made a mistake and done something on the spur of the moment, nailed him and the PBG inside here, and she would have had her target in the snap of a finger in loosening her own load. At that moment I really didn't want to start liking her anymore as I realised the nature of her job, and my inner thermometer went from warm to cool in a flash.*

In the forced reassessment, I determined that under that shiny dark coat was a physically strong woman despite her petite size and slight frame. Three-quarters legs, long fingers with no long nails, red varnish today, blackish-purplish mod Mary Quant haircut, face wearing a lot of foundation now but could change her appearance to fit the occasion, early-30s, a permanent provocative sulk, and the cynical face of a big city girl. To my active mind the sexy classic female assassin with a Russian-made "lipstick pistol" – it could fire a single 4.5-mm shot from close range into your ear while she smiled promisingly into your eyes, arms clasped around your neck dancing. She had travelled outside Bulgaria this one to buy the finer quality make-up she wore. *And while I no longer fancied her I sensed something creepy crawly about this miss as if she was a human black widow spider.*

But I'd seen enough already of "Potato Head", "Knobby Knuckles" and "Cleopatra" so I prepared myself to leave. I was just someone who was stopping in for a quick thirst-quencher before heading home. I tipped the bottom of my glass slowly and drained it to see through the glass around me. If anybody was watching me, I wasn't giving them a lot of time to idly sum me up. But I'd come in and evaluated the target in the half an hour I'd needed to familiarise myself and to tender a lay of the land report, when it was asked for.

At that very moment "60" staggered out of the loo, fidgeting with his nostrils repeatedly. When he did it the third time I saw his left hand's little finger's nail was curled and longish while the others were well manicured. He'd had a snort of white powder in there, no doubt about it. That was why he appeared so distant, even from across a room. Contradicting his in-your-face behaviour, he had looked at himself in the mirror before he came out. He must have tidied himself up in there, wiped his skull's sheen, maybe splashed water on his mug to remove any tell-tale coke. Standing near to him and observing him I could not escape the notion that this unsavoury character did not give a monkey either way because he was in a special place, beyond where us mere mortals were to grasp the importance of his position. Granted his act was so overplayed that a person of my culture found it acutely embarrassing. It was like watching someone parade around shamelessly, waddling around with all the aplomb of an overweight vulture.

I was just now beginning to understand H/BUL/OPS' first ever comment about "60": Everybody wanted to get this guy and nobody would miss his loving company when he suddenly went bump in the middle of a dark night. Very clearly he was a man who pissed off those that were previously "un-piss-off-able", me being one of them. I'll log my findings via Pouladvand, next it was a question of where and when, then I'm going home to where my heart was.

I was quite happy that I didn't like him at all from the word go; I really didn't, which justified my impending involvement all the more. He gave me the impression that his mind was enclosed in blackness with no shadows, a type of man who drained the oxygen out of the air, even sucked blood out of bodies like a vampire does. In fact, when I was back out up in the night sky and wandering along the street, unusually for me, I realised *I actually hated him intensely.* The world would be much better off without the likes of his kind. Good riddance.

After this run-through of a reconnaissance I'd already decided what my preferred method of his grisly death would be, if it was left to me, but it wasn't my call to make. I was only the point man. But no amount of paper planning elsewhere can decide that ahead of time, old chaps, because you only do what's best at that given moment of opportunity.

Act like a hunter and you are the hunter.
Act like a target and you are the target.

Yet by the time I reached the place of abode I was asking myself logically, 'But who really stood to benefit from the demise of "60"? What's really going on here?' In between us and them there is an almost imperceptible no man's land and that is primarily where I operate best in. But my instincts struck me that this situation was presenting a wide open field with a lot of players still to appear. An odd feeling that I didn't know the answer to but felt that it would come, soon.

Where there is smoke,
people look for a fire…
but it could be a smokescreen

or a message sent into the sky.

Chapter Nine

I was swimming backstroke alongside a dwarf of undetermined sex against a riptide in the monsoon rain. No land on the horizon in any direction. Every time I turned a shark's fin broke the surface then dived, coming closer each time. An unseen eunuch's voice from the clouds with little tonal variation hissed, "OK, here, look down the front sight and aim to hit him in the number seven area. Yes, just like in target practice."

"You mean shoot him through the heart?" I spluttered, nervously watching the ripple effect on the water advancing. I was thinking of a better way to do it.

"A-ha, yes, I want him dead. I want nothing but a red zero on the left of his floating torso..." Suddenly the sand had parted the waves and I was a beached whale flapping there. No oxygen, I can't breathe...an albatross dived and snatched the midget, screaming into the endless sky until they were quivering dots...

Pouladvand's pensive mug was above me shaking me awake. I nearly punched his daylights out in fright. Pidgin French and Russian rained on me, "*Mal nuit.* Bad night, *Koba, prosypatsya!* Wake Up!" I felt embarrassed that I missed him coming in and mumbled incoherently as I bolted upright, ruffled my hair, then went to take a pee and then rinsed my face awake with the cold only water.

When I came back in he was rearranging the contents of my breakfast that was on tray on the table, like a waiter in room service does.

"*Koba?*" I was finally in today's world now. "Wasn't that Stalin's sobriquet during his revolutionary days? Why did you use that word just now?"

He didn't miss a heartbeat in answering, "Certainly it sounded more like an adopted name for you, yes. I don't have a name for you so this is what I will call you, while I know you. You speak Russian very well I see, even when sleeping. It is the name designated for you."

I didn't mention that he'd pronounced another Russian word not in the wooden tongue that Stalin insisted people of Pouladvand's generation spoke in but in the short abbreviated style, pinpointing him to having learnt it in recent years.

"In Bulgaria one can understand Russian well. There are only three less letters difference in their respective alphabets...*mais, oui, c'est le nom* I am to call you. I commend you on picking up so quickly on that nuance."

"Who really decided that name for me?"

He stopped what he was doing to look at me like he quite didn't understand me. I noticed that his choice of English words had seemed to vastly improve. "We are questioning each other?" He then smiled gently, "I don't know. When the person gives me the brush pass (swift exchange of an envelope by sleight of hand), it has 'Koba' typed on it. But there is only one person I am giving it to anyway regardless of what name is on it. You."

"Typewritten in Cyrillic or Roman letters?"

"Bulgarian. Written English would draw attention to me, if seen, obviously. Around here." His hands waved around for the world at large out there.

"Why, are you dealing with another like me too?" I was more than curious. "You don't have a problem speaking it though."

Pouladvand shrugged, like I was supposed to know but clearly I didn't. "Yes I am. I collect from this person by brush pass and they give me the envelope for you. I take it out of the other one first, of course. The money is for me."

"Is he from my country too?" Now I was piqued, grabbing at every word.

"*Oui*, I am assuming so even though I do not know yet what country you are from though I can suspect which. But it is a she not a he."

That momentarily threw me. "Oh, how long has she been in Bulgaria then?"

"Since one day before you that I have been dealing with her." He hesitated, and then hunched his shoulders, slightly frustrated. "If you are going to ask me what she is doing, the answer is I don't know. I swear I don't even know what you are doing in Sofia. I am not supposed to know nor do I want to know. All I do know is that, I think, you are, a *razvyeadchik*."

I believed him. Everything about him told me so. His use of the

Russian word for "scout" instead of "spy" was interesting. The Soviets and their eastern bloc partners liked to infer that they were merely "exploring" us while instead we were "watching" them. I had noticed the same when we used the word "killed in action" they preferred "destroyed" (*razrushenny*). Besides it was now the third time he had knowingly used a Russian word in my presence. I wondered whether that was consciously or sub-consciously intentional but didn't say anything this time.

And I noted he never answered about the spoken English probe. A lot of things were starting to not add up. I was beginning to feel like Alice at the Mad Hatters Tea Party. Or was I getting paranoid, which was unlike me?

But the whereabouts of another deep cover Briton was never mentioned at any time during my briefings either, at least not in my presence anyway. I thought my messaging system originated from H/SOF or SOF/1, if there was one. It struck me as more than just odd that it stank and screamed at me. *I know the infiltration is supposed to be compartmented but this op is slowly shaping into something else entirely.* But I knew from instinct it would somehow. It was no use getting on this low-key bloke. He wasn't going to know and wasn't supposed to know either despite getting paid well. I slumped down to eat, a little rattled myself.

I talked with my mouth full. "Does the female party know of my existence, from you?"

"Not to my knowledge. I have not told her because we have not spoken yet. If she would ask me I would say you are around though, just like she is. But I will answer her question truthfully. To anyone else I will lie."

I was thinking quickly. "Do me a favour, tell me if she asks you anything please?" I looked up at him for clarification.

He bowed fractionally like a maître d'hôtel. "If you wish."

I finished the meal hurriedly without tasting the food, wiped my mouth and stood up abruptly to hand him back the empty tray. As he stepped forward to take it in his hands I held on and intoned, "I request her code name, if you don't mind. If you have one for me then you must have one for her as I'm assuming you brush pass the other way as well. Your messages for her."

He must have been aware by now that I never ever said his name out aloud at any time as protocol demands of a NOC in such a situation abroad. Why identify whom you're talking to for those listening in, and vice versa, if they indeed were.

His black marbles were right there level with mine, so close this time I could have easily head-butted him. He didn't seem at all bothered by our dialogue. No emotions of fear were transmitted or at least I wasn't picking up on them. He thought for a fraction of a second.

"Nilats, N-I-L-A-T-S," he responded firmly, almost whispering as he spelt the letters. The slight hesitancy before replying bothered me a wee bit too. I was naturally suspicious of anything now. Any space of every kind occupied me as I weighed it up.

"What the fuck does that mean? It's not a Russian word. Is it Bulgarian for something? An acronym?" That was really puzzling.

"If this is even Belgian or *Byelorusski* (White Russian) or Beninese, I do not know what! But I think perhaps too many words have been said now. It would seem to me that you are not knowing or did not know of her involvement. I am not happy about this. I am sorry I gave you this information. Now I am implicated in something that is clearly not factored." He bowed and I let go of the tray.

I wanted to assure him of otherwise but I felt the same as him. My gut was churning in the pit of my stomach though I couldn't get a handle on where his intuition was. Then I started to shake my head at his dumb straight morose face about in which language it may have been, very accidental tongue-in-cheek that was. Then I smiled to myself. Naturally, for me to seek humour at such a bad time I knew my nerve-handling mechanism was starting to kick-in.

But he was already shuffling half way out of the door now.

"Thank you for that dialogue," I called hastily after him, not too loud.

He turned then and did his little bow again and slid out. I was half inclined to rush out and follow him but my sixth sense told me not to. *'Play it safe, Anderson,'* that safety valve voice from within had advised. *Just tap the cricket ball back to the bowler or go for one short run at a time. Don't go for big hits, keep on batting, try not to get yourself out, keep your end up and let the other batsman take the risks'.* I even acknowledged it by bobbing my head once ever so slightly in response to nobody else in the quiet room.

But my adrenaline was thundering its roaring guns big-time. I had to think hard. I'd always paid attention to the subliminal, when it made an advent. I almost never suffered from nightmares, but because cognisance doesn't always work I believed that it was my own way of filtering important information through. It was something that I hadn't picked up on at the moment it had presented itself. I consciously listened to myself more in such rare instances. It was a survival bell. But what was it? I'd have to rewind my inner tape. It was possible I was blocking information, too.

I opened the latest envelope that Pouladvand had just left there. I'd been too pre-occupied with other things up to then. He must have removed it from the one marked with my code name on it. Suspiciously I held it up to the dull sunlight to see if any hand-written imprint had pressed through but clearly the name had been typed, as he'd indicated, before it had been inserted.

It contained a single unfolded sheet of water-soluble paper of an update with a hand-drawn map that included from/to hours to be present. I got the impression the diagram was indeed prepared by a female and was marked with the location, the times and directions for this afternoon. Men aren't usually so meticulous. I began redrawing it into my memory bank because I had to destroy it in any event. I knew that the uniquely manufactured invisible ink is sometimes scientifically programmed to kick in at specific hours, days or weeks after being written. But I didn't know when this particular specimen's blank was supposed to commence or even if it had been expertly applied.

Within a few minutes and after a couple of deep breaths my blood started to calm down, thank goodness. My heart's pumping gradually decreased, and was now perceptible only to me. It felt like walking up the staircase backwards and in slow motion. After being whammed with a sledgehammer to start the day it told me my brain was taking charge again. One can perform better in this modus operandi.

Pouladvand was the kind of bloke that if he told me something far-fetched, I'd still be inclined to believe him. I'd already discounted him from my alarm bell theory that couldn't be explained verbally or easily documented to another person, even if I'd tried. Besides he would rot in hell for what he was doing if they caught him. And if he wasn't valued he would be taken to the woods for a speedy appointment with the firing squad, last cigarette offered or not. *Or he was a good liar.*

I did next what I was supposed to and ran the paper under the tap. I then went and sat down again but the endless drip of fear pervaded. To give my constant drumbeat time to come to a gradual end I went and tipped out the canvas bag of tricks, specifically to inspect for recording devices. In an act of reassuring myself, as I hadn't remembered to do that earlier, was now doing so from within the bag itself and the bag's inner linings, turning it inside out. I found nothing. Picked up the TV and felt under it, may be something inside…

…then, suddenly, it amazingly occurred to me that *Nilats was Stalin*

> *Entering a world I don't quite understand yet*
> *but where I have been before,*
> *a single-minded resolve begins.*
> *I have to go beyond my possibility, always.*

* * * * * * * * * *

She was relating a tale as if sneaking a peek through a door left open while covering her slightly goofy grin with her expressive hands, so as to prevent more words from spilling out, while continuing a conversation with someone out of view.

I put down the stand-alone SUSAT telescopic day sight that had been included with the assortment provided by SOF/1 in the event it might become useful. (SUSAT stood for Sight Unit Small Arms Trilux, with four times magnification, which can be attached on top of a British Army sniper's gun.) The problem as I saw it was that this unit looked like it was taken off an Enfield rifle's bracket, made in the UK. It could lead investigators to look towards us if anything went wrong. I was starting to think absurdly: *Maybe they want something to point to London?* I began to look around in the same way that a small bird does after pecking to ensure it doesn't become a morsel itself to a roving predator. If anybody was paying attention to their surroundings even a birdsong stopping in mid-repertoire can divert interest this way. Sitting there on the grass I detected nothing in the forest wall of dense green around me. *Why is it the presented obvious outside but the never presented inside unobvious that prickles me? Am I looking for something that's not there? Am I a part of a bigger game plan to create a distraction perhaps? Am I here for another smaller reason even? Bigger one perhaps?*

I returned my focus to Liudmila Zhivkova. It was almost a voyeuristic angle of looking at things in a cracked way because she wore only a white towel with her back to me as she was applying make-up in front of a large mirror that allowed me to see her face. I was trained on an image of a diminutive woman with her hair up in a bun, dark eyes, straight nose and small breasts, nipples visible through the fabric even through the viewfinder.

From three-quarters of a mile away, beyond the low fence, her room was one floor off the ground in this tastefully done stately mansion. It was quite a contrast to the stern communist architecture the rest of Sofia presented. I concurred that wherever this woman was then primary target "60" wasn't going to be that far away from her, at least during the hours when she attended public functions. One was recently scheduled to commence in less than an hour from now. I was also thinking a secondary thought: She was going to be late at the rate she was preparing herself for it.

Scanning around the perimeter, a black very unusual-looking saloon car driving slowly came into view, did a lazy U-turn, before it stopped at the main entrance to the place, which was to the right just below her spot. Two very security-type men in dark suits – one size too big as usual I noted so the pieces can be worn comfortably – confidently alighted from each side of the vehicle's front doors, then stood around aimlessly, for once not covering their private parts in their usual stance. They were obviously awaiting her exit. Neither one belonged to the pair that was with "60" in the beer cellar the previous night.

Suddenly I felt a scintilla-moment, a very gentle tug on my inner existence then. It was ever so slight, like when an eyelash loosens and you dislodge it from the rest. Only you know it's moved, of course, and nobody else would remotely notice the vibration you are susceptible to. It had dawned on me that I was informed she was right handed and she was using her left…or did the juxtaposition in the mirror reverse the image?

Adjusting the cumbersome range lens from the fixed wide view to the finer closer range, I returned to her window above the close protection pair waiting down there. How many times could she apply her lipstick, again and again? I still hadn't confirmed my thoughts about her hand. Suddenly I was convinced it was a bloody flick I was seeing and it wasn't a reflection! Why would anyone want to re-run footage of a film starring oneself?

Then another strange thing happened. The double doors on the ground floor were suddenly opened outwards by "60" and his bodyguard "Knobbly Knuckles". No sign of "Cleopatra", though. Then a fully clothed Liudmila hurriedly walked out down the few steps towards the car. Simultaneously one BG opened a door for her while the other, the driver, hurried to his side. All five got in and the limo rolled off across the gravel to the gate somewhere out of my sight around the trees.

To say I was confused was an understatement but something told me to keep close watch on that window. I returned my focus to that spot and kept it for several long minutes, maybe an eternity of four or five passed.

Just as my eyesight was getting watery, amazingly a woman that I could have sworn *was* a haggard Liudmila again hesitantly came to the lip of the balcony, looked around and closed the curtains. She wore pyjamas of the kind that hospital patients do and I could have sworn she was limping but won't swear to it. She stood there only fifteen seconds then she slowly turned back inside, that glare of film of her was still running behind her when the curtains joined again.

With now a blankness to stare at I shut down the telescopic device, looked around momentarily, stood up creakily and stretched to release my tension. I was in half a mind to go and bang on the embassy's door and demand to speak to the faceless SOF/1 or even H/SOF, if he was back in town. Were they aware of this strange activity and besides who was the other assumed British subject and what was her function?

Walking quickly back down the same country lane that led to the main road, I was in a quandary as to what to do next. To say that the goings-on were highly unusual was a massive understatement. My mind was racing. Nevertheless, I decided to head back to my den where I could decipher events with a clearer mind. Besides Pouladvand and his dinner delivery were due in less than two hours' time.

En route, I absentmindedly snipped two daffodils with my hands from the hundreds along the side of the country lane. When I got back into that lonely room I placed them in a cup of water. I could use their company to break from the monotony of solitude and they may be even able to help me with my thought processes. I went to lie prone on the mattress and missed a heartbeat...the yellow flowers looked identical in angle, size, bloom...yet...

The girl at the bottom of the steps in that bar was no doubt the same girl that was the decoy for Liudmila...suddenly the realisation came to me...a change of wigs and clothing, and we have ourselves a body double, bloody hell. But Liudmila had *je ne sais quoi* (a certain something) that charms everybody; the other girl absolutely didn't possess an ounce of that indefinable, elusive quality. That was the difference between the 'twins' even from distance – the twinkle factor.

To myself I noted a second odd assessment:

Sometimes one's hobby comes in handy. The large dark cardboard box of a car I had never seen before at Zhivkova's residence was, I think, a 6-door FSO Polonez Strona. (For a brief moment I had closed up on the clearly Polish-language insignia) it obviously had some sniper-resistant and anti-bomb special armour-plated work on it and was probably fitted with dual-purpose shatter-proof and removable windows for an emergency exit. The several antennae on the back end of its roof were a dead giveaway in many ways as to the communication value of its contents. One of the BGs had messed around with moving from one place to another of an elongated instrument featured a handle with a mirror attached to it at the bottom. It was probably used to search under the chassis for any unwanted attached explosive devices. I'd memorised the licence plate but the vehicle was so strange-looking I would have recognised it anywhere. *Why then use a car that was so uniformly different to so attract attention to its every movement? It begged to be noticed. Or maybe that was the idea to let people know Zhivkova was out and about?*

* * * * * * * * *

The bright spotlight of hindsight in an upside down world!

It didn't arrive at a destination or start a cobweb. Looking up while lying on the bed I don't know how long I'd been watching the little house spider choreograph its way around the low ceiling. It seemed to pas a deux with itself with its many arms and legs in slo-mo, and almost in tune to the soft classical music that was filtering through from above. I felt I had something in common with it though. I, too, was ambidextrous, multitalented and could dance to a variety of tunes.

Suddenly I could hear Pouladvand's distinctive scuffle coming in a little earlier than normal time. I sat upright.

"Good evening, you are early." I'd decided to get a dialogue going with him, no matter what. His arrival had got me wondering about hidden surveillance cameras now. I made a mental note to discreetly take another look around after he leaves as something could have been planted while I was out today. Or ask him point blank. Could he have known that I was here already?

Seconds later we were facing each other but there was no food tray in his hands this time. Instead they were held out resignedly as he simultaneously shrugged, "After this morning I realise you would wish to talk, so I have come to do so."

Nothing like the meeting of the minds I thought. Good. I invited him to be seated and wished I could have offered him a choice of drink. I sat and without saying anything I signalled with my eyebrows for him to begin. I noticed his clothes were rumpled like an unmade bed and imagined that perhaps he had been doing the same as I had been.

"My stomach tells me you may be wondering of what country I am from?" I nodded in agreement. We can start from wherever he wanted to.

"With borders realigned in the wrong places, my town of birth is Orumiyeh, which is in Iran, but my father is a Turk and my mother a

Kurd."

"So what does that make you, by your own choice?" I asked.

He looked at me with that now familiar quizzical expression that seemed to say that the answer was obvious. "I am first a good Muslim and second a bad Iranian Turk but I feel Kurdish most of the time. I am trapped between three identities."

We smiled warmly at that. Intended witticism or not still thought he was an enigma, no matter what, and knew I was a conundrum to him by the very fact I was there. He defied being boxed into any pre-set category. So did I.

"Sir, for your own protection and as a man I believe you would protect me given the opportunity as well...so I would like to educate you on why I *think* you are here and also why I have to speak to you about it. Even though I swear on my children that I have never spoken so forthrightly to the people I have been protecting in this safe house for the past 10 years I have been doing this work..."

"OK," I injected, "first off, is this place bugged and under surveillance?"

"No, not at all. But I can understand why you may think this, of course. I sweep it regularly. I have the equipment to do this under lock and key. I live very close by. One minute away."

"Dangerous, if found," I said. I made a motion of the gun to the head.

There was a brief moment of silence between us and I indicated for him to carry on. The amateur DJ beyond had changed the record to opera to fill the void.

"As you must know Pope John Paul II survived an assassination attempt in The Vatican just two months ago."

Boy, I admit that really whacked my senses and I almost missed hearing the next sentence due to the internal drums rolling as I half-lip read Pouladvand say, "I know everything about this attack and more." The percussion was banging loudly inside my head.

I tried to control my knee-jerk reaction but failed. Judging from my facial response, it must have been screaming at him. I was sure I lurched forward.

"Why would you want to be telling me what you were not going to say?" I uttered weakly. I was trying hard to buy a little time to control my nerves.

"Because I trust you. Nothing more or less than that," he shrugged. "And that is because Bulgaria is systematically trafficking Turks and Kurds in this country and I wish to stop this human humiliation. I am half of one or both after all."

"Are you saying that what happened in Rome is linked to this disgraceful policy you refer to?"

"Yes. And more."

I held up my hand to stop him. "But this has nothing to do with my being here, if you must know."

"You don't know that." His voice had taken on a harder edge as he stared at me. "Your being here is far too coincidental. To come to Bulgaria so soon after."

We spent time gazing into each other's pupils. Even the opera singing on a gramophone player somewhere else had stopped vibrating dully through the thin concrete walls surrounding us. I didn't realise it until it was quiet. The loud silence was eerily fluky. No new sounds emanated, like it was an intermission.

I finally muttered, "Are you sure you want to tell me whatever it is? It may compromise you?"

All he did was shake his head sideways in a series of denials, almost as if fighting with himself. Then he accepted the moment then sighed, "It is my destiny to inform you. The local authorities, specifically certain members of the Bulgarian Politburo and the workers under them, like the intelligence branches, are allowing certain other ethnic Turks to smuggle hashish and heroin from the east and weapons from the north to pass through Bulgaria to the west. Of course, they get a handsome cut for allowing this rite of passage. Hypocrisy at its worst. They kill them sometimes and love them other times depending on their needs."

Capitalism at work inside communism I was musing. "Is this under the umbrella of Kintex?"

"Ah, so you know of this shell company then?"

"But so what," I held my hand up. "What's it to you if this is going on under their noses?"

"What you must be interested to know is that certain members in the British Parliament are doing the same in partnership with the Bulgarian Politburo. In turn representatives at international MI6 and domestic MI5 are being paid to turn a blind eye from these illegal activities here. They are also the same ones heading the offshore corporate entities that are importing the goods!"

I was thunderstruck for all of a minute as I tried to connect the dots and understand all the ramifications in my poor fizzing head. I had suspected it and now here was the unconfirmed confirmation. I still needed to uncover evidence. What I would do with it I hadn't the foggiest notion. I didn't trust my own side, not the ones at the top anyway. *I questioned their loyalty above all the other issues.* Finally, I offered, "But how do *you* know all that?"

"Bulgaria is the central point of commercial distribution and bartered exchange of all kinds of arms for my Muslim brothers in Afghanistan fighting the Soviet invaders. While essentially being under the control of Moscow's communist rulers it also recognises the advantages of playing both sides against the middle…itself being precisely that and profiting handsomely from both ends, front and back.

"For example, through the business channels of Kintex the west will buy the world's finest poppies produced by the Afghan opium farmers. But the west knows full well that these poor people are barely eking out a subsistence in growing this crop in order to feed their families. Yet they cannot deliver the finest opiates to market without first importing acetic anhydride, a key and restricted chemical made in the United States that is used for the conversion of morphine into heroin. That is where Bulgaria's secret capitalists come in with their underground laboratories and worldwide distribution system. All right here in Sofia.

"Without the machinery of the global media, manipulating the common man on both sides of the political spectrum to fuel ideology, it would not be possible. In this respect the main proponent in this game of twisting the mind and of emptying the pocket is somebody who runs a worldwide communications empire in your presumed country – I believe you are British – who funds all of these activities. Unfortunately, I am not knowing of his name, but he oversees it.

"To answer your question though. I am the local PKK* representative, a semi-official post. The Bulgarians know what I do but don't interfere. Am I legal to them? I don't know. We are involved in distribution in the drug trade for them and from the profits I am sanctioned to buy substantial weaponry back from them…so they tolerate me. But we very much disagree with the smuggling of slaves for sex. It has reached a point where we are uncomfortable with this participation. It is against our religion and our culture to be involved."

---

* *Partiya Karkerani Kurdistan* (Kurdistan Worker's Party) whose objective was to establish a fully independent Kurdistan. Kurds live mainly in Turkey and Iraq with small pockets spread into Iran, Armenia and Syria.

* * * * * * * * * *

The next morning after breakfast I went outside into the old town's street for some fresh air. It was sprinkling a bit with rain and I immediately got an odd feeling that I was being preserved on film or being watched, one or the other or both. *The thought I dreaded the most about revisiting Bulgaria came trickling like thick blood slime all over me again.*

There are people coming and going as it's the local morning rush hour. I slow down and pan around to get a 'perspective on the weather today' and spotted no one that could be shielding a camera or looking my way. Most are on the go. The hunch is still there though, sixth sense clinging like shrink-wrap to me now.

So I strolled around some more and stopped again to look into a suitably large framed shop window displaying knick-knacks. I focused on the glass' reverse image of one stationary individual at a time behind me out of the half dozen within my field of vision, all the while adjusting my own angle to get a better sight. Each clear surface metal item of interest in the window as part of the double examination process appeared in my shutter. I shunted quickly from one object to another with the uniquely shaped surfaces presenting me with a different slant to observe who was behind my back. The fifth subject, a hooded figure with a small frame seemed uncomfortable in its body and was beginning to move away. Not a smoothly practised person, or new in this kind of work. To run after him will make him run away, therefore attracting attention to myself. I chose to make him come to me and to find out if this person was part of a team.

I moved off again. Window shopping-mode now ended. The no agenda approach of simply crossing the road. The guy appeared again. *The human camera is locked securely onto the subject now.* A tingle effect overcame me. I tried to pick up if any others were involved but nobody came close. This one must be working alone, I was convinced of it. I speeded up and the distance between us grew purposefully, actuating in me the SIS reverse dolphin surveillance method (see all the time, then disappear).

Within minutes, through a freak of geographical dexterity using a modern shop's entrance and exit doors being different, I bettered myself and found myself behind him. The way a person walks is like a puppet on legs, almost like a tree with limbs gesturing. You can learn a lot if you observe the subject: it will transmit a vocabulary of movement, of habit, of preference, of condition, even its defects. Everyone's body is an education, a conduit-producing nuance, and other forms of connection…and this one was effeminate and slow moving.

Intuition made me advance quickly upon the subject from the rear. I was subconsciously beginning to feel confident when I saw the anxiety of losing me appearing on the face…and it clearly was that of a worried looking older woman's, fringes of silver hair peeking, and I knew she wasn't a Bulgarian.

I decided to make an approach and started walking alongside her, saying nothing. She glanced over at me, turned away and then looked again, jumping back startled. She had a face that tells the story before you hear it and she was going to betray herself as well as possibly suffer heart failure. I held her arm forcibly and we kept advancing. In a nervous, perfect middle-class British accent, she said, "Please. My name is Mrs McBarton. I'm English, like you. Don't harm me."

A minute of harrowing silent walking passed before I pulled her into a suitable passageway and pressed her against the wall. She started to babble. I shook her firmly and replied in Russian, which she clearly didn't fully comprehend, so I repeated in English, "Get a hold of yourself, missus. I'm not going to harm you. Why were you following me? Who am I to you?"

Holding her rock steady there, my face in hers, her frozen wide cobalt eyes never leaving my brown, she began to blink rapidly then attempted to compose herself by taking deep breaths. I decided to feel hard outside her clothes down her back slowly, her bottom, briefly across her vagina, inside her inner thighs and her breasts. I expected to find a radio, a recording device or an already cocked piece of equipment but I found nothing. The feel down had made her gasp faster, her pupils widened again, followed by her lips opening. I got a quizzical distinct sense this was the closest she had come to making love for a long time, with her clothes on. Even in the shadows you could see that she had been pretty in her time, a very southern English countryside blushing rose type. She must have been about twice my age, like my favourite auntie. Don't know why I couldn't have seen that fact faster from afar, or maybe it was the speckled water reflections from the rain that clouded my judgement. But I could see that she was already going to freely give me the answers to the next questions I was going to ask.

I whispered, "Is there anywhere to sit down nearby?" She was completely in agreement. I put my arm inside hers and led her back to the street. "Let's go there. Take me to it. Try to collect yourself. You look like you saw a ghost." She was leading us to a public garden ahead.

She smiled timidly, "Well, I actually just *did* see a spook…*spook* is

Dutch for ghost, you know, and you really did spook me. You remind me of my husband, we lived in Holland for a while. He's dead now."

I smirked at her answer, boy-like, like a younger family member brat does, while I was thinking to myself, 'An eccentric in the unexpected British behaviour mould…what the hell is she doing here? This is a spy?' We said nothing again as we strolled slowly to the green area that appeared ahead. I was almost propping her up as if her legs had gone wobbly. She was momentarily leaning on me for support now. By the time we sat down on a bench a few minutes later, her panic had done its lap and she was back at the start line, in control of her emotions and balance like a bitch bulldog. The sprinkling rain had tapered by then, on cue, too. I wiped the seat surface with my elbow sleeve then we sat down on it under a large sheltering tree.

The first thing I said in a grinning mocking tone was, "The beatings will continue until morale improves." That seemed to break the ice as her eyes rolled sexily and her face visibly relaxed at my irony. "Your turn to speak," I prompted.

"You say your words in a forward fashion," she replied. "Positive, in light of what you do for a living."

"And what do I do for a living?"

That made her big blue eyes widen again and stare into my face, as if taking me in for the first time. It took her almost half a minute to respond.

She finally stuttered, "I know enough to be franker than most."

"Which is what? What does that mean exactly? I am not here to amuse anybody, as you can see." I looked around for any surprises coming our way.

Then her shoulders slumped in defeat, which triggered her mouth to move. Her yarn to come was incredible. The answers finally came together for me, the back joining the front. "I, I wanted to be heard but now I'm lost for words… It's an inconvenient truth."

* * * * * * * * *

The heart is the engine that keeps us going forward.
The soul is the spirit that goes beyond.
The brain thinks and arrives there.
The nose detects where.
The eyeballs see it.
The key moments.

No procedural normality this. Prior to being privy to this wisdom I came from a world where I was fashioned to want to gain meaningful assurances over internal controls, risk management and governance processes where the discharge of responsibility is of critical importance to us all. *All I knew thus far flew out of the window and kept spiralling in perpetuity into a dark hole.*

What a sharp learning curve it was. When truth doesn't make sense anymore from a forward and horizontal angle, you look at it laterally and expand outwards to anywhere where you aren't. Almost everything during this operation was superfluous that it required superimposing a different thinking and response. *I understood that little house spider's message now.* It had eight eyes at most, main eyes and secondary eyes. Most people on this planet have two eyes almost always looking in front of themselves to where they're going. I was nothing but a red herring, a cog in a bigger wheel of deception, which was already in motion. I had already sensed the pretext but had to find it, to understand which wire spoke I was in the spin of things. I had to utilise my other observations, the less obvious ones, obey my instincts. What I was focused on wasn't what it was but I knew so.

Being a student of my environment I developed a rare ability over time to simplify and readjust my own mind set, even to adapt rapidly to changing situations. I never bought into the apparent so why did I do so up to now? As time progressed I realised that the stated reason for my being here was the opposite of what I was told back at HQ. It had gone from a would-be physical action into the psychological.

Living on the edge of this precipice existence, in the end my brilliant sarcasm and optimistic pragmatism led my soul to ask this: *Why does Mankind's inquisitiveness always seek the correct answer? Why can't some things remain a mystery and be left untouched? Do I really want to know the answer? And the contradictory riposte was: I do indeed want to know! There's a slow realisation that history is always written by the most scandalous of biases...and we the people are suckers for believing what was fed to us. This system of governmental control must change. I had always thought that. What was going on here was the left and the right were not working. There had to be a third way to explore where the top and bottom mutually benefitted.*

I had to professionalise my thought process, so that margin of error was minimal and the deduction remaining is then maximised. I prepared myself better this way for what I knew I was about to absorb.

There were sharks from all over the world swimming in the small cesspool of Bulgaria. Double-dealers that played both sides of the moral and unethical fence, and in doing so profited in the millions in any currency that was selected in the preferred foreign exchange rate of the day, in itself an obscene tool of profit. Their only constancy was to the god of gold and themselves.

Of course all these shameful shenanigans couldn't be achieved without the knowledge, acquiescence and even cooperation of government officials from both wealthy and poor nations, regimes, banks, hedge fund managers and insider trading with unlawfully gained privileged information. Favourable treatment, embargoes, "special relationships" and other artificially created financial instruments would be exploited brazenly for a piece of the pie. Stock markets, futures exchanges and derivatives trading could be manipulated almost at will. The credo in short was: You can cheat, lie, circumvent and essentially do anything illegal for as long as you want but if you get caught we knew nothing about it.

It was a similar world in my game and that's why I recognised it at once. It's a contest of big money played by the big enterprises. Crucial information gained is used to boost investment performance, by executing trades designed to inflate the value of a stock or dumping shares and then buying them back at a bargain price after the predictable panic and selloff by the public. One hand washes the other knowingly but these activities are always expressly denied. Confidentiality requirements were routinely ignored and avoidance of due diligence became a norm. Exploiting tax-free loopholes on a worldwide basis or conveniently not collecting duties was practiced so long as it was beneficial to the few that were above the law, who were ably defended by their legal and accounting teams.

Security agencies with a remit of defending their nations' sovereignty were used towards the serving of that end, too. Sadly, the younger intelligence officers like me were not always aware of the shady practices and thought we were striving towards nobler causes. *Now I do know otherwise. There's even a descriptive term for it in my government: Perception Management. PM was an acronymic euphemism to mean the deliberate creation of untruths for gain.*

Meanwhile the bunch of knaves, punks, scallywags and rapscallions weren't doing it for country or honour and were only in it for the "moolah" it generated.

* * * * * * * * *

"You are a dangle," were McBarton's first words. I had already sensed that. It was jargon for a double agent op in which one intelligence service sends someone to meet a rival intelligence service to try and gain insights into their ops. In this case neither apparently subversive, leaning more to subservience for the common good of the common people.

"I see," I muttered, "who are the other lot then?" I was convinced she was going to say the KGB.

"A representative of the people of Bulgaria." She paused to look into my frowning face before continuing. "I am their messenger. They have a lot of internal problems that they'd like to address and have requested the help of the British. Please understand that just like in Britain there are good and bad persons in every organisation, and they have theirs. In London there are the preserve and promote democracy proponents and then there are those who want fat pockets for themselves in championing their causes. In Sofia one side of the political spectrum wants to maintain staunch communism while another faction from within wants deep pockets for themselves, a goal in direct conflict with its advocacy."

I smiled, "It's in direct conflict to ours, too, I may add. Phew. What a frigging mess. Pity we can't all be what we want to be while everybody benefits, instead of one or the other. There's only so much you can spend in 16 hours a day anyway while we sleep eight. What's your codename?"

"I don't have one that I know of except that I am the designated go-to person between the parties in this country. I am British but have lived in Bulgaria a long time – decades – so I see where both sides are coming from and going to. They perceive me as neutral. And they trust me. I own an English-language bookstore here in town so I've plenty of time to study the volumes on the subject and cultural behaviour. The west and the east each set a separate system that they expect everybody to fall into line with. They don't understand anyone that attacks that one-track mind. We are standing on the fault line and nobody wants to fall into it when it cracks open, so we have to build bridges."

"For answer to part two, see part one. It's still more of a frigging mess," I gibed. "Dangerous liaisons for you, even if one goes down wrong."

"I don't know if you mean to be funny ha-ha or what but I find you are, very much so, all delivered with a stoic straight-face."

"That's because when I'm between a rock and a hard place with nowhere to go, it's how I deal with it internally." I tapped my forehead for qualification.

She smiled weakly, then her mouth went even wider moving her high-cheek bones higher. She touched my hand lightly. "Well, I operate from the point of view, as naïve as it may sound, that no harm will befall me since I do not possess any evil in my heart."

I hesitated, then I finished off my train of thought, "Assuming, therefore, that I have at least a few seconds to ponder the impending result of your incredible stupidity: If and when I die will it solve the question I've often wondered about, which is: How will I die?"

"You see, God, you are so dry! Living here so long I don't get to hear this kind of ironic gallows humour often. It's the language of my youth in England."

I didn't know if she was too preoccupied with thinking she was in a comfortable space for her mind to pay attention to what was really going around her, but I was all eyes while chatting. I needed to get off the fine print into the solid words. I didn't want to read through the whole manuscript of her to learn the epilogue.

Eventually I said in keeping with her opinion that I was a bit of a jokester, "Being alive is worth celebrating just by itself, miss… Right, well, the comedy routine preamble is now over. If you must know I always thought I was mentally ill for the second half of the first 30 years of my life, doing this kind of work. When am I supposed to meet the other side and to discuss what? And how can you assure me I am meeting a likeminded individual and not the enemy? Or is it a *dukhi* (ghost) too?"

Mrs McBarton's eyes always met mine first and they told a silent story of truth, as she knew it to be, before her mouth said it. She owned a book shop so I had to read the pages of her as they turned, often in the wrong numerical order, but they told the story she wanted to tell me. She said I would be dealing with the good side. I didn't believe her but I didn't say a word. But rolling the dice to see where it would lead to was a part of my personality.

In many ways Mrs McBarton was saying the same thing as Pouladvand was from the other side of the divide. *There is an existence of a parallel structure.* We the people are on a level down here living our lives trying to survive another day. Then there are a few others existing on another level up there benefiting from our wilful ignorance and making obscene money in the process. But I sought the evidence and it hadn't been presented to me yet. I was only listening to heresy so far.

* * * * * * * * *

The next morning Mrs McBarton was driving me out of Sofia heading south in a basic Lada model. The early road signs read towards Blagoevgrad. Landscape was hilly. She said she wanted to first take me to see the "real person behind the running of Bulgaria" but wouldn't tell me who. She was afraid I would refuse to go if she did. She said it would be about five hours there and back with an exclusive one-hour audience granted to us. She calculated we'd be back by late-afternoon. Within five minutes I knew it wasn't going to be Liudmila Zhivkova or her "twin" because her place was in the opposite direction. I went along with the risk anyway, which was true to my form, because her statement had intrigued me and increased my curiosity.

We went through Blag without stopping. The scenery was getting more picturesque thereafter. Macedonia was over to the right of the *planina* (mountain range in Bulgarian) running parallel to us. If we'd kept going straight at the higher wall of peaks ahead we'd be crossing into northern Greece. My Romanian passport didn't have a visa for either country. At Petrich, the last town in Bulgaria, she pulled off the main road. Obviously she knew the way as she had done the trip before. We were driving alongside a pleasant slow moving river to a village that could be seen ahead. She said there were nice hot springs around here and ordinary people came to this corner spot from all over the country for their holidays. We got out of the car and headed to a house that was somewhat larger than the typical houses in the village. A number of sombre women dressed in black blocked our way to the door. I don't think there was a funeral going on though.

We were shown in by a similarly dressed woman while another stood in the background. McBarton and the door opener obviously knew each other. It was fake spooky in there. There were candles everywhere that reminded me of a crystal ball gypsy's den I once went into to amuse myself one night in Blackpool, a northern English resort town. I'd gone there as a trainee intel officer to report on a two-day communist conference. It cost me two quid to hear instantly forgettable nonsense. That and the spiel during the day from the podium was tedious, too, costing £20 a day to register. I don't know what fried my brain to a crisp the most.

True to the setting a witch appeared and sat down in the shadows. For a moment I thought it was a Halloween costume. But when she came into the light she was blind as a bat, shawl around her head, dark garment. I'd put her in her seventies, white hair that may have been blonde when she was younger. It got a bit creepy then, air got discernibly heavier like being inside a tomb. Mrs McBarton translated back and forth into Bulgarian and English. She said I had come all the way from England to see our hostess (which wasn't strictly true). She stupidly told the old girl what I did for a living, most amazingly. I wished she'd asked me upfront about that disclosure as the price was too high for calling it wrong. Apparently I was in the esteemed company of Baba Vanga (Grandmother Vangelia), one of the world's greatest and most accurate predictors of prophecies, I was told. I looked over at the elderly Englishwoman sharply when she said that. She didn't see me roll my eyes but the crone did despite her sightlessness.

Turned out she was Macedonian and not Bulgarian. She made McBarton and me in turn promise not to interrupt her thought process save for the interpretation into English, so we agreed, or should I say, I went along with the rules established. The old enchantress seemed reasonable enough, bit of a high speaking voice but had a pleasant demeanour. I could see how she could seduce some with her vision, excuse the pun. She had a magnetic human dimension to her, timed her space between spoken words well like top actresses do even though I didn't know what she was uttering. Her words carried weight and kind of sucked you in. The British lady was totally entranced to be in her presence. Ga-ga might be a better description.

Baba Vanga commenced with words that she knew I doubted her psychic ability so she would only offer one foresight in conclusion. She would not lapse into any clairvoyance and would only address what she was directly told by others. "Conversations from the path of life left behind" were the exact interpreted words. You had to let your imagination figure out what she meant. I was thinking why always me at the time but let her continue. I wanted to see where all this would go.

She immediately made me sit forward by stating Istanbul was not the separation line between the west and the east but that Sofia was the real crossroads. In the centre of Sofia was a company that was raping the world of its sensibilities and its name began with a K. The letter K would feature prominently soon but she didn't say whether it applied to the universe, to Bulgaria, to somewhere else, to Mrs McBarton or to me. Sounded like a prediction to me even though she had previously said it wasn't so. PKK had two K's in it I was thinking. Kintex had one…

This corporation was a trade exchange centre and a clearing house for the left-wing politics in the east and the right-wing politics in the west. It all got fudged in there was what I presumed her to be saying. Fucked up might have been more apt. One of its masters was spreading propaganda that our enemy is our enemy but in Sofia our enemy is our friend. They function on the same side of the coin. This is harmful to the good of the world. The common people lose. This information could have been passed to Baba Vanga by any insider, indeed even by McBarton herself. She herself, in her translating mode, never alluded to the fact that she knew this already. Glossed over it beautifully, credit to her.

Baba said her good friend Liudmila, the daughter of the president, had come to see her privately very recently. For a moment I was wondering if a body double could have duped her but thought not, not by the timbre of speech surely. Liudmila then informed Baba Vanga that her fate had already been decided officially and behind closed doors. In short she had a brain tumour and was dying. McBarton gasped then, as it was new to her, it would seem. Then she wheezed again when Baba Vanga confirmed that Zhivkova knew she had been poisoned slowly and why.

It was because she was going to expose the K company's shenanigans to the global media shortly. But Baba Vanga said Liudmila would only last the week alive. McBarton and I looked at each other speechless. I wanted to interrupt and ask who did it but it would cut her line of thinking off.

Our hour was almost up. Baba Vanga through Mrs McBarton asked me to stand up and come to her so she could cradle my head. I had nothing to lose. These things happen to me all the time it seems. I had joined chanting Mayan priests making offering to the gods from ancient temples in Central American jungles. At another time I had agreed to requests from Hindu swamis in the worse slums of India to hold children's foreheads so as to bring them luck in life. Even the non-denominational Christian chaplain at London Heathrow Airport, after a rather bizarre incident took place, once asked to bless me in the middle of the terminal. Me the atheist who doesn't believe in any of the medieval goobledygook but plays along with the charade in the name of keeping the peace. And so I stumbled to my feet and took the humble few steps to her throne to kneel.

After a full minute of silence, I only heard the electricity in the house hum its surge for a few seconds and her breathing. Baba Vanga next pronounced that I had "psychological characteristics and attributes that gave me innate knowledge about Mother Earth, that I was cautious and careful with a noble heart as well as a warrior with the purity of spirit" – McBarton's voice was saying so from behind me. It all sounded nice but generalised.

Then she added that I was "troubled about the life of a woman I loved". *That shook me, it really did.* Vibeke was sick at home with a mystery illness, the prognosis was glum because nobody knew what it was. There was more…that "her soul would wing to the sky from her present illness and that I would mourn on Earth where she would lie". I bit back emotion in my throat then and returned to my place silently to hear more of her sermon. I wasn't taking much in after that.

It ended with the old woman refusing an offer of money from McBarton and wishing us all the fortitude to tell the world the story of this outfit named K.

We got back into the Lada without looking or talking to each other. Somewhere along the road there was a small restaurant so I asked to pull in there. The absurdity of what had just taken place was making me smile inwardly. My first words were to calmly say, "Like Baba Vanga respectfully suggests, please allow me to speak without interruption. So that, to your mind, was the real person behind the running of this country?"

She was staring ahead of herself then slowly gave me her patented big blue eyes look. "I knew you'd have your doubts but I've lived here a long time. I'm a committed communist. I believed in the cause so I moved to live and breathe it. Officially there is no religion. Politically it's hard line Marxism. It's not utopia. Nothing is perfect. Like back home you don't know who to believe. But that old woman speaks the truth publically and often, so much so that the heads of different nations come to see her to ask her opinion. Instead of being sceptical you should be grateful. You had an hour with her. Millions wish they could but don't."

"Fair enough," I replied. "What now am I supposed to do with that information? Go back to London and tell them what she said? I'd be laughed out of the building, likely demoted, maybe even sent out for psychiatric evaluation. You know that full well, too. In many ways everything you told me theoretically yesterday just got blown out of the window in actuality. This kind of thing loses you credibility in the real world, you know."

McBarton gripped the steering wheel, hesitated then looked away. To the windscreen she said, "I don't know your real name, probably will never know it. People in high places in Britain were approached about coming here, to look and see what's happening, to assess the situation. It was of international concern. Out of all this frantic manoeuvring behind closed doors, arrives this fresh-faced young man, the scout riding ahead of the pack presumably. When I finally met you yesterday I knew I just had to put Baba Vanga and you together. What you do now with this, is up to you. I can't do anything more than I already have." She heaved a sigh then started the engine up.

"And I'll say one more thing," she added, looking at the road ahead. "Too many people in the west are just too comfortable and think any and everything can be rationalised through science. When you're born in the east and south you are raised in a world where there's not enough to eat. Then suddenly strangers appear to provide your daily bread and needs. That's when it's easier to put things into perspective and realise that we cannot explain everything especially miracles and the outright inexplicable. The same applies to Baba Vanga's imparted wisdom."

We sat in solitude motoring back up to Sofia. Somewhere near Blag I said, "Tomorrow, you take me to Kintex. Show me the place. Tell me all that you know, okay. I have to be convinced obviously. Some documentation would go a long way towards proof. Then afterwards, let me meet the *good* Bulgarian I'm supposed to meet. Then we go from there. You want to conquer this thing then we have to climb it methodically whether you like it or not. And I can be in defiance of logic if it's not effective. But the rendezvous has to be under my terms seeing that I'm the fish out of water here."

Mrs McBarton, glanced over at me, smiled briefly and simply nodded. Later on I noticed she wiped a tear discreetly. And a little bit later on she said, "I'm sorry to hear about the woman you love. I heard about the impending loss of my husband the same way."

* * * * * * * * *

Chapter Ten

I got off the tram at the Oborishte stop wearing the tight clothes I'd borrowed from Pouladvand. I thought I looked ridiculous in the cloth cap he produced for my use. In my mind I mimicked the way I watched him stroll the first time I saw him, like I belonged. Comrade McBarton was already there waiting. I had to stumble into her by design to make her notice that it was me. I had already told her not to greet me but to start walking one minute after my alighting at a medium pace towards wherever Kintex was. A lot of what I was going to do had to be improvised because I didn't know the lay of the land. She was also informed the day before that I could abort at any time of my choosing and she would have to accept my decision. It was my life after all that was on the line, not hers.

I followed her from a safe distance and let her walk about 75 yards ahead of me. It wasn't that busy as most people had arrived at work by now. The street was cobblestoned, lined with trees – quite sophisticated this part of the business sector of Sofia. I noticed various misspellings of what seemed to me a quasi-French and English name for the road: Boulevard James Bouchier. A plaque I passed and read quickly stated in several languages that he was born in Limerick, Ireland, and was a trusted advisor to Tzar Ferninand of Bulgaria. All that had occurred way before I was born. I thought it was totally out of the ordinary for an Irishman running around here in those days. Very much like this entire op, I concluded. And here comes an Englishman in his footsteps doing the same mad thing.

Meanwhile what was also interesting about her meander ahead was that she had stopped for all of one minute looking at a nameplate then walked back over. I passed her on the return and, bless the old gal, she didn't pay me a glance, then she went into number 76. I walked on to see what she was gazing at and it was Kintex's building at 66. No armed guards, dogs, cameras, sensors, nothing that would signal its importance. Suits coming and going, a reception desk in the foyer. I thought I would go and check across the street to see if there was anything over there worth observing.

I walked on a bit further, then crossed the street over the tram tracks. I retraced my steps in the opposite direction to get a better view of the modern building. I walked parallel a few yards in the direction I'd come from and then traversing over again. Apart from the policemen further down lecturing some poor arse about something he'd done wrong everything else appeared normal.

I was now outside the building of the Bulgarian Red Cross with its prominent logo displayed in Bulgarian and English, where McBarton had gone in. I leaned on a nearby tree for a while absorbing the geography and getting a feel of my surroundings in the manner of a local working man taking a morning break after an early start. I wasn't going to go in and willed her to reappear.

Fortunately, in the down time I saw two older model Mercs' park, most certainly once stolen from Western Europe. One was on my side of the street and the other on the opposite side. I could discern three bodies in each. Then Pouladvand got out of the car on my side, lit his customary cigarette and casually leaned on the bonnet. No acknowledgement of each other. *I felt very safe then.* Criminals or terrorists affiliated to PKK these boys would protect my back.

After 10 minutes a frowning Mrs McBarton came down the steps, looking around for my whereabouts. I came up behind her, startling her. "You keep doing that to me, please! Our friend is inside waiting for you. If you prefer him to come out he's willing to," she declared. I was reading her emotions for any warning signs but all seemed to be in order. I elected to follow her in. The reflection in the glass door showed one man from each car alighting, both wearing a long coat, and starting to come towards the front of the building.

On the ground floor we went into a rental office space at the back. Upon entering an elderly well-groomed but balding man with thinning white hair and a Captain Ahab-style beard stood up to shake my hand. I was much taller than him. He had a nice western-made suit and tie on. The first words he uttered were in English, "I am Raiko Nikolov, ambassador for Bulgaria in Rome. Many years ago I secured your release from my country. I wanted to meet you. I specifically requested your presence here. You are a brave man for returning to Bulgaria considering the circumstances the last time."

There's not much one can respond to an opening line like that. I didn't know whether to believe him or not. I may have mumbled some hazy, profuse and embarrassed words of gratitude before sitting down across from him. I needed to be seated where I could see anybody come in the door. Between us lay a thick file stuffed with paper. Mrs McBarton sat at the end of the table between us, as if presiding over a meeting. She was very quiet today, literally taking a backseat. I looked beyond her for any discreet cameras, but saw nothing of note. Nevertheless, I assumed I was being bugged. There was a walled garden with many flowers in bloom outside the fixed window.

Nikolov smiled pleasantly at me, then put on a pair of spectacles while opening the folder. He then raised his eyes to look at me full in the face again. "First you must know that I am a staunch communist, a hardliner. I believe in the system wholeheartedly. It's my life's passion." He let that sink in and then continued. "What Bulgaria is undergoing through Kintex next door is against all the principles of my existence. And indeed the opposite of your society's stated objectives, too. I want to stop this madness before it ruins us beyond repair. But how to do it is very difficult because its roots are deep into the ground now."

I took the cue to volunteer, "I know already mostly what they do and who is in league with them. What I don't know is what is being planned for the immediate future and the future beyond that. Perhaps you may enlighten me, sir? It is in this area where we can perhaps make better preventative inroads. I agree that what's already operational is much harder to stop."

"Well, I'm glad to hear that," he looked grim, "because what's coming shocks me to the rotting core. Makes me lose faith in mankind altogether."

"Ply me with the details, to the best you can Mr Nikolov. I can only do my best thereafter to deliver the message." The truth being I *didn't* know what to do with it but he didn't need to know that part.

He began by showing me various documented projects aimed to supply Bulgaria and the Soviet Union with advanced computer technologies that furthered Big Brother control of text data over its people. "This is also earmarked for expansion to Western Europe and North America, and eventually the world," he grumbled emphatically. It was paid for with arms sales.

He diagrammed how Kintex's many illegal commercial dealings circumvented embargoes in place. Very complex. Needed a drawing to follow how elaborate the schemes were. Who they invested with and had stakes in was head-spinning. The scale of money laundering, names of upstanding well-known people on the bribery pay list and those getting on the bandwagon, truly appalled the senses. I assumed the information he presented me with was factual as I could only take his word for it. The papers I saw could have been counterfeit.

At this point I asked, "Am I receiving this file afterwards?" The answer was that I wasn't. Thereon I did my best to memorise the information. Obviously a high ranking diplomat in his position had direct access but he had to return it as is.

I saw names of clandestine companies operating abroad, including in the UK. I tried filing most of the British firms with easier names in my head who were the beneficiaries from the said Bulgarian proscribed activities. Revenues were deposited in foreign bank accounts, of which The Vatican featured prominently and Lichtenstein to a lesser extent. One statement showed mid-seven figures in US dollars in transactions over various odd-numbered instalments sent to Poland and marked "for Solidarity, as needed"…except the name there was simply K.J. Wojtyla, which Nikolov reminded me was the Pope John Paul II's birth name. The money chain started with the Bulgarian State Security's First Main Directorate, who were the primary managers of the funds. The cash was then channelled through a local military computer research outfit named Stara Zagora. Annual funds reached a staggering US$1 billion, tax-free. This being 1981.

A few years earlier a special directorate had been set-up within Kintex that was also known as the "hidden transit" directorate. Its function was to barter or double-deal in smuggled arms, narcotics, the illegal trafficking in people, and to a lesser extent in stolen objet d'art of historical value. In every case one pre-determined value was paid off against the receipt of the other. This operation was above and in addition to the aforementioned dealings already in place. Kind of stepping up a gear, doubling its profits by forming a sister operation that specialised in heavier shit but without actual money being exchanged. It was harder to track the activity when there was no tell-tale trail left behind.

"This is really alarming," Nikolov was shaking his head as he handed me a photocopy of a bill of lading. He must have noticed that I received the paperwork between my forefinger and middle finger so not to leave fingerprints. Attached to it was a list of items and their quantities in container loads due to arrive by sea in the Bulgarian port of Varna. The three-necked flasks, reflux condensers, funnels, et al, I understood. But I didn't know what the chemical-sounding names of tropinone, ethanol, distilled pyrrole and ecgonine were used for.

"Sounds like products for a lab but I don't know what kind," I shrugged.

Looking into me hard, Nikolov stated bluntly, "Ecgonine comes from coca leaves and is dissolved in the ethanol to eventually manufacture cocaine. Seeing Bulgaria is already producing heroin it is going to do the same with coke. Import, make and distribute it. Various South American nations are air transporting the fresh leaves to drop zones in South Africa and then it makes its way by private jets to here. We know to where and how already. It commences shortly."

Finally, a recent photograph of "60" appeared out of the stack. Sure enough in the background were his star assistants: "Knobbly Knuckles" and "Cleopatra". Except they were looking very dapper and conservative at an international business conference, much like he was, in smart business suits. The woman really had a talent to look so different on a new day.

The ambassador must have noticed a giveaway glint in my eyes so said, "We'll come to him in a minute. But before I want to address a situation that I find myself closely connected to." I nodded for him to proceed. I was all ears, trying not to lean forward too much in anticipation.

"Just over two months ago a Turkish madman attempted to assassinate the Pope in the Vatican in front of a big crowd and live on television. You must have seen it wherever you were at the time. Naturally the conspiracy theorists purporting to being observers of The Holy See and with the pontiff coming from Poland commented that he was on record that he would organise resistance in his homeland against the Red Army, *if they invaded.* Illogical logic. One prominent investigative journalist even came on his national channel and exclaimed that Bulgaria was connected to the Soviet natural gas and electricity grid since 1972. To me this was no secret at all but they were making it sound like it was a new news.

"Sitting in our embassy there in Rome suddenly the global media were parked outside the building screaming that Bulgaria had organised this crime of the century on behalf of its Russian masters. A picture was being painted that these things had something to do with this botched job by a known petty criminal. Even one of our state airline employees at Leonardo da Vinci has been arrested for some support role that has been dreamt up. I know he is an innocent man.

"It made me sit back and think what was happening? One big reason I have concluded is Kintex's brazen business model of supplying weapons for war to third world countries, its non-deniable involvement in the drug trade, and add in all the other ugly badness that it does and it becomes easy to finger a scapegoat. *Even if we are guilty or innocent.* I decided then and there to get actively involved in dismantling this cancerous negative that harms Bulgaria in the long run. True or not the furore surrounding the reasons for the attack on Pope John Paul II was way too far below the belt of humanity, really scraping the muck at the bottom – from our perspective.

"If it continues the way it is, where it becomes de rigueur to blame Bulgaria for just about anything one feels like, it is unacceptable. We do indeed have a long history of smuggling, yes, but these new activities are making us beyond uncomfortable, even to ourselves now. On the other hand, our experiences also shape our character…and with luck we will gain our strength from those experiences…"

"So far you are describing what is called perception management, inventing an unquestionable big lie to achieve one country's own agenda but what that goal is in this case, I haven't a clue as yet. So where does this fellow come into the equation then?" I prompted him. I was tapping "60"'s photo.

McBarton and Nikolov exchanged glances. The older man asked me, "Have you ever heard of the Grey Wolves, who are known as *Bozkurtlar* in Turkish?"

I had, but only in passing, so I shook my head. I wanted to hear his version. "The Grey Wolves are Turkish right wing Fascist extremists. The man who tried to kill the anti-communist Pope was a member. What they support is the exact opposite of what Solidarity is trying to achieve. Bulgaria likewise is a very communist nation, as far to the left of the spectrum as you will find. We don't endorse this kind of totalitarian ideology whatsoever. But Kintex is playing a dangerous game of attracting everybody and anybody regardless of their political affiliation. *This is precisely what makes Bulgaria look like a hypocrite.* True communists don't mix with any system characterised by right wing dictatorship and repressive nationalism. The most extreme organisation of all is called Gladio, of which the Grey Wolves represent the Turkish sector. This man is its head of Eastern European operations. And he lives right here in Sofia."

I stared at him, giving my brain time to think. So I picked up his sheet of paper with the diagram on it and turned it over. Upside down on the blank side they could see it appear as I drew a circle and cut a line through it from top to bottom. An arrow going left from the pinnacle around the length of the curve. Repeating the same on the right. In the end lowest slice of the pie nearest to them I darkened it. I concluded with, "But if you are an extremist left or an extremist right it's the same thing – its extremism and nobody of sane or responsible mind wants to go there. Anarchy in any form is to be avoided at all costs."

I let that sink in. "So what's his name? And please give me a brief on Gladio in your own words. Quickly though, within Turkey, am I correct in thinking that the PKK are the sworn enemy of the Grey Wolves?"

"Yes, historically, yes, a bit like your various factions in Northern Ireland fighting for notoriety against the constabulary and army. Only much worse, more violent and representing extreme opposite ideologies. One is Socialist seeking freedom for its people and the other is Fascist and wants to control them. There's more to it than that but that's a brief explanation."

He next dug out two pages stapled together from his pile. Four pages in English, nicely formatted and professionally typed. "For your eyes only."

Four photographs of "60", as he had aged as each decade had gone by, appeared across the top of the first page. Even in his youth he was a difficult man to have sympathy for. Underneath were 10 names or aliases he went by. They ranged from the Ukrainian, Russian, Bulgarian, Hungarian and Turkish – two from each. There was a disclaimer under them saying they were all likely names stolen from his victims. It could not be verified that any of them was his real name and he rotated them constantly along with assuming random others. One of the Ukrainian names had a double K if initialled, interestingly.

The report by persons unknown to me was compiled from extracts of limited conversations he'd had over the years with third parties known to them. He was born 64 years ago in Odessa, the Ukraine. As a young man he became a constable in *Ukrainska dopomizhna politsiia* or the Ukrainian Auxiliary Police finding himself stationed in the capital of Kiev. Circumstances saw him guarding the Syretskij (local name) or Syrets (German name) concentration camp and he was recruited into or ordered to join the annihilation gangs that were responsible for the deaths of untold tens of thousands Jews, Gypsies, mental patients, Ukrainian nationalists, et al.

The Soviet Red Army liberated the camp and later used it to house German prisoners of war. At some point around this time, perhaps as part of the Nazi retreat, he made his way via Hungary to Italy where it was assumed he presented himself as a war refugee. As millions of displaced persons did at that time. While there in the border town of Trieste, in a camp for several years, he managed to alliance himself with American decision-makers that were in the process of forming Gladio. For the past 30 years he has become responsible for its Eastern European network.

Sordid reading. I looked up at my pair of guests who were facing me and let out a breath of air. I then handed the paper back with my crooked fingers.

Nikolov took over the mantle, "Gladio, as you may well know, is half of the word Gladiator. Its motto translated from the Latin into English is: 'In silence I preserve freedom'. It was sanctioned by the United States' National Security Act in 1947 for 'stay behinds' after World War II. The US' purpose was to have a paramilitary organisation in place prepared and ready for the Soviet Union's projected invasion of Europe to start World War III. *Its other objective was to conduct covert false flag operations in the meantime as a pretext for helping the anti-communist cold war military industrial complex peddle their American-manufactured arms.* It was a high-level authorised right wing strategy of creating tension by using plausible deniability to discredit communism in any way possible. In actuality it became a secret army at the capitalist illuminati's beck and call with a licence to create mayhem. It is still in place as we speak.

"The Gladio funded business trading arm was set-up in Sofia in the late-sixties, which is in itself a contradiction because its long-range goal was anti-communist. Do you see now how Bulgaria has become a charlatan? To all the world we say we are Marxist collectivists striving on behalf of the people to have a fair living but behind closed doors we welcome with open arms the free market capitalists, the opposite of our ideology – one that disgusts me – so we can make obscene revenues for the few. This exactly pinpoints why I am losing faith in mankind. I am ashamed."

A few hushed seconds passed. I put my hands up finally, palms showing in exasperation. I contemplated then spoke. "This meeting is likely to last only a couple of hours. You are telling me inside information going back decades. I am only one man. What am I to do with all this…what can be labelled as heresy because I have not been given evidence that any of it can be authenticated. You must know that, too. So, please, why don't you tell me what exactly it is you would like me to do?"

As Nikolov and I gazed at each other a voice in-between us whispered, "You are an officer of what was once known as Section D at SIS, am I correct?" I turned to look at Mrs McBarton's tense face.

I replied, "It has no name that you need to know – it has a media name that is the flavour of the month, which keeps changing. Its last one was 'Revolutionary Development Support' or 'RDS' in short – but we can refer to the unit as 'OSB', if you like. For 'Operational Support Branch' but that is not its name either. But it was briefly officially called Special Political Action at one time, yes. Insiders tend to refer to the colour seen on its personnel's files."

McBarton's big blues were penetrating into mine. Her face was simmering with thunder. "Their involvement would solve a lot of this problem. You can organise it, I believe."

"That is my understanding also," piped in Nikolov. "You are the deniable ops team for MI6."

"It's not my call to make," I murmured defensively. "And we don't do political killings on a whim. There's due process to PK and orders are dispensed, verbally. In extremis laws may be disobeyed if said disobedience is deemed legitimate and in furtherance to the cause…a British cause I may add. This is a Bulgarian issue."

"This is an *international* issue that we've asked your country for their assistance with, seeing that the criminal mastermind is behind it all is a naturalised Briton. Politically you are just as embarrassed as we are about these developments even though some of you are profiteering well from the venture," volunteered Nikolov.

"Decisions like what you are indicating are made at a ministerial level," I responded. "Then it takes planning. If it ever came to pass, given what I know already, it would be made to look like an accident and not take place on or near our island. That is if you are referring to the intended termination with extreme prejudice of this gentleman," I tapped "60" photograph again.

"Nor within our lands either," Nikolov offered. McBarton was nodding in agreement. "Plus we would like to see the man and the woman in the picture with him never come back to Bulgaria again, as well. They are the primary brains behind the new barter division."

He hesitated before continuing, pointing at "Knobbly Knuckles'" image, "I regret to inform you this man was your chief torturer when you were in jail in Bulgaria for 11 weeks, if you must know."

I think I must have had a red mist come over my eyes then. I know I wasn't aware of Nikolov and McBarton for a few seconds as I transposed myself back to that hellhole for a nano-second. Yes, I know now why he seemed familiar to me in the bar. I remembered his hands, those cruel protuberant hands with the same gold ring that left indentations all over my body and scars in my mind. I'd blocked the notion filtering through to my cognizance because I didn't want to know.

I came back into focus with the pensive faces of an older diplomat and a grandmotherly bookstore owner looking intently at me.

"So they are not from Bulgaria? Where are they from then?"

"He is from the Karakalpak Autonomous Soviet Socialist Republic, a part of Uzbekistan, preferring to say that he hails from *Oaraqalpoghistan*. Speaks a Turkic language but fluent in Russian as I know you well know, as well as passable Bulgarian and English. He is responsible for Kintex's dealings with the Islamists, of which he is one himself. He will take charge of all operations east of Sofia when the old man moves on. A teetotaller. Observes his faith to a degree but doesn't observe its finer religious messages, especially its material-related aspects."

"And the girl?"

"Irish. Dubliner. Failed actress who joined the Provisional IRA. In time graduated to Kintex's weapons supply unit and is in charge of her compatriots' account and others like the ETA Basques, Baader-Meinhof in Germany – European wing only. Both these individuals double-up as the personal close protection to their elderly benefactor for social and public occasions. It serves their prestige well as he introduces them to contacts."

I shook my head. I waited for my scattered emotion to return to normal before proceeding. My jaw muscles were grinding. I spoke slowly for emphasis. "Back to me. You should know, you've said so yourself, that certain clique-y circles in the UK are making handsome income from these dealings. It isn't going to be approved so easily – if it ever will be – and I wouldn't know who to trust on my side… Fingers will be pointed at me within SIS for my involvement and it would never get off the ground. Career suicide. *How you or I would go about this privately is another matter entirely.* It would have to be done in absolute secrecy… But I have an idea…you fund it, I'll steward it through and I have a third party with grudges I'm pretty sure are more than happy to involve themselves in the task. Two month minimum to three months maximum from commencement until completion. That way everybody will be happy and justice will triumph. What'd you say?"

They looked at each other partly victorious and partly quizzical but wanting to know more.

"But first I have a question though that I've been meaning to ask you Mrs McBarton. I hope you can answer it." She acceded. "When you say it was 'of international concern' and the next thing you know is me coming here. Who were you dealing with to get the ball rolling?"

"The British Embassy here," she answered promptly. "They know me and I have known them, for many years in fact. It's their idea. I was brought into it by them."

"And," I continued, "who tells you about the brush pass information to forward on to me and vice versa?"

"The same source. The head of station. I believe you may have met just before you came here."

"So you don't know who that brush pass person is, I take it?"

"No. I've never seen him before in my life. Several days in a row I tried following him and I got lucky on the fourth attempt. He's not exactly a fast walker and he disappeared down that alley way. I returned there the next day. I saw you appear from there eventually. I didn't know if you were who you were so I just followed you. And here we are."

"Why did you do that?"

"I was curious. I found it all rather exciting. Different to the usual hum-drum. Got my adrenaline pumping."

"Why did you want me to check out Liudmila Zhivkova's dwellings?"

"I didn't. The fellow at the embassy thought it would best fill in some blanks you would have in your head. I only drew the map as told."

I turned to Nikolov. "Sir, when we first met, you stated that you 'requested my presence here'. Whom may I ask did you tender that wish to, please?"

His answer was the same source. They were introduced by the same source. The same source informed them his office manager was killed by an unidentified party in Bulgaria. They didn't know that man. A lot was riding on this source's say so. The same source told them about my connection to "OSB". I promised them I'd get to the bottom of it. *For my own sake.*

Nikolov and I set-up a method for the sending and receiving of future coded transcript, teller to receiver only. He confirmed that substantial funds would be found but didn't say from where.

There was a light knock on the door. Upon his bobbed approval a nondescript middle-aged female secretary entered and shuffled across the floor to Nikolov. She whispered in his ear and returned whence she came stifling a sniff. Nikolov took off his glasses and said to the fixed space in the wall behind McBarton and me, "The lady came to let me know that national radio is reporting that Liudmila Zhikova has passed away."

I drove back with Pouladvand and friends. On the way I took the opportunity to ask him how it had come about to be trusted to operate a safehouse on behalf of the British and brush pass messages?

He was very candid in answering. "First I clean houses for wealthy people. One Bulgarian person was a manager at the British Embassy. They are maybe 20 working there, two-thirds of the entire staff are nationals of Bulgaria, 10 British, including the Ambassador. Then over time they say this person and that Briton could use my services. I build up my clientele good over many years. One of them was the Deputy Head of Mission and one day he asks me to help with something like what I am doing now and afterwards he was happy with me. So it continues from time to time. There is trust between us."

"Did you know the administrator that was murdered not so long ago?"

"Not personally. By face only."

Does the Deputy Head of Mission know what your other job is?"

"No. This I would never tell him. I think he would not like it."

At that point I started to outline a job prospect for excellent pay with all expenses paid in South Africa for four PKK fighters. It would help their political cause greatly. They were very interested and wanted to know more. Their involvement would have to be approved by someone called Apo in Turkey, which they told me meant Uncle in Kurdish. I supposed it was the nom de guerre of their leader.

They later dropped me near the Deputy Head of Mission residence. I spoke to them as if I knew him well so they thought it was no skin off their nose to take me there. Well I did know him in a way but I'd suckered them into disclosing his home locale. I would find my own way back to the safehouse afterwards.

Waiting there in the shadows for an hour, there was a lot of evidence of mourning for the deceased Liudmila Zhivkova. Flags were being flown at half mask on state buildings and houses with many cars displaying her image in their windows. She really was loved by the younger people. It was the stodgy elders that found her offensive.

Soon after dusk H/SOF came strolling along the road. He did his normal trained routine and then went in through his front door. Before it closed I had forced my way in behind him making him gasp loudly. His breathing was pumping hard. I detected in his reaction that he thought he was about to be shot in the head based on his rapid blinking and twisting of his neck. Like he wanted to see it coming at least. As I didn't know what to expect when I went in so I had to perform it silently. But everything looked all clear – no dogs, no wife, no housemaid present, no security alarm bells ringing. I switched the hallway light on.

When he saw my face, he sobbed and dropped halfway to his knees in relief but I pulled him back up. "I haven't got a lot of time. I followed you home. Nice cover title you have," I lied. "I just want you to answer some questions then I'll be on my way. Sorry to startle you like that. I'll deny it if you write me up about this visit."

He was quick to regain his composure as we stood there in the hallway. "Don't be silly, I wouldn't do that. We're on the same side I'm glad to see. Fire away old chap. Ask me what you want. You're doing a splendid job so far. I may write you a commendation though."

"Right. Back at Century House I believe you said you had a 'so far dependable Bulgarian source' who was passing you information to you? 'A third hand witness' were your words, sir. Who was that?"

"Your answer is or should I say *was* Liudmila Zhivkova. You must be aware that she died today, reportedly a suicide. I don't believe that. But I never actually met her. My administrator that was murdered was our go-between. When her security people found that out they did him in. Decent fellow, didn't deserve that."

He hesitated a fraction. "Look, I've been in this world's second longest profession a lot longer than you. I selected you because you reminded me a lot of what I wished I was. I thought I had it in me but I don't. I'm not suited to this part of it, what you're doing now. But the punch line is this particular scenario cannot be solved by diplomacy or reasoning. That's why it has a 'run interference' designation – kept away from certain people on the totem pole. It *has* to be an 'OSB'-type op. Just for the record H/BUL/OPS in London is part of this Kintex bunch of cowboys in that he receives pay-offs regularly, to look away at certain strategic situations and to distract at other times. He's not the only one at headquarters. I can't prove it all to you right this instance so you'll have to take my word for it. The man was present when we met last so I had to speak to you in the manner that I did for you to grasp things weren't perhaps quite kosher. I think I may have succeeded."

The older bloke stopped to take a deep breath. "I've already tried to take internal action on Kintex but Robert Maxwell and his cronies' tentacles are wrapped tightly around some key decision-makers balls back home. I've been vetoed a lot. I'm sure you're like me, you're not sure what to believe anymore and who to trust. Welcome to the club. If you want me to say it out loud I will: This lamentable situation has created a backlash. Your part in the jigsaw is you organise this FPA (focused preventative action is SIS code for assassination) with or without 'OSB' participation and overnight the world becomes a better place for it."

"So simple that it's fucking bullshit," I hissed. "Within days they'll have their replacements appointed who would be carrying on per normal. Besides it's against the law twice over and your bit about 'run interference' could well be applied the other way – kept away by the bad from the good."

The older Englishman stared at me momentarily, "That's absolutely true what you say but we'll get them anyway, showing them that unknown renegades from within are just as capable of hitting below the belt. It'll slow down the process, make anybody think twice before stepping into the empty shoes that need filling again. It's the lesser of the evils. Meanwhile the others legislative, diplomatic and business processes will be working by then to stop this Kintex madness from another angle. Take my word for it, I will protect your arse till my dying day. Others won't know, will not know, while bringing in the necessary support for the end games that will come from this action. And the least people involved the better, I say."

"Why are you so wrapped up in this seemingly lost cause?" I asked.

He grimaced before answering: "The problem with this country before it became Marxist under Soviet rule was that it was a monarchy with pro-Nazi leanings. One extreme to the other. But the King stood up to Hitler and refused to deport Bulgarian Jews to the death camps. So Bulgarians are not all bad. It didn't see much action during World War II as it was. Now is the time again to stand up to the likes of Kintex..."

"That's a reason?" I queried. "Or are you also saying you are Jewish?"

"I am indeed. But all things considered this cancer has to be cut out and fast. If anything for the sake of humanity and justice. Too many are content to just sit on the fence twiddling their thumbs collecting pay stubs. As usual it's down to the unsung few to pull it off. Have you seen enough stinking crap already? Want gorier details? I can get them to you. But as time passes more of this goddamn poo gets dumped on an unsuspecting world. I'm like Nikolov, it's finally time something was done about it. *I care.* So I want to know if you can devise a strategy of elimination? I'll be your protector dealing with the in-house politics and believe you me there's a lot of back stabbing going on."

I was looking into his fervent eyes, feeling his passion. He truly believed in what he was doing. "I've decided already," I replied matter-of-factly. "Working back over. I know who will do it and an approximation where we need to lure the targets to, subject to further information being received. But I know I want to get out of here as soon as possible, the same way I came in. I have a deeply private matter to take care of first at home – a fortnight off. Meanwhile in the downtime you figure out why I need to be sent to South Africa for two months. Maybe three top. Also devise a lucrative sting to attract the flies to the light where the sticky paper lies. I'll work with you on it, with Nikolov. Then hopefully it'll be accomplished and everything gets back to normal."

* * * * * * * * *

I got back to Berne via Bucharest and Geneva. Vibeke hadn't improved. The live-in caretaker elderly Swiss lady I'd paid to take care of her needs was at her wits end by now. I gave her extra for her troubles and bought a nice cake for her husband and her from the patisserie. They lived in the same street fortunately.

I looked at my lovely girl lying there sleeping in bed wasting. I did something then I'm so happy that I did: I gently cut off a lock of her golden hair and placed it in my passport for transfer later to a nice box. I also decided to take her home to Denmark because I couldn't stay and look after her. I hated myself then for being a slave to the demands of my job.

Her mother answered the phone. Kind of anticipated it really. Yes, everything was ready at their farm. The bedroom she had as a child was hers forever, she'd said. I remember the awkward space that followed, fizzing with meaningful emotion.

I packed up everything I could think of that she would have wanted with her. Her dolls as a kid included. I dressed her and as I was doing so she woke up. The most beautiful thing in the world that content smile, that realisation I was home, that strong grip of my hand that slowly let go. No words were whispered and she never opened her eyes on that occasion.

When I carried the bigger doll of a girl to the car the sun shone on her face momentarily. The tears were rolling down me by now and my heart was heaving. *Whatever happens that love of ours would never die.* We talked a little on the trip – her eyes wide open now enjoying the sights – but it was mostly lovely sweet nothings of the memory of certain things. I was glad we had that precious time of bonding even more tightly. We'd even chortled at the crows on the road ahead playing Russian roulette in possibly misjudging our excessive speed. "Birds don't react to cars' flashing full beams, silly," she'd laughed. But she slept like a baby most of the way, front passenger seat back in comfort. Every time I looked across at her angelic face it seemed to have a different light shining rays on her.

I'd driven this return trip a couple of times before. There was a foreboding sense in me that this was one way. *I was facing up to the impact of her leaving me already; and the irony was I was the one leaving her.* It took a while on the winding roads to get out of Switzerland. I drove through Germany the fastest I'd ever done. Thank goodness there were no speed limits on the autobahns. At the time, I remember thinking I'd actually travelled the length of Deutschland in exactly 10 hours border-to-border. It was another two hours to Thisted, in northern Denmark from there. The Danes had set a sensible speed limit given the propensity of black ice to form on the road due to its flat surface and lack of natural defences from the elements.

The parents and younger sister came out into the night air when the Audi entered the long driveway to their farmhouse. Such huggable respectful nice citizens. Strangely I could see only then why Vibeke had escaped them to join the national airline as a stewardess, to climb out of the stifling closeness of the closet and go and soar to discover the wide wonderful world out there. Not sure how mum and dad were in their younger days but the sister was an ordinary homebody, so opposite to the once wildly mad crazy funny girl I loved. It was almost a handing over ceremony, not just a homecoming, a return to her roots…the moment I laid her on her bed.

I stayed nine nights in that room with her. When she was awake, which wasn't often, we relived our time together magically. It was spellbinding what we could recollect that we had done together. We enjoyed those sessions a lot. I don't think a lot of people would understand the pleasure it gave us, just to lie on a bed and chuckle at the most stupid of things we'd experienced. We were a quirky couple to the straight and narrow types, and we'd long known that.

The local family doctor came by a couple of times and could not get a handle on what it was that ailed her but his prognosis was grim. He would soon bring his good friend here from medical school, who was now a well-known doctor at the big Copenhagen hospital, to see what he knew. It was the least he could do. Lovely guy. But he repeated what Swiss, French and German medical specialists had already diagnosed: She had suddenly got a blood disorder and her immune system was so compromised by now that they were unable to restore it back to normal. None of them had seen this kind of condition before.

I had to be leaving soon. The father and I had a deep man-to-man chat in the large kitchen by the stove after the girls had turned in for the night. A typically stoic big Dane with a light beard who had been a pig farmer all his life, like his father and grandfather before him. I'm glad we had our quiet connexion over a couple shots of akvavit. Each time he said that word I kind of injected it instead before ingesting as being snaps, which they also call it. I'm not certain it occurred to him that it was derived from the Latin *aqua vitae* and literally meant "water of life". We were in essence toasting the beginning of the end of his beautiful eldest daughter's limited time on earth – the love of my life. And we shed tears together without shame. He'd agreed I could leave my car there in the garage and he'd take me to Copenhagen airport in his in the morning.

I told Vibeke I would be back as soon as I can, in about 8-10 weeks' time. Her diamond blue eyes gleamed as she smiled that knowing smile that I loved, and coughed, "Ah, but then you always say that." To which I responded, "Ah, but I always do come back to you, too." We had both grinned knowingly like kids one more time. It said something to us about our free spirit. It was our wee maxim between us. Just like we'd always sit next to each on the settee in silence holding hands whenever one of us was going be away for a while. It was a custom the Eastern Europeans observed and we had adopted it, only we didn't do that this time.

Outside the door I think the threesome standing there thought we were both nuts to be finding humour at a time like this. I think in a nutshell that was probably what they never got to understand about her all along, but I did full well comprehend that she was a loveable nice nutter from the beginning to the end.

* * * * * * * * *

(Understand, please, that this had evolved to being an unapproved op in South Africa. Whether we were just as bad as those on the Gladio-Kintex side of the fence or not is debatable. The saying about 'two wrongs don't make a right' is an old wife's tale. All aspects considered, it had to be done. So many ticks in the boxes of wrongs and none in the other column. "60", "Knobbly Knuckles" and "Cleopatra" had got away with murder in more ways than one for far too long. Their come-uppance was coming. And I was risking my career by being involved but I'd got to a point where I didn't care about me anymore. In telling this story the unexpected ingredients that popped into the mix far outweighed the rather predictable plan and end result.)

> *This is the eruption of the end.*
> *So that the thief expires.*
> *This is the final struggle.*
> *The people want only their due.*
> *Let us group together, and tomorrow.*
> *The earth belongs only to men.*
> — *excerpts from 'The Internationale'*

When I received the proposed game plan it was pretty straight forward but nevertheless creative and very international in scope and coverage. The Bulgarian in Rome had quickly obtained a donation of US$1 million from an undisclosed foundation for the party being planned – read that as non-refundable. The Kurds in Turkey approved their participation on the spot. They had a score to settle with the Grey Wolves as it turned out and wanted to send double the number of operatives. I managed to persuade them that four was enough, and less was better. The Englishman in Sofia had set up a unique and creative sting operation. It involved the owner of an extremely profitable South African gold mine who wanted to put up the company assets in return for profit-sharing in KIntex's wider global revenues. This appealed greatly to their greed factor and it "fitted" into the expanded barter system coming down the line. The logistics of the South American aerial drop-offs of crates of ingredients from coca at night in designated zones at the nearby Kalahari Desert would have to be worked out so as to benefit the enterprise.

Most of South Africa's gold mines are about 49 miles (80 kilometres) west of its capital Johannesburg. Keep heading due west and the barren lowlands of the Kalahari Basin appear. Dead reckoning westwards still and the arid Kalahari Desert sands come into view. Jo'burg to the fringe of the desert was 250 miles (402 km) one-way. I know because I drove it in a rental car under the guise of being a tourist on holiday. I did so as part of my cover as a temporary official posting there to follow up on leads for the new cocaine delivery route to Europe and Asia.

The flight plans of pilots of small planes started from Angola to the north, staying due south on the Namibia-Botswana border to west of the town of Ghanzi then they turned southeast to their destinations – all uninterrupted airspace. Not wanting coke flooding its cities the Soviet government ordered military satellites to track the aircrafts from Angola who was a long-term ally. The findings were forwarded to the Bulgarians, and now we had the data in our hands. It was useful intel towards my final report to SIS who would in turn tender it to the South African authorities for their immediate action.

I opined that I thought the threat of *muti* (use of human organs for magic cures by tribes), as a strategy to pull the targets away from perceived safety into the set trap, was ingenious. After being eaten alive by a predator, man's second worst nightmare was the criminal use of his body parts in others – in the west anyway.

I met Ivan (his real name), the gold mine's owner. A little fellow in his seventies, slight frame, thinning blonde hair with the most stunning blue eyes. We got along well and the two of us had dinner on the balcony of his large house served by his friendly black staff who happily lived on the premises with their families.

He told me he was Jewish and had lost his entire own family in the Holocaust. His surname was now of very Dutch-German-South African origin, as was his heavy *Suid Afrikaaner* accent. He offered some more information about himself to me: "Just before and during World War II when I was a young man I was head strong and went to join the Zionist extremist organisation, *Irgun Zva'i Leumi*, in Palestine. For you it would approximately translate to National Military Organisation. This group fought the British mandate and campaigned for the establishment of the state of Israel. But I was captured, treated reasonably well in jail by your countrymen, which resulted in me modifying my views. I was released after the world war was over. When I went home I couldn't find anybody I knew…when I should have been there for them…"

I never found out from him where he originated from in Europe and never asked. Nor how long he was incarcerated for. He never returned to Israel because, I'm guessing, he lost his passion for terrorist activities and saw no reason to kill British soldiers anymore. As a wartime refugee he probably was admitted to South Africa. But there must have been some old connection or favour owed and that's how this acquaintance was made. I'm quite sure he never married and had kids of his own. He seemed content with the family of others he had around him now.

Normally not a person striven for payback, he said the opportunity to engage in this sting was too attractive to refuse. He would be the smiling businessman 'front' who wanted to participate in the lucrative Kintex global profit plan. At this point I told him about my Uzbek torturer in Bulgaria. After hearing my account Ivan concluded very matter-of-factly with, "What goes around; comes around." I was impressed when he added that he didn't want to toast to that, not now and not ever. Then he went on to say in finality, "The Torah strictly warns against taking revenge; yet some Jews believe pre-emptive violence is acceptable. I previously never really had a personal reason for being involved. But your experience only makes me more resolved."

"Yes, but that's moving the goalposts to keep the rabbi happy," I smiled. He roared with laughter on that insight and hugged me like the son he never had.

There was only one problem. "Cleopatra" never showed up. Only the two arseholes with two of the BG's that I recognised from my brief visit to Liudmila's grounds. I was there discreetly at the VIP airport with my binoculars ready when they came down the gangplank off the Yakolev Yak-40 private jet that carried Bulgarian markings. It was possible that the Irish girl could spring a defence with more BG's from behind our backs, so I made a note of that possibility. I wished then that I had the extra four Kurds at my beck 'n' call but I didn't.

The limo took them to a luxury villa not far from Ivan's gold mine. After a night of pandering they would be taken the next day to see the facilities by the old geezer himself. Then if satisfied – Ivan assured me they very much would be – they would spend the day after going over his accounts to discuss further business opportunities. It was that same night that Ivan would then return in alarm to say the local tribes were on the war path for human organs and to 'escape' to his mine's grounds for protection where he had around-the-clock armed heavily security, which they'd already witnessed.

The night 'security' team being the Kurds that had arrived after undergoing a brief training exercise in the Kenya bush. I was on hand to see their separate arrival at the international airport on four different flights. The drivers taking them to the hotel being the key. Interestingly "Uncle Opa" had chosen those who had non-ethnic Turk appearances. I was impressed. I was informed later that all of them were furnished with false Greek-Cypriot passports courtesy of my country and from that I presumed they each spoke good English to South African immigration.

Ivan had given me a licensed pistol for my needs that I had welcomed. At all times I stayed in the distance monitoring proceedings and keeping an eye out for any support crew they may have mustered. But my suspicions were unfounded. As the hours counted down I was strangely calm. The bodies would be disposed of down a recently shuttered deep mine shaft afterwards.

I can't tell you what a strange and utterly unpredictable world we live in. Even the best laid plans go astray. The team of Kurds stationed themselves in preparation outside the gold mine's perimeter barbed wire fence with its spotlights on. Ivan on cue turned up at the villa at the designated time screaming to get in his car. The "guests" did as they were told but instead of jumping in Ivan's car they decided as a security precaution to find their own way to the mine in the pitch black darkness of the night in a rental car they'd just hired. Not good. We hadn't factored that.

They never ever arrived at the gates of the mine which puzzled us. We warily went back twice to their luxury villa and found no trace of them there either. The lights were blazing and their belongings were not packed. We figured they'd got lost. The mission was deemed a failure that we'd have to reorganise.

At dawn's first light we went looking to see what had happened to them. Their car tyre tracks had ended where a massive sinkhole had suddenly naturally occurred. Their bodies were swallowed in the muck and were never found despite a search by the police who recorded their deaths as accidental.

It was a bizarre op. Nothing made a lot of sense. And what a strange finale that was – who would have thought that would happen.

I'll end on an apposite remark by a South African security guard from the gold mine, who knew nothing about the dead's backgrounds nor what had transpired leading up to the shocking discovery. He stood at the edge of the bottomless hole in the ground, and almost to himself, muttered, "It looks like it leads to the doors of Hell. What had they done to deserve this fate?"

I could only smile knowingly to myself.

* * * * * * * * *

Chapter Eleven

You can punch them but their dignity will remain,
and their desire to retaliate increases.
You can kill them to eliminate the threat,
but their family and friends will replace them,
and then their neighbours will join the cause.
A fiery moving picture with its celluloid corners curling
…you are only living to exist in the inferno.

The Lebanese capital of Beirut was a viper's nest inside a crate reeking with mongrel cats and a pack of rabid homicidal canines slavering outside it. A scratching, biting, hissing, howling crazy dark hole that the farther down you ventured, it became an endless screeching tunnel of more clawing, eye gouging, spitting nightmares of the worse kind – with pong and psychosis in the mix you can't possibly imagine. Fires burned nonstop every stinking day, the coughing smoke clouding judgement of all those stuck there, me included. At SIS it was called situation ROR (red-on-red). In modern history it was the first example of asymmetrical warfare: More than a dozen heavily armed parties simultaneously fighting each other in an arena where the Cockroach Theory was in full effect, which was, 'Where there's one, there's many.' *Everyone who wasn't on your side was the enemy, and even worse including some fringe elements from your own side. Like scum they'd scurry away when the blue light came on as I shall explain:*

My team was UNIFIL (United Nations Intervention Forces In Lebanon), featured nationalities who mostly were French, Italian and Irish (from whom I was issued bona fide photo ID) and we all wore and were known in the streets as The Blue, also The Blue Helmets. To get the full picture of the farrago it's worth understanding what other parts of the multi-coloured jigsaw comprised of: The Yellow who were the fundamentalist Hizballah (Party of God), the Lebanese Shia militia Muslims of south Beirut suburb of Dahiyeh in their distinctive headbands who saluted like Nazis and were originally founded by the Iranian Revolutionary Guards; The Green, their rivals for the control of the religious Shia population, were Amal (Hope) who were based in southeast Beirut; The Black & White were the PLO (Palestine Liberation Organisation) who had been uprooted from their homeland and had parked themselves in the southern suburb of Fakhani in this city – most people didn't know that it was a multi-party confederation that comprised of 8-12 Palestinian factions of which* Fatah (Victory) was the largest; The Grey who were clearly the largest and most visible sponsor out there was the Syrian Army (Jaysh al-Suri) and its government backers with their official party line of half-truths of 'two countries, one people.' Their special forces made occasional guest appearances at an early stage wore blue shoulder lapels and red berets – who was not yet officially involved but their intelligence officers were obviously operating from the Beau Rivage Hotel downtown; The Pink of Sourriyat – let's just call them the secret female Syrian undercover unit; The Red were the Druze who called themselves the "people of monotheism" were allied to the Syrians; The Black were the Christian Maronites and their Phalange militia who controlled East Beirut; and pockets of others in some ominous shape or form and dye were mid-table further down the league pecking order. All battling for position in the top flight in the urban sprawl of Beirut and the surrounding countryside…and just from the confusion of colour one can already see it got dizzyingly psychedelic out in the actual field of ops, especially with the orange explosions as a backdrop to the music (gunfire) playing and angels (killed in action) flapping their wings in tune to the hymns and arias heavy metal-style.

Then away to the east of the capital was the second division of

---

* Arabic is read from right to left, thus the reverse acronym Fatah comes from *harakat at-tahrir al-watani al-Filastini* which translates to the Palestinian National Liberation Movement. Up to this time they had caused more friction among the PLO then they had to any other group or nation. To address the specifics of each faction within the PLO is impossible. Simplified generalisation is needed so best to describe the union as *asabiyya* (solidarity to keep power) for the Palestinian *shatat* (diaspora).

combatants, which played their games in and around the Biqa (Bekaa) Valley, but were ready to promote themselves if anybody dropped out. Everybody who was a wanna-be had a dingy dressing room in the central town of Ba'Labakk – a wasps nest in the cedar tree that had many branches (Iranian, Japanese, German, Armenian, Peruvian, et al) – where a selection of the big city's back-up reserves lined-up too. Some who played in the same designated colours and indeed some of those considered themselves affiliated in name only who opted for invented ID tints of their own – their respective squads' spawning the British equivalent of dirty bastards, muckers, wide boys, spivs, hard cases and rogues of varying bunker and wolf-pack mentalities. The players (the code name for terrorists) knew the price of everything and the value of nothing…especially someone else's cheap life. If there was one thing that all they all had in common, to be fair-minded, was that *to maintain dignity Arab culture demanded that they self-destruct.*

I missed out the most obvious largest colour combination till last and that was of the Israeli Army – internally called "our pale friends" – who also wore <u>Light Blue + White</u>, and as far as everybody else were concerned that made us at UNIFIL and them both part of the same squad, which we were in a club sense but not in practice. *"Bashert,"* the Israelis would tut-tut in mock Yiddish and shrug apologetically and be occasionally sarcastically about this link of colour coordination, then would follow the word in English with "…it was meant to be."

Then looming large on the fringe was the non-involved South Lebanon Army (SLA) or Jaysh Lubnān al-Janūbi, the remnants of the original Lebanese Army after its break-up soon after the chaos started. To the best of my knowledge they weren't known to be involved in Beirut or Ba'Labakk but may have come up from their southern base in Marjayoun and taken a few look-ins. For the record they wore <u>Red & Black</u>, were allied to the Israeli Defence Force (IDF) and were made up of both Shia Muslims and Orthodox Christians. So they straddled two religions while subservient to a third. Interestingly SLA soldiers wore IDF uniforms with the markings stripped off.

And six months before I left Lebanon both the US Army and the US Army's Special Forces were deployed to Beirut. To really now confuse everybody their berets were respectively <u>Black</u> and <u>Green</u> with the occasionally seen Rangers wearing <u>Tan</u>.

Lastly, almost like a wealthy gambler with an unlimited account at what remained of the casino for anonymous telephone bets, was Iran. Not actively there but involved in financing various long-term productive fundamentalist-disguised programmes to the extent of hundreds of millions of dollars. They kept quiet and never uttered a word, unlike loud bragging western governments who were consumed with self-gratifying public relations campaigns, coupled with short-term thinking and zero sum games, of which I was an unwilling servant. So let's label them as <u>The No Colour</u>...though they had a big say on how The Yellow spent their donated monies.

As for the presence of Russians in any form...I was always puzzled by their physical absence in Leb and wholly expected to run into one eventually. After all everybody bar UNIFIL and the Israelis used Soviet-made equipment. Even Hizballah's anti-angel track (armoured personnel carrier on treads) gunners used the ultra-modern (then) Red-designed SPG-9 recoil-less rifles that fired 73-mm's at an effective range of 1,000 feet. Where were they getting it from? Somebody was selling it to them. *Hizballah had only formed as a resistance group to defend Lebanon after the Israelis had invaded yet had all the needed gear available to them immediately...this possessed tremendous insightful pre-planning.*

It ought to be pointed out also that it constituted to a war crime if soldiers opened fire while dressed as the enemy. International law states that it's okay to pose as the enemy as a tactical deception but to actually fire while so camouflaged is a breach. *So like in a football match the ball has to be over the line 100% to be out or in, so it was all in the eyes of the beholder.* In my field of specialty, being an undercover NOC, it was a problem to consider when one was or was not operational and it was an occupational hazard of existence.

There's a common saying, too, among military personnel who have seen combat that "there's a fog and fiction in war". What's also factual is *when the intensity increases so does information tend to lag,* and it later becomes an acceptable military excuse when things go wrong (whether whatever got screwed up was "accidentally-on-purpose" friendly fire or otherwise).

Then the longer the snafu goes on it evolves from being true into an untruth then becomes a lie, like shifting sands from what was white through grey into black, like a pendulum swinging across in front of your very eyes in slo-mo: From everything being alright to fucked up quite quickly through no fault of your own happens, and you have to accept it and keep moving. A bad production of a pantomime, it seems.

Ordinary peaceful Arabs would naturally have preferred to endure *hudna* – a continued cessation of hostilities, but it wasn't going to be. It was an absolute mishmash of misinformation in a badass lawless land. *Al- haqiqa* (the truth) will never really be known when there's total anarchy.

So with this invisible asterisk disguised in the form of a paragraph I'll let you figure out what's written between the lines hereinafter, bearing in mind that *in war the first death to be recorded is always going to be The Truth* anyway. So it's not good to often find yourself in between a jagged rock and an even harder place with nowhere to go to hide. As for my own problems I was frequently being told to make a dead cat bounce (perform short lived recovery actions), which is well nigh impossible when the shit is rapidly deepening, all the while standing in it.

But to guys like me who had an odd sense of humour a line often came to mind from the spoof movie *Airplane*, which was popular at the time that kept me sane, whereupon the aircraft is finally touching down safely and the landing strip lights are recommended to be switched on and then an air traffic controller says, "No, that's just what they'll be expecting us to do." Yes, the whole Lebanese war was like that, a total farce of a lot of irrational things, with non-existent rules of engagement.

* * * * * * * * *

An adequate pretext for war had been served.
No glory embraces to you in a pressure cooker.
Only a will to force the door open and flee like the wind.
The absence of hope comes when the law is not preserved.
Sectarian violence on steroids is like dancing with a broken doll.
When your soul doesn't want to be inside you anymore, it pirouettes.

Idly observing the show of bravado of what remained of the Lebanese Air Force as its rapidly depleted British-made Hawker Hunters zoomed overhead, here on the floor my eyes fell on the obvious trafficking of something going on down in the little fishing port in the Christian corner of Beirut but it was being ignored by all denominations of Beirutis alike. It had to subsist on some means and illegal was accepted as legal in this part of the world. You quickly learn that in the name of being forced into a continuation of subsistence that people did not necessarily lie but they don't actually tell the truth either.

Defying excessively dangerous moments regularly is not a sign of courage…it is stupidity. If I ever had to get out quickly one day it was an avenue for me to escape via the sea, across to either the UK island fortress of Cyprus probably a full day's chugging in a fisherman's boat or many hours in a semi-circle down to Israel, a recognised US enclave, by the same mode of transport – plus a mound of cash for the brave unmarked boat owner willing to risk drowning in avoiding the hostile underwater mines, navies, fighter planes and not to forget the insane high waves on storm days. Plus, the coxswain had to return, too, if he wanted to. Right, so I had my Plan E for exit sorted out. Now I had to work next on fall-backs D for the desensitised stage, C for the cock-up and B burnout stages. A for adrenaline was in action already.

In my muse mode, and feeling like an invader from outer space, I glanced down at the half empty bottle of local ouzo I had consumed sitting alone on the beach. Shards of memory were zigzagging in the fading sunlight, so sharply that I had my palm over the sunglasses. Earlier in the day I had received a double-whammy of information: Reading the station's telex I learned that a week previously an old school friend who had joined the Royal Navy at almost the same time as me had died half way around the other side of the world in the Falkland Islands when HMS *Sheffield*, a type-42 destroyer was hit by an Exocet missile that didn't detonate but the resulting fire killed 20 British sailors. My mate was one of the unlucky souls who had perished. The ship sunk eventually. This was my toast in silence to the watery grave of the likely lad. He was from near Sunderland, a northeast English town, where we had grown up together. Saturday nights "glassings" there were common with the main reason given to police that the "victim was looking at me"…warranted a vicious smashed bottle full into the face. In that respect there wasn't a lot of difference between there and here, then and now. Only one used another kind of bottle to Britain's in Beirut – bullets and bombs, even bloody Molotov cocktails bursting, which I could occasionally hear in the distance, real or imagined. This mixed with, most strangely, my pal's face miming soundless verse that didn't rhyme with our school's anthem ringing in my head: # *"Non nobis domine, not unto us o lord"* – I hadn't remembered those words for decades…what an idiotic choice of words to reflect on the revisit to the latest Knights Templars' Crusades in real time here. Then I laughed out loud to myself, when I recalled that I had once accused him for being so absolutely fucking normal a person in everything he did!

Our joint paymaster was the UK's Ministry of Defence. In the west when we used the military term "Defence" we actually subtly mean "Attack". It should really then be called the Ministry of Attack! I sardonically smirked to no one.

Listen to your own eyes. Smell with both your ears. Feel with the pit of your stomach the bile that can be tasted in your mouth. My intuition would be based on my dearest chum's demise hereon out. The message was my cavalier attitude could well be my enemy too. Just survive buddy – ignore this breath of doom on the hairs of your neck

With the inner discussion over I finally agreed with myself that it was a discernible enough a feeling in today's Beirut. Everybody carried an air of displacement, a stifling transparency clinging around our minds. Lebanon was a slow motion train wreck waiting to happen. The wobbly locomotive's wheels were slackening off again, the carriage's windows were smashing, its passengers shrieking, the brakes were screeching, the air smoke-filled and the concrete beneath my feet trembling from a temblor that never came. I felt like a man at the destination's platform looking back at the black tunnel with distant headlights inside it, not looming, unmoving. But it was going to be hit again soon, I could sense it in my gut, like everyone else could and that was why I was here in my cover role as an armed international observer for the United Nations' peacekeeping initiative. UNIFIL had arrived on 23 March 1978, over four years ago, and done sweet fuck all in the general scheme of things.

Specifically, I had to determine who was screaming in anger at whom and who was for harmony and who was coolly manufacturing hate, with all things in-between and beyond considered in their various shades. The word 'Observer' – my official title on my ID papers – too, often mentally rhymes with 'object' because you knew that because of your designated capacity you will fill someone's viewfinder from afar at some point, and if he's a sniper and whether he fires or not is another story, reminding myself how precious life is in the balance for us all.

Then I exhaled deeper because I had always thought it ironic that the UN were bloody good at keeping the peace but not so good at stopping a war...while that impasse called "peace talks stalled", continued. *Public policy holds back so much advancement of people*

Arabic speakers called the French, Italians and Irish among us *Nisranis* (Christians – those from Nazareth). Knights faithful to the catholic pope in white with red crosses of our god astride magnificent snorting steeds descending from the hilltops in cavalry formation did not fantasise in me...# *"Onward, Christian soldiers, marching as to war, with the cross of Jesus going on before..."* receded in my head...

I went back to staring glumly at the glare. The other piece of bad news I had received was that my DEROS (date of estimated return from overseas) had been cancelled and the tour of duty extended indefinitely...and I was cursing blue murder at the cloudy skies for some more time. Then I smashed the unfinished bottle on the rocks in frustrated finality and headed back to camp, bongos playing on my skull bones.

* * * * * * * * * *

So I was in Leb longer than I wanted to be. Originally I was sent there to assume the role of IR (information reporting) to officially follow-up on leads and monitor events as they unfolded. I'd send my reports in to the Irish government I represented who then forwarded them onto the British. I was their joint man on the ground. But as time went by I also ran in behind enemy lines depending on what was needed to be done. Everybody that was supposed to know knew what I did. It was a secure secret that became an unsecure secret. I was the conduit between many. And I knew I was a potential valuable hostage to some.

There were infrequent incidents where I would introduce myself upfront as an Irish intelligence officer for UNIFIL, whereupon my intended brazenness surprised the perceived enemy. Often I would say, words to the effect, "Look, my job is not to believe you so try convincing me instead. You have to understand that I'm only the messenger. Together though we have to try and compromise, attempt to solve this issue the best way we can. Everybody must win, advance from where we are now. Best then to work with me, please, and I with you." It wasn't trust but it was the next best thing. And I was straight as a nail with them and they knew so.

Meeting local political movers 'n' shakers from all the sides in their offices had a particularly intense focus. Every syllable and body movement carried meaning. At times I was so wired that I was able to detect lies through human involuntary changes in speech timbre. A cough or clicking of the tongue would also be willingly translated to mean a positive by friends while foes interpreted it negatively and I had to consider both angles as to what was meant just by that sole sound.

Mad as that may be the aura I created often worked well in a kind of built-in bubble of steel protection around myself to prevent been taken as a captive. I also projected a 'don't even think about screwing me' look when I sneered the bullshit back into their faces. What was really effective out in the field was that I made it clear that armed others from my side were in close proximity to come and get me out if I encountered problems with any group colour that wasn't my own Blue…when factually there was nobody behind me most of the time.

But there were only so many bridges you could burn in that modus operandi and I got into credit a few times, which I paid off as quickly as possible by trading exclusive minor information of mine in return for further details on theirs. There was a lot of give and take, tit-for-tat. Regularly and purposefully placing your personal being in the crosshairs of the opposition and then reversing the focus on to them in order to then understand what their primary objectives were and intended methods of achieving it. To later tender the information gathered in a report to others without betraying the source.

Many times I knew disinformation was also being dished out but my mug didn't betray the fact to their faces. Time can freeze everything out there, while you try to remain flexible and slowly gain their confidence. I was productive. I was making inroads. I protected my informants. Sometimes even meeting their family. We didn't have to be thrilled in each other's company, instead we had to have a certain common regard for where the other person was coming from or even going to. I got inside the belly of The Beast (as Beirut was often called). But effecting change takes a tremendous toll on the changers. The burnout was high.

I had arrived there at the end of January 1982. Though I had been in-country many months already the profound reality of crash test dummy living really started this day on 2 June 1982. I remember it was a Wednesday for no particular reason whatsoever, other than it was the dreaded day I was told to stay in-country, that the HMS *Sheffield* sinking was still on my mind, and that the football club from that English city carried that day of the week in its name. It's a strange thing how matters get catalogued in the filing cabinet inside one's head. Six months in the deep end getting shot at on a regular basis isn't a normal way to live one's life and I had trouble explaining the phenomena in my feedbacks. I wasn't the complaining type so I largely dealt with the situation within but I knew deep down they couldn't care less about my predicament anyway. It was par for the course in an alternative war zone that the British public wasn't informed much about via the media.

Something else most Britons inside the governmental machine itself didn't have the foggiest notion about was that the very next day on 3 June 1982 the Israeli ambassador to the UK, Shlomo Argov, was shot in the lobby of the swanky Dorchester Hotel in Park Avenue in Central London. He survived and while no actual evidence of the deed was uncovered by the British authorities Fatah were immediately blamed even though they didn't claim responsibility, which was what they normally did, so that was a bit odd and very coincidental given the day before I was told to hang around longer.

Select seniors in the SIS I have supposed must have had some inkling of some blip of bother appearing on the radar. I had occasional access to several high-ranking members of Fatah in Beirut at the time so I connected the dots that it was *the reason* for my leave being cancelled – they needed the lines of communication kept open. Then when the Israeli Air Force symbolically bombed Lebanon nationwide on 4 June 1982 killing untold numbers of innocents I knew something much bigger was up.

Two days after that along came the answer: On Sunday, 6 June 1982, at 11:00 hours Israel invaded Lebanon's 63-mile border in Operation PEACE FOR GALILEE. Over the next 22 days 22,000 soldiers and 220 newly-made Merkava tanks crossed the border. I always wondered how so many numbers could be activated so quickly because if you have any concept of logistics it takes many weeks to mobilise and launch a large scale assault such as this one.

The stated reason for their invasion was "in retaliation for the attempted assassination of the Israeli ambassador in London". Meanwhile the PLO to whom Fatah belonged had observed a cease fire for almost a year – according to UNIFIL – but the Israelis all of a sudden disputed the claim. *Classic PM functioning or perception management – the creation of the big lie.*

Then on 13 June 1982 Israel's Minister of Defence, Ariel Sharon, publicly stated in a radio news announcement that the Israel Defence Force "would stop at the Awali River, 35 kilometres north of the Leb-Israel border". When I heard that I gazed across at all the Israelis milling around in what was left of a once beautiful Beirut. *It was already under military siege.* Either the man was lying or couldn't count the number of rivers he'd already crossed or he could not read his mileage metre counter well.

The Israelis ended up staying for nearly two decades and later that number of men increased to 38,000 and 800 armoured vehicles encamped in Leb – and not to mention later on when the bulldozers and wagons worked around the clock to truck the finest Bekaa valley soil back to Israel.

None of these facts was given much space by the rest of the world's press as the campaign to regain the Falklands Islands (codenamed Operation CORPORATE) was the international news editors' choice of the moment.

* * * * * * * *

The large signposts in capitals stating "UN ZONE: ARMED

PERSONNEL DO NOT ENTER" were routinely ignored by all, including myself. The reverse side of the sign was completely blank. If challenged, I could always say that I came from the other side and didn't notice the warning.

Granted UNIFIL hid behind the Israeli lines thereon after their arrival but I often had to get over to the other side of the Green Line to see my cascons (casual contacts) and agents so I knew where the safer holes in the walls were. It was the official separation dead centre in the many lines of the kaleidoscope where all the factions' colours collided. But in actuality there was no marked border of paint in the ground in its six miles between West and East Beirut.

The name referred to the excessive foliage there as both sides of the street featured grey ghost-like bombed-out buildings that were long deserted. As there were snipers of all denominations congregated there one thing you didn't do is go through the same place two days in a row, so I had at least a dozen different routes to choose from on a revolving basis. Barricades would change by the hour and who was manning them. Many were left unmanned on purpose and had visible carelessly planted trip wires so you had to not tread like a clod on bouncing betty's (a mine with two charges, one explodes at waist level and the other fires upwards – Hizballah had obtained cheap caches of them from the Vietnamese who sold leftovers of still effective US ordnance – or at least one Islamist-owned garage we had broken its door down had plentiful in stock, much like items for sale on firework days).

Two blocks east of the Green Line the French troops rode around in Leclerc APCs (armoured personnel carriers) and, after the Israelis arrived they tended to stick to the Hamra business district in the city centre while the Italians patrolled the Ayn Muraysah mosque close to the burned out St Georges hotel along the seafront. When the Americans came later they stayed mostly around Beirut airport (BIA) at Khaldeh, eight kilometres south along the coast. The Israeli Defence Force (IDF), meanwhile, had practically parked permanently in their numerous APCs one block away from the Green Line. IDF's mobile tactical headquarters could easily be ID'd by its massive array of antennas, like a sea urchin on wheels. If I could get to talk to whoever was in charge on the day, I'd tell him to log it that it was my intention to cross shortly but they'd always advise not to as they could not guarantee my safety. After a while I didn't bother completing their time-wasting taskers (job request form) and took my life in my own hands. I didn't always put on my bullet- and shrapnel-proof Kevlar vest either as speed of foot was the key.

When approaching the toe-curling line of control (beginning of the demarcation zone) the senses never failed to heighten to extreme alert status. Street warfare doesn't provide handy maps to indicate where tonight's fighting is going to be. No billboards advertise it and there's no television channels to advise you where and when not to go. What's an important part of this entrance-exit strategy is paying attention to the sound of any bullets fired as it contains a peculiar pattern of information like where they were fired from, aimed at and even how many. After a while I became fluent in the language of gunfire and could tell which group was pulling the triggers, friend or foe. There were quite a few times I could have popped somebody myself with my semi-automatic Walther PPK pistol but I didn't as it would attract attention to myself. With all the adversary machine gunners with bandoliers (belts of ammo) walking in small groups *(firquats)* at port arms position (across chest) and ready to retort it would have been an instant suicide wish. I stayed lower than low when such happenstance occurred. A sustained burst from AK-47's can hit its target from 1,500 meters and highly accurate from zero to 750 meters cutting a person in half. But in reality most of these fighters didn't have basic military training. Instead of aiming their guns properly they'd fire on automatic from the hip believing that Allah or God would guide their bullets to the enemy. The *Armée de Terre* (French Land Army) and the IDF could easily have shot me dead, too.

I should add that I could tell, too, who was who from the weaponry they had. Even when the younger PLO factions took off their headgear and pretended to be a Christian or a Jew their old "Tokagypts" brand of choice gave them away. It was a 9-mm recoil operated automatic pistol normally made in Hungary and modified from the Soviet Tokarev TT-33 but a special licence had been granted to Egypt. It was very noticeable because it had a finger-support on the magazine hanging down. In the west it was called a Firebird. The silly thing about the *fedayeen* (men of sacrifice) – fights at the front were by the chosen disposables – was most experienced operators like myself knew that they could be found hiding on floor *chamza* (the fifth) as it was their lucky number. Their tracers were indeed green, the colour of Islam.

By the time I'd done it the tenth time I was already thinking it should have been called the Red Line because the UN/US tracers always glowed red. And that a red line has always to be crossed to proceed in life. Occasional red spatters of fresh blood were observed on certain active days.

Understand, too, that some groups used rapid succession of shots at nothing in particular to send messages like the Red Indians did with smoke signals into the sky.

Night or day the smouldering etched its sombre designs on the canvas above. I'd read my own missives into them while passing time for the right moment to get from one spot to another. Once I was fatigued mentally and in the gloom a black presentation from a burning tyre resembled a question mark, which naturally made me stare and think why. I came to realise that my own steps in the dust on the ground represented the footprints of imperialism and I felt marooned out here in the rubble of the ruins of Beirut.

Star shells tore holes in the night sky but helped illuminate the streets so I could see where I was going. I knew from being a former heli pilot that those few in low-flying choppers hated the free light bulb as it always invited a burst of tracers at them. The French flyers tongue-in-cheek coined it *sous la lune de Renoir* (under the moon of Renoir, which meant there was a spotlight on those watching the painting). When finally deciding to kick-start the heels with adrenaline in the tank full to the rim and on the breakneck blurred hurtle between ruins and into open spaces, every sound, object and colour would be spinning wildly. Paradoxically, it made me deeply present, appreciating the moment to the fullest, making every single second of my existence count. Totally karmic.

In spite of that many others found it was where they finally rested in peace. Carcasses rotting there were a regular occurrence and the ravenous mutts would feast on them ferociously. This kind of fairground arcade game wasn't the way I wanted to go so I triple checked everything I did before doing it.

It is frequently said that when in solitude one finds himself. It may be true but I developed an excellent understanding of myself in high-risk and stressful situations. I discovered that the faster the world moved the slower my eyes saw it, almost frame-like. I was Panglossian with a hint of a Savonarola in me – optimistic in the face of adversity yet mercilessly unforgiving – upbeat to creating possibilities but to those who were blind and ignorant of the obvious I didn't suffer fools gladly.

Eating a date one day in the countryside that I'd picked off fresh, standing there chewing it, I heard the whine of a mortar and actually saw it whizz over my head, a wee black blur between the tree tops. There was no time to react. It's a lottery of life even in quiet places.

I vividly also remember sitting as a passenger in the front of a car just before the Israelis invaded, driving about a mile behind another vehicle on the outskirts of the capital on a mostly deserted stretch that hadn't seen any fighting yet, when we heard a piercing heavy drum thumping sound coming louder our way. My Lebanese Christian driver, Joseph, yelled "STALIN'S ORGAN!", ducked and veered madly into a ditch. From over on our left we got a glimpse for a few seconds of a SAM (surface to air missile) as it screamed in our direction insanely trailing sparks looming large then saw it smash into its target ahead of us. What a helluva bang! By the time we'd reversed and approached the severely burning wreckage there wasn't anything but the wheel, a metal frame in bits with four bodies in pieces – and the 100 yards radius around it completely impacted with fuel-smelling smoke and small fires.

After we'd slowly circumvented it some 20 minutes later – an ambulance or a police car siren could be heard approaching – my "chauffeur" said, "If you hear a shell whistling like that it's the sound of it going by you on the way to *not* where you are. But you should duck anyway because the shock waves will knock you over if the shrapnel hasn't already passed through you." I stared at him as he continued, "The sound, *habibi* (my friend), is the difference between living and dying or surviving with serious injuries from the blast that sweeps over you. That's why I drove into a hole back there. When we temporarily lost our hearing that was the sound surge zipping over our heads. Any vehicle our size is an automatic homing device for a ground-fired heat-seeking missile. It's a tinderbox ready to flare at a flick of a switch. I should know since I was in the Lebanese Army's counter-intel *Deuxième Bureau* (Second Office) before the war started. I regard myself nowadays as an expert on all things to do with Islamist sympathisers."

I was to learn from him that a large 122-mm Katyuska (an endearing Russian form for the girl's name Katie) SAM has an inaccurate range of 12 miles. The smaller version warhead was 82-mm. But you stand no chance when it's fired from less than a mile away. Psychologically traumatic the pulsation of the blast reverberated for a month in my head and it would wake me from slumber in the morning. And the reason for the bad dreams was because I knew the IRA had personally taught these bastards how to improvise the Russian-made multi-rocket launch platform into a home-made version to reduce the range and as a result be more accurate. Yet we short-sighted British didn't do anything to stop the export of knowledge at the time, thinking it was somebody else's problem to deal with. It was also the first time I'd heard that shouted expression "Stalin's Organ!" – I still don't know if it refers to the Russian despot's body part or a musical instrument – but I got to hear it a few more times afterwards, never failing to be panicked by it all.

What sticks in the memory isn't the whooshing or the noise but the silence that follows, then the screaming.

To really compound the guilt at around that same time a half-burnt British driver's licence still with its plastic case melted on it had found its way to my attention for dissemination to my superiors in Dublin (and on to London). It was discovered by one of our allies in a hastily abandoned campfire. In those days they didn't carry a photo and it had the name missing but clearly through the browned-out green paper I could read the full address in Glassdummond Road, Crossmaglen, Newry, County Down. That town was the centre of the IRA activities in the heart of the Northern Ireland province of South Armagh. I duly forwarded the information but retained my opinion on national culpability*.

Inside a warehouse in the Beirut suburb of Ghobeiri, my French UNIFIL colleague called me to say that his troops were following up on a lead. In doing so they had surrounded a location and inside found a Mercedes lorry's cab booby trapped with its wheel base rigged to the trailer behind it. The vehicle appeared ready to transport a system full of explosives to an unknown destination. The three launchers packed inside its hold each held 40 missile pods, half with 68-mm rockets having a range of up to three miles and the other half with 85-mm with a range up to four miles. One of the smaller shells could punch a fist-size hole in a thick concrete wall so it was mind-boggling what 40 multiplied by three strapped together in one truck could do, if utilised. It opened our minds to future possibilities to counter, especially when learning that the numerous smaller crates lining the walls inside the HGV (heavy goods vehicle) contained thousands of nails – but the notion was absurd. It seemed then that the arsenal wasn't being shipped elsewhere for storage purposes. My co-worker had a crazy thought. He was thinking that a kamikaze driver could ram its target loaded to the hilt with this booty to become a human bomber and would become a martyr in the process. I dismissed the Frenchman's verbalised wild imagination point blank. But when I went there to look for

---

* In 1981 an Irishman named Denis Donaldson was arrested by French police returning from Beirut. He had already served time in 1972 and became an IRA turncoat providing the SIS and its French counterpart DGSE with plentiful inside information. A French intelligence officer and I were tasked to check it out on-site.

myself I observed that the external giveaway to the weight of the load was that the tyres showed considerable strain on the hydraulic pressure. Once moving slowly it groaned noticeably. But, no, nobody in their rights minds would do what he was thinking but he won me over with his argument. Up to that time no such incident had occurred in Lebanon but from our findings it was logical that it was possible. My French colleague and I reported our findings in writing forthwith.

It was from my forthright team mate I learnt the word *racaille* (scumbags), which I've now incorporated into my own vocabulary, including *baisie vous* (fuck you) and *pauvre con* (prick). When you live this kind of life on the edge it helps to let off steam in any language!

Especially so when we later learned that the property the loaded lorry was found on belonged to the mosque where Sheik Mohammed Hussein Fadlallah preached, the Shi'ite spiritual guide of Hizballah. Not good. He had a bit of a reputation as a rabble-rouser but of the intelligent variety, which made him dangerous. I saw him in the flesh once surrounded by his plentiful push 'n' shove armed goons. Stocky man, medium-height, dressed in black with a matching turban, dark sunglasses with a straggly salt 'n' pepper beard. He threw off a demeanour then that he despised anybody that wasn't from where he was, and this discovery kind of confirmed it. Sprinkle stardust on his followers he did not do; it was soot. You'd think men in his esteemed position would take the flock forwards but he went backwards. Hypocritically he'd say one thing publicly and do the exact opposite behind closed doors. Fadlallah wasn't the only one that took the worse negative line leading their children to drown.

Then you had his alter-ego on the other side of the crowded boxing ring: Ariel "Arik" Sharon, the IDF Rottweiler of the Israeli Prime Minister Begin, the Zionist hardliner that hated Palestinians in any form and who was deeply committed to a militaristic agenda. Not good. Fadlallah and Sharon, the terrible twins, each as bad as the other, and running amok in Lebanon. What was scary was that both had that inalienable right about themselves that they could do no wrong. Yet that's exactly what they were doing. Sharon already had the dubious reputation as the father of Israeli illegal settlements on Palestinian lands, erecting 64 in four years during his tenure of Minister of Agriculture starting in 1977. I think Ben-Gurion said it perfectly of him in his diary: "If only he would be cured of his weakness of not speaking the truth."

Around that same time in Leb the village of Ein Arab at the bottom of Mount Hermon was abandoned. Joseph said he was present when the IDF flattened it just for the symbolism of it being already empty. *It sent a message of 'if you weren't already dead you weren't safe'.* Not good. As for me I'd seen the Israeli Air Force's silver Kfirs (that closely resembled French Mirage jets) and the F-16s they'd got from the US dropping cluster bombs on innocent people. It is to me the biggest of all the crimes. From afar they make a distinctive repetitive sound of popcorn. Their 155-mm shell's warhead opens with a single plop 50 meters above the ground and sprays hundreds of small darts. Earlier versions contained nails. Always resulted in maximum damage. I don't care what one's religion is or nationality, to once like I did, inspect its gruesome impact afterwards…it's beneath shameful. Little children don't deserve to be butchered into bits of meat.

The Pallies weren't angels either but in my capacity I dealt with them since my arrival. Often with Fatah themselves. I'd always smile knowing that Yasser Arafat's special protection unit Force 17 got its name from their extension number at the PLO headquarters in West Beirut. The women in the camps would serve up home-made bread dipped in *zaatar*, a powder made of oregano, thyme, marjoram and sesame seeds grown from the land, after dipping it in olive oil. Very tasty. As if the damsels knew a better way to your heart was through hospitality, not via all this horrible thuggery.

There's too many acts of revulsion that took place in my last six months in Leb: car bombs, massacres, a quartering by four cars witnessed through binoculars of a Lebanese villager by the *takfiris* (fundamentalist Sunni Islamists) just for having an Israeli shekel in his pocket as it turned out. Madness on the rampage everywhere you looked.

You'd think a sense of balanced view would come into the humanity of it all but it was always hatred being spewed: *You hate me, I hate you, we hate everybody…results in making a huge hole bigger and everybody loses. Retaliation, reprisal, revenge, retribution and chain reactions aplenty. In retrospect Mahatma Gandhi got it right with his policy of restraint when he said, "First they ignore you, then they laugh at you, then they fight you, then you win." Many times I cried on the inside in despair. But war never kills hatred.*

* * * * * * * * *

In my downtime I was privileged to receive week-old newspapers from around the globe. When you're in the referenced shithole itself what governments' wants their public to think and perhaps grasp is what most *sahafis* (journalists) are not permitted to tell them. The maddening irony about ever changing words in print is while fighting on paper for one clause (read also as cause), another prevails, only for the original to be installed again…and none of it has anything to do with what's actually happening by the time you read it. It was a like a surreal mirage, you'd read the article then look away at the skyline that tells a different story.

And there were some truly head-shaking humongous spin! The number of times I talked to correspondents who quoted "news" to me that was written before the "event" happened and apparently pre-dated Greenwich Mean Time and US Eastern Time told the real agenda in itself.

In Leb there were many injustices changing by the hour. The reporters that bothered to get themselves off the barstools at the Beirut Golf & Country Club and deep into the real bunkers out there managed to relate reasonable legitimacy between the lines, the rest just got drunk on deceits. They'd come in-country, collect their Lebanese government-issued press cards at the Hotel Commodore and in five minutes you knew who cared to tell a fact as it was and who did the opposite. Among the latter it was a routine "we're the good guy; our enemies are evil" regardless of what went down at the time. They were knowingly the tools of propaganda with a pathological ability to fabricate.

How many of them were black PR (paid media) I'll never know. My eyes smarted on sight at some of them because it was bullshit and they knew it but what was worse than that for me is believing in your own bullshit.

If only some photojournalists had recorded the mass exodus of the population from the devastated ruins of Beirut, then more would have known of the pain of its people. If only one shot of one car with one family evacuating with everything they owned piled up on top of it…it would have told a powerful story. I fight tears when I write those words. I'm ashamed we at UNIFIL and the world let them down.

Then the arithmetic was chronically wrong. If you added up our side's count of "enemy killed" they'd be no more people left and we'd be fighting nobody. That means everybody that wasn't Blue. Meanwhile UNIFIL's losses were described as "light". Seeing the Red Cross and air force transport planes departing at all hours to destinations in Western Europe, knowing that they took the body bags home or the seriously injured – military or civilian – in need of immediate surgery, told another falsehood.

I felt that I never stopped caring. I knew full well my own intel reports were ignored in the name of a bigger picture being achieved, whatever it was I would never know. Actually I did suspect what it was then but I couldn't tell anybody as I'd be in trouble if I disclosed it. I do confess that since that time I have willingly looked away from the past – I beg a temporary meltdown – but it was decades before I returned my gaze, only to then realise that I must not lose against myself again and that I must tell the story as I know it. I have long realised that truth is regarded by many only as a commodity side-lined in today's rolling news. But it's flat wrong. The difference between writing about it then in cables versus now in a book is that back then there would have been no spaces in-between my words – they'd be all joined together – …and even now while they still trip over each other I am somehow able to breath pauses.

* * * * * * * *

Being a macro thinker I often wondered what was at the bottom of all this religion-induced craziness. Could people really be so blind as to endlessly knock each other out senseless? Inside UNIFIL there was an underlying strategy at play that *winning the war was straightforward but to not to ever lose the peace.* One day I mentioned that to Joseph, my regular driver. He was quite forthright a person, and he responded in anger, "When the ones who own aircraft that shape killing patterns in the sky say they were not prepared for the refugees yet their warplanes bomb the towns to accentuate the flow, what can one say to that? It's says we can afford the war but we can't afford the peace?"

Joseph knew I was an atheist so I pacified him by saying, "Faith is knowing without proof. Belief is knowing with proof." He looked at me aghast then broke out into a grin and back-slapped me. "You are *jahili* in Ireland, spiritually ignorant."

So where did it end, what was the reason, why did a lot of things happen? He and I were on the streets a lot seeing situations unfold with our own eyes. It was billed overtly as Democratic Equality versus Islamic Dictatorship but Joseph and I surmised that even the liberated and the theocracy must be smarter than this shambles. We agreed that *military occupation by force is completely incompatible with freedom.*

I began to ponder where the money was coming from to sustain all these factions? Who paid the gunmen's salaries? It couldn't all be from all the crimes committed. My job permitted me to get around the country and I did. Almost all my focus was in Beirut and on a secondary level to the east and south. To the city's west was only the Mediterranean Sea.

One summer day during the latter stage of the Siege of Beirut we headed north to investigate the rumour that Hizballah had a training camp for underwater demolition on the border with Syria. Looking at the vastness of endless water tells you exactly that and as no thermal imaging instruments had yet been invented to search the sea bottom from land-based points. Despite following a couple of leads, it came to nothing.

But I could see some rundown rust-bucketed vessels anchored within sight of land. Through my binoculars I spotted three cargo ships idling high in the water (no load evident), none flying their flag. One I could make out from the stern hailed from Dortyol, a port in Turkey, with no crew activity aloft discernible. I asked the ever present Joseph what those were doing there and he made some enquiries of the locals. We were directed to a ramshackle oil refinery on a peninsula with a long quayside snaking out to the water. There two old but shipshape small tankers were docked, all hatch covers battened, yet were low in the water (laden). Both these vessels had the Lebanese flag fluttering, Sidon being their registered port. No human life present at all, no gangplanks even. The sign at the locked gate in Arabic stated that the secure plant was called the Tripoli Oil Installation but our queries revealed that trade was sporadic but still active. But if the natives don't want to talk about it then there's not much else to gather. Nevertheless, as we sat in the car looking at the TOI oil refinery we had stumbled across, Joseph grinned over at me and said, "It is for me these moments we live for, huh." It wasn't the crude oil we were marvelling at. It was *the new drilling equipment* on the decks with still some by the cranes dockside that prompted his conclusion. I took photographs of it all.

In *my head I heard the SIS country officer for Lebanon say, "If you don't read up the files we give you, you'll be more afraid of what you don't know." Liar.* I didn't know whether to log my findings because in my pre-brief before being deployed to Leb there was no mention of the Karkūk-Bāniyās-Tarābulus (Kirkuk-Banias-Tripoli) 30-inch wide oil pipeline that snaked 546 miles (880 kilometres) from the oilfields of northern Iraq to the deep water port in Syria with an added spur to Lebanon. It was what the old man in the nearby restaurant had told us – you did not see roasted songbirds in pomegranate on any menu in Beirut – where we sat for lunch. His son worked in the refinery so he was well informed. But I was intrigued! These vessels were shipping the crude black stuff in barrels the extra 50 miles as the crow flies into a war zone as needed because the pipeline had been shuttered recently. Who was behind these petrodollars? As a teenager I had once worked on oil and gas rigs for my summer holiday in the North Sea off Aberdeen in Scotland. I knew what all that drilling apparatus was used for. My curiosity was further piqued.

But we had found the cash injection into the vein to Lebanon's hidden economy and likely it financed certain warlords' operations. More so because it was an island of tranquillity here, *far away* from the depths of misery that was in full flow south of there – that being only one and a half hour's driving (52 miles/84 km) away. This scenario was likely purposefully controlled, without a doubt.

I think Joseph got it right eventually by quoting his favourite Arabic proverb in scorn, "You know that when a cow dies, the number of butchers always increases. Well this is the opposite of that."

* * * * * * * *

I learned a lot from Joseph who was 10 years my elder. He didn't talk much about what he'd done in the past but he knew a lot about the future, where this was all going. In that respect he and I were likeminded. I don't know what I would have done without him. He never called me by my Irish name, as if he knew. Instead every sentence ended with *habibi* (buddy). I still occasionally use that word and when I do I think of him.

One day we drove all the way from Beirut south to Tyre (Sūr). From time-to-time unexploded rockets stuck out of the ground pointedly. *They looked like signposts to anarchy to me.* On the way down there he told me more than UNIFIL collectively knew. As we went along he'd say, "We have just left Maronite Christian-control into Druze", like it was another country and he'd entered it illegally. And then later, "This now is mixed denomination here but soon we will be among the Shi'ites where I am not safe. It is where Hizballah also calls home. Not just in Beirut."

He was a bible about the Litani River area just before reaching Tyre where we spotted an armed UNIFIL contingent of Nepalese Gurkhas neatly turned out. We waved at them but their discipline didn't allow them to return the compliment. Then we saw what looked like a whole Irish battalion. They, too, didn't appear thrilled to be where they were, and I knew if I had spoken to any lad from there he'd know instinctively I wasn't from his island but from another one next door, thus blowing my cover. A quick scan through my binocs and I could see that both the Gurkhas and the Irish had their fire power locked and loaded on full auto, ready to go, the selector never on semi. *No battle plan survives the first shot regardless.*

Joseph told me that facing them in the AO (area of operations) was Hizballah who had 1,000 full-time fighters in the region. The Israeli Army had 1,500 troops and the South Lebanon Army more at 2,000. By now he also really had it in for Hizballah, telling me their tactics variously included concealed small roadside bombs inside cheap plastic rocks bought from garden centres and nurseries in the west; the construction crews were

Shi'ites and that they buried heavier bombs under recently laid asphalt that would detonate when newly arrived Israeli tanks rolled over them; and that kids were practiced in the art of putting small explosives under fresh roadkill for the same purpose. "Hizballah will run farm animals across fields to confuse motion sensors while its fighters were among the goats." Whenever we heard about some atrocity he'd say, "Hizballah like to film all its attacks for distribution to news stations. We'll see it tomorrow on the BBC or TF-1 how they did it."

My favourite answer of all I got from Joseph when I was asking about who exactly he was talking about among the newsmen was, "You know, the one who has the perfect teeth that was born in Britain." Anybody who has spent time among foreign natives who speak good English will testify to this kind of speech, it's very charming. We once had a heated discussion about a transliteral interpretation between Arabic words to the English when he concluded with, "Is it now okay to do a little *Sesame Street* pronunciation segment like Hermit the Frog does?" Very funny! I saw him take a dip in the ocean once, even naked in his swimming pants he exuded security. I was happy to have him next to me. A pillar of support.

It was him that also told me that the reverse acronym Fatah spelled forward to *Hataf* means death in Arabic.

* * * * * * * * *

It's only when you've been away from her for a few days and upon returning to Beirut and the once lovely Martyr Square that you notice how badly pockmarked her face had become. Her once beautiful naked body bore the dark starbursts as if she was in the late stages of a terminal cancer. She was still breathing but was in danger of becoming a corpse from an over-abundance of shellfire into her fragile skin. All the men that claimed they loved her bore responsibility for her dismal state.

It had become a surreal human swamp before our eyes. Craters were everywhere on the streets. She obeyed its own carnal law whatever it was. The kind likely operational inside a prison yard of sorts. Certainly a boxed-in mentality. A capital city without normal recognised regulations like traffic lights functioning, parking restrictions, speed limits and road signs. Every other person had a gun at the ready. Fender benders could result in somebody getting shot. Right of way at a junction went to the driver who fired a warning bullet first.

Worse of all were *hajiz tayyat* (spontaneous checkpoints on the move) by groups of thugs who carried the most firearms at any given moment. If you were perceived as foe you died there. Likewise, *al-qans mashi* (sniping in progress). Knowing where *khat altamass* (the line of contact) was at any given day was important. Joseph and I knew the backstreets of the city centre well. *Had to.* It was important to pay attention to these vernaculars when they came your way because if you didn't you could pay the price for it with your life.

Government services had spluttered to a halt in Beirut by now. An estimated 17,000 Beiruti civilians killed in the fighting just in the time I'd been in-country. If a baby was born, a couple married or an elderly person died naturally, nobody except the immediate family would know. Such breakdown signals the start of the end of civilisation.

Yet some political bodies based in lands afar were afraid to describe it as a "civil war". So other parts of the world made do with describing it as "non-international armed conflict". Apparently a bureaucratic difference when, in reality, it's the same thing. And while the words are fluffed and warbled more innocents died. That number was more than 100,000 since this whole mess started in 1975, seven years previously.

* * * * * * * *

Chapter Twelve

Death was in charge in Beirut.
We the living, were the servants.
The stench of it permeated everything.
But it was the stillness that I remember the most.

Shameful interventions, pure fabrications by world powers, rabble-rousing and brainwashing were daily occurrences and they had become the norm. Reverse eugenics continued to hide behind partisan one-upmanship coupled with blind religious hatred. Albert Einstein's famous definition of insanity was *doing the same thing over and over again and expecting different results* was spot-on. It definitely applied to the "euthanasia programmes" – there is no other descriptive to use – *en force* in Beirut as the bodies piled up higher. The ideology imbrued isolation from reality. The black humour on the street was 'when it starts to eat itself you knew then that would be the finish line at the end of Lebanon'. Something had to change and it did for both the better and worse.

* * * * * * * * *

One evening I was invited to Joseph's flat to meet his pretty wife and two young children. We had dinner – I was going to kip on their settee for the night – and after the kids were put to bed, his lady left us to talk. He got out a bottle of *arak* (anise liqueur).

It was my opportunity to ask a question that was long at the back of my mind as I was always distracted in the field to pop it to him: It was the fact that Saddam Hussein's Sunni-led Iraq had agreed to supply crude oil to Syria and Lebanon where the Shi'ites were the majority. The dictator had stepped outside the norm in doing so, so what were his thoughts on that?

His response to me was in actuality the Arab version of perception management (PM): "I can't really speak for the Syrians," he said, "but we Lebanese usually manage to screw things up. Instead of focusing on what's ahead we're always thinking on how to stab each other in the back. So the world's largest suppliers of natural energy like the Soviet Union, Iran and the local big boy Iraq know how to twist our heads around to look in the wrong place. It's a cultural deficiency that they exploit time and time again. And we blind, deaf and dumb Lebanese fall for it every time. We don't learn. It's not about our religion; it's about profit for them at our loss.

"After a while, I can see why the rest of the world thinks, 'What a bunch of social inadequates these fellows from Lebanon are'. I mean when you compare us to others' mentalities.

"What really gets me deep down is that it's clear what the political objectives are from the onset. When you deal with liars you don't deal in honesty with them. But, no, we Lebanese will swallow their hook, line and sinker, no problem.

"To address what you asked specifically: Since our discovery in Tripoli I have chatted to some of my Lebanese Muslims friends. Sadly, the general consensus is we have people in this country who can only see as far as the fact that the oil came from Syria, their religious brothers. But the other fact that it originated from Sunni Iraq is not part of the equation. Amazing isn't it? This select short-sightedness…"

Joseph was a committed Christian but I could feel he was walking a tightrope between duty to his country and his conscience. I didn't interrupt his thought patterns and waited for more that he clearly wanted to express:

"Here's the strangest thing. *Sunni* in Arabic means 'one who follows the traditions of the Prophet Mohammed'. While *Shia* is 'a supportive party of the people' though its correct name is *Shia-t-Ali* for 'Party of Ali'. What's the difference? When the Prophet Mohammed died in 632 AD in what is now known as Saudi Arabia, power was passed to someone capable of continuing the job, so Abu Bakr was made the Head Caliph. But the Shia believed leadership should have stayed within the family and handed over to his cousin/son-in-law Ali bin Abu Talib and not to any imam. *That is each other's bottom-line argument and willingness to kill over centuries later.* For both these sects their religion is Islam and Allah is their god, and they each observe the five daily duties as good Muslims. But they'll fight each other tooth and nail over a *promotion* that went to someone else that happened before their great-great-great-great grandfathers were born. When you know that it doesn't make any sense, habibi."

"Well before you get into how goody-two shoes the Christians are," I injected, "I cut my teeth in the Troubles in Belfast, Northern Ireland. The Roman Catholics and the Protestants believe in the same concept of deity, scriptures, Jesus being the son of god, how he died and where, et al. Oh, and they both agree that the Prophet Mohammed was false. So what's their argument?: *They see sin differently*, plus some other minor minor minor minor points that they are at odds over. Even though Martin Luther created Protestantism in Germany in the 1500's, King Henry VIII's created the Church of England, allying it with Protestantism. He separated from Rome because the Pope wouldn't agree to him getting divorced and he wanted to have sex with lots of different women."

Because I'd delivered the line with a straight face Joseph laughed so hard at that, almost going blue in the face, that his wife came out to see if he was alright. And her concerned expression made us guffaw again.

I continued. "When I was there in the Falls Road, the dividing line in Belfast between the Catholics and the Protestants, a hard boy teen once asked me what my religion was. So I told him I was atheist. Can you believe the little bugger then proceeded to ask me if I was a Catholic atheist or a Protestant atheist? I stared at him for a second then told him to fuck off."

That made Joseph titter again. "Well here in Beirut, there are people who can't bring themselves to say the words Jews or Israelis in their vocabulary so instead they refer to them as *abna al-mawta*, which means children of the dead. Israel is a monotheistic state, *tawhid* we call it. They believe in only one god, and for them there is no human messenger in the middle like Jesus or Mohammed. Some people get their knickers in a twist over the pedantic."

I added, "In my Oprep, just before coming here, it was stated that a Jordanian delegation in 1980 had told the UN Special Political Committee that, in their view, there was 'no distinction between Palestinians and themselves since they had all originally had been natives of one country – natural Syria.'"

"Yes," nodded Joseph, "that's true, the Syrians, Lebanese, Palestinians and Jordanians all speak with the same dialect. Blood brothers in a sense."

"Well you heard it here first," I muttered. "I'm *al-kufr*. I have unbelief, as you know. But it was factually translated from the Ten Commandments that 'Intelligence is a dirty affair, done by gentlemen.'"

We toasted to that. "But, habibi, why are you?" asked a quizzical-faced Joseph.

"If you have undertaken readings of the major religions – I have read the Bible and the Koran – they are littered with intolerance, racism, discrimination, violence, hatred and human values. So when a person says 'they believe', they are indirectly saying to me they are in support of all these medieval wrongdoings continuing in a modern world. I am proud to be an unbeliever, to be actively against this fundamentalism of the ancients. I have long moved ahead and left it behind. I decided that at the age of seven. What I am saying is that I am neutral. You can't do this job being biased. If you want to believe in a faith, it's fine with me but don't hate or kill someone else just for that sole reason. It's dumb."

"Well, habibi, Saddam must know something we don't," concluded Joseph.

* * * * * * * * *

I received a long awaited package from the UNIFIL courier office via an SIS front address. I immediately took it to my quarters to peruse the contents. It had been sent to me by a close friend that worked in the international oil and gas exploration industry. Actually he was my London apartment's long-term next door neighbour and I'd requested this from him in a phone call. He had no idea what I really did for a living only that I was absent for long periods. Still I liked him and he liked me, so he kindly obliged.

According to publicly published figures Lebanon in the early-80s had a Gross Domestic Product of around US$56 billion. Same as everything else, you read that and look out the window and see nothing but an eyesore getting worse.

The short timeline was in the late-60s the first Lebanese oil and gas exploration was onshore. By the early-70s several wells had been drilled across the country. Nothing substantial was discovered. In 1975 war breaks out and all developments ends. That was the officially recorded version.

Elsewhere though, while they were knocking each other out on land, it appears that the Russians had found offshore deep reservoirs in the Levant Basin of oil and gas buried beneath the Eastern Mediterranean. But no drilling had commenced as yet. Colour photocopies of maps and depths were included for my viewing. The field's north boundary started just north off the coast of Lebanon giving Syria minute access by chance via a freak of a geological funnel; its west boundary was some distance from Cyprus; and its eastern and southern boundaries above Israel's Sinai desert. The port both central and nearest to the illustrated area of 108.11 square miles (280 square kilometres) in size with untold riches below it was Sidon in Lebanon. Altogether it was estimated to hold 1.689 million barrels of oil and 122.378 billion cubic feet of natural gas. Based on 1982 current prices, those reserves were worth trillions of US dollars.

My British buddy had gone through a lot of trouble to explain next about the United Nations Convention on the Law of the Sea (UNCLOS), which governed the use of maritime resource. To compete in offshore drilling a country must first pass an exclusive economic zone (EEZ) law, submit it to the UN, and then work out treaties with any neighbours that might have competing claims. A state can claim an EEZ up to 200 nautical miles (370 km) off its coast and would have to negotiate with any countries that have overlapping EEZs. This meant that Lebanon would have to have treaties with both Syria and Israel. *But the kicker was both Lebanon and Israel were not signatories to UNCLOS but Syria was.* And so was Iraq.

It was highlighted by my colleague that the United Nations does not act as a mediator in disputes and that the involved parties have to work out a deal between themselves. *Also adding that the find was almost exclusively in undisputed Lebanese waters.*

I sat back and let out a deep breath. It was politically then perfect for Syria to allow Lebanon and Israel to knock each other out senseless while it secretly dealt with its long-time ally the Russians, the technical drilling experts, who would need access to their deep water port of Banias that had refineries at the ready. So my eyes did not betray me at Tripoli where all the offshore drilling equipment could be observed! They were already moving ahead quietly at sea while the huge perception management big lie took place on land.

The Soviet Union's other commercial partner in the Middle East was Iraq. So it was a case of you scratch my back now and I'll scratch yours later. We'll give you the oil and gas from our field that you need now and we'll share in the spoils from your field later. But let's keep pouring fuel on the fire for the religious warmongers to distract them from what we will mutually benefit financially.

I always knew something was underfoot and here was my proof. Well it was undersea actually. I decided not to tell Joseph about this because it would only make him even madder.

* * * * * * * * * *

There were a lot of incidents that one like me who was there could address at length. The main event, in my opinion, that changed everything discernibly for everybody was the horrific massacre in Sabra & Shatila on 16-18 September 1982. A clear line marked in the ground of memory. The 4Ws are well covered in the history books. Regardless of anyone's zeal this kind of craziness is unjustified even in war. There are those few brave warriors that have faced unimagined terror and have witnessed the most appalling scenes created by man on another man who regard this act as beyond justification. My direct experience was only on the morning of the 19th, to go there and end up in total shock thinking, 'If they hadn't been shot then they would have drowned in all the blood'.

What's never been addressed is the fact that the very people that may have defended these innocent victims – some 1,500 PLO fighters – had been evacuated only a week earlier to Tunis by the US 32nd Marine Amphibious Unit and the French 2nd Foreign Legion Airborne Battalion on chartered Greek ships, taking Yasser Arafat with them. Altogether 6,436 Pallies of all ages passed through the checkpoint out of Beirut port. I know so because I was among the multinational personnel assisting in the task from 25 August to 10 September 1982 and that was the official departing figure by the Italian military responsible for the harbour administration.

What I personally don't like is the fudging of these numbers: I have seen data that 15,000 PLO left Lebanon at that time – a zero was added. No it was under half of that figure. The apologists for the Sabra & Shatila crime will say it was 762 Palestinian dead – that's a corruption of statistical plagiarism in itself. When all the bodies were lined up in clear plastic bags I personally stopped counting at 3,000…and I wasn't at the end but the longer it went adding up I couldn't go on convincing myself that any final tally made any sense whatsoever. So my report stated: 3,000-*plus*. It had taken 38 hours of nonstop executions committed by 300 to 500 Christian criminals to slay all these defenceless children, rape and kill the women, and castrate the men leaving them to bleed to death. The pendulum of madness had gone into the point of no return and the needle of remembrance got jammed there. The overpowering smell, the nonstop sobbing, the pain felt and the guilt of non-action by those that could have done something left its mark on me and others for a lifetime.

It was during this freeze frame moment when I stopped counting and reminded myself of the promise to get out this game in about four months' time.

More and more violence rained down from the heavens, tumbling into chaos, a lot of people were walking around on the ground in that deadened state, like zombies. I wasn't at that stage yet but I could see that it was possible to be desensitised. There's only so much shit one can take before starting to ignore it.

The Lebanese government was in shambles as nobody was running the show. Meanwhile like flies drawn to a light Beirut kept attracting ever larger numbers of internally displaced persons (IDPs). They came in all religious denominations and, in a sense, became future cannon fodder. Victims of crime are predominantly the poor and the marginalised who are often also forced to participate in it.

Then with 90 days left to my self-imposed deadline, in October 1982, Joseph, my French investigative partner and I met Elias Nimir.

* * * * * * * * * *

Elias Nimir was 27 and hailed from a large Shia family near Tyre in the south. He was a sleazy wise guy with a weird sense of humour who wanted to be a hero. He had nothing and had no prospects, so anything gained was a plus for him and that included all the free beer we gave him that he sucked down like a fish. The fellow wasn't the sharpest knife in the drawer but his immediate boss was, who was using him for his own ends, which was apparent from the first time I met him. Nimir was a used tool.

Namir had got my name from doing some low-paid errands at Force 17, which was within Fatah's office where the PLO was based in Fakhani, his neighbourhood. He thought I was brazen to go in back then and disclose that I was an UNIFIL intel officer. Rather liking my candour he divulged to me that some of the Pallies higher-up hadn't had anything bad to say about me behind my back, and that had drawn him to me in the first place. But now that they had all left for Tunis he had joined the newly formed Hizballah, like a large number of the newly unemployed had.

Joseph had screened him alone first then my French intel colleague went along the second time. The third time I did. The message that hooked them on Nimir before I met him was that he had some brazen information of his own to give me in person. So we all met in confidence at a place and time of our choosing and Nimir was each time given a full body check for any equipment he may have carried. Some uncammo (no uniforms on)

French UNIFIL troops were the ring fanned out around the bar.

And what you do think Elias wanted to tell me? He was proud to say that he was one of the chosen few suicide drivers for a spate of truck bombings to be organised! In essence he was a would-be traitor. Did we believe him? No. But set another couple of meetings we did, just in case. It wasn't everyday someone spoke forthrightly like that and in a way it was my own strategy working back over. And it wasn't because of what we already knew pre-Tunis from finding a loaded Mercedes lorry in a warehouse in his neck-of-the-woods. But since then a whole lot of changes in the local landscape had occurred, especially with the moving over of Fatah's Lebanese employees to Hizballah's offices. We needed to keep tabs on them and Namir was offering us a way to do so.

Turned out that a guy younger than him named Imad Mugniyah, age 20, who had been a personal bodyguard for Yasser Arafat had struck up a friendship with Nimir slowly earning his trust "to gain more inside work". They were from the same home town after all. Then his once-in-a-lifetime opportunity to be a martyr presented itself and Namir had immediately accepted.

All he knew at this early stage was what the first target was and that was hugely important: The US Embassy located on the seafront in West Beirut. It would be planned for daylight hours, too, which wasn't saying anything startling in the general scope of things. Namir was intent on telling us that Hizballah's role was to defend Lebanon and not Syria or Iran. From that seemingly learned statement there was a distinct implication that *they were indeed involved* in the planning stages otherwise why go through the trouble of denying it upfront.

So we knew *who* he got his orders from, *what* the objective was, *why* – to be noble to their wrecked nation, but not *when*.

Namir actually also gave us details where he could be found after work, if we had to contact each other before the next scheduled meeting in two weeks' time at another location.

Seemed all too easy to get this kind of information or disinformation all dropped conveniently in our laps without asking for it. If I ever felt a stooge in my life it was then. All delivered free by a beer boozing fool. The others felt exactly the same way. Was it even worth meeting again?

If it was then the most probable conclusion was that it was false. What dictated our next move was who Elis Namir reported the outcome of our meeting to, if indeed he ever did: Imad Mugniyah. He already had quite a reputation for extreme violence on the streets on Beirut so it was worth following up on.

* * * * * * * * *

By the time I met Elias – "please call me Elie" – Nimir the third time, I noticed he invoked his mother quite a lot in self-composed quotes. Like he had a Mum complex. He didn't seem to look at pretty girls walking past but then he didn't do it to good-looking guys either. For a while I pondered whether it was some kind of code of his for self-justification on what he said he was going to do. As time went by, some of the titbits of information we'd fed him actually came back with meaty punch lines. One by one the questions got answered. We slowly figured he was a bit mad but he was real. What convinced me was that a heavy goods lorry would be too noticeable and less flexible so his boss Mugniyah had elected not for a car or pickup truck but for a delivery van. All our meetings were duly filed in detailed reports at UNIFIL.

Simultaneously it turned out that Joseph was organising his own escape from the madness of Beirut. He had an uncle in Boston, Massachusetts, in the US willing to sponsor him, and he had applied for a visa to get his family out. The paperwork was slowly being processed but while inside the embassy building and grounds he did his homework on the logistics of what Nimir was saying. It was indeed feasible. I was thinking then that intelligence officers would make good terrorists. But if Joseph could check it out then Hizballah could too.

Turns out on one visit Joseph had struck up a conversation in the hallway with a US State Department fellow he'd once met way back. The key piece of information he had gleaned from the chat was that their SEP wasn't functioning properly. Naturally Joseph then asked what that stood for. The answer was: Security Enhancement Program, which was a computer linked to the data of all the other multinational task forces who were present at the time in Beirut. So as far as he could gather it answered a question of our own in that we always felt that our reports were ignored. So perhaps it wasn't a wilful action but an inoperable internal system glitch that wasn't receiving or accessing UNIFIL intelligence reports. It was on the tip of Joseph's tongue to tell the executive about our findings from Nimir off-the-record but he didn't. Upon learning of this snippet of information I filed that learned discovery about SEP with UNIFIL too – just to be on-record about it. In non-bureaucratic language it was CYA (cover your arse).

One day Elie Nimir got into a bit of a rant over propaganda. It was above his station so I figured it was a subconscious repeat of Mugniyah-speak he'd heard or was told to say. He proclaimed grandly, "This war in Lebanon is not just against the Shia Lebanese but against humanity as a whole." For him that was a major statement. Prompted with beer he disclosed how Iran and Syria were supporting Hizballah with funds and equipment, and how it comes through Ba'Labakk after it had crossed the nearby porous border. For me to get into oil and gas exploration with him would just blow his mind completely so I didn't go there.

What was doubly interesting from that same meeting was "technical support services were still provided by people from your country, Ireland." He went on to tell me the two Irishmen's names he had just met.

The suicide bombing target month was set for April next year, 1983. So now we knew three and half of the 4Ws. We still sought an approximate date. At the next meeting Elie Nimir said it was going to be a Monday because that was the day deliveries were mostly made after the weekend was over, making them less noticeable. It definitely now would be a delivery van, not a lorry or pickup or car. He confirmed it was down to him or two others for the job. He prayed to Allah five times a day that he would be the one chosen.

I wonder where his head was on that last part? If he'd told us it was going to be him he wouldn't have made it out of that bar to go and carry it out, even if it was an untruth. We would have apprehended him immediately. He was nuts that lad and the alcohol loosened his mouth wider.

Circumstances play a huge role in destiny. My French colleague answered the door one night at his secure residence where the French troops were in abundance. The man at the door aimed to shoot him in the head but missed, grazing his temple, before sprinting off. But the bullet ricochet into his spine. Still he lost a lot of blood and was airlifted to Paris on the first flight out. We never said our au revoirs. He is still alive but he has spent the rest of his life in a wheelchair so that's why I've never used his name.

A day later Joseph's US visa was approved and I went to his farewell party. We cried in each other's arms and for our suddenly departed French friend, hoping that he would live. His last words to me were, "There's no point in having the word 'truth' habibi." His voice reverberated in my head for some time afterwards. I believe he still calls Boston home now and fathered another child there. I'm happy for him.

Two brave bastards gone from my life within days of each other. Suddenly it felt very empty to be in an already bare Beirut.

My own year-long planned escape was nearing fruition. I feared for my life now more than any time ever before.

Elias Nimir never showed up at our next meeting.

I went to my favourite spot on the beach to contemplate everything. I came to realise at that precise moment that not for the first time my own steps in the sand represented the footprints of imperialism. I, again, felt shipwrecked on land out here in the vastness of the sea that lay in front of me.

I gazed back at the broken city behind me. Quixotically I started to feel like a gamecock in a cage, which I had just fought another to the death and won, but the capitalists humans outside don't remotely understand my pain for I am seen as a chance to win more money. It's a safe bet that the more times I do this numbers game I will eventually become another statistic. The minutes and hours were not to my advantage. I was going to leave in a few days' time with what was on my back plus my passport and wallet.

I took out a large photo of Vibeke out of my pocket. I had brought it with me from my quarters instead of a bottle this time. I looked at her smiling inside a large metal picture frame and concluded that it didn't properly recount her life lived, which was so free spirited like a bird. I wasn't going to leave it here and I couldn't take it with me. She appeared locked in there so I took it out of the four corners and threw the casing on a nearby rubbish dump. I read with a smile the inscription that had been scribbled on the back by me an age before. It was a windy day so I kissed it and held it up above my head. Within a few seconds a beautiful breeze took it to wing into the sky to now see everything through my eyes. I have never regretted that imaginative transposition knowing that her ambition was to carry on as before albeit in the afterlife that I didn't believe in. For me she lives in peace in the blue yonder of water and air. As I watched it drift away I thought again of the words by the French philosopher, Blaise Pascal, that I'd just read:

The heart has reasons of which the reason knows nothing.

* * * * * * * * *

I was writing my story and I was the lead actor so this is how it had to end. But there's a wee bit more icing on the cake:

The brave young Lebanese fisherman and I motored 24 hours in calm waters in his boat to Cyprus and freedom. He wasn't going back either and he found someone in me that would pay him towards his own liberty. No matter what his god was I was a godsend to him.

En route in a north-westerly direction we saw two Soviet warships on patrol around a flotilla of various hammer and sickle-flagged vessels at anchor. In my 12 months in Lebanon I had often wondered where the Russians were. It looked to me like the oil and gas drilling was about to commence while the war continued.

I did my best to tell it like it was.

* * * * * * * * *

Accretions

Elias Nimir – He wasn't the one chosen by the Shi'ite Lebanese Hizballah to drive a delivery van packed with 2,000 pounds of TNT explosives into the lobby of the US Embassy in Beirut on Monday, 18 April 1983. The suicide attack killed 63 and among the 17 Americans who perished 8 of them belonged to the Central Intelligence Agency. Despite numerous warnings issued by UNIFIL stationed within the same city, the danger signals were not detected due to computer problems or were deliberately ignored. Nimir *was* picked up soon after though and rightfully accused of being implicated in the bombing. The CIA then wrongfully chose Nimir for repeated and senseless torture and as a result he died of his injuries in his detention cell. They should have served him beer to loosen his lips instead.

I write that last line because despite all that went down, that same year on Sunday, 23 October, another suicide bomber drove a Mercedes lorry loaded with 21,000 pounds of TNT into the American barracks and killed 241 US Marines. That same day, almost simultaneously, a second attack targeted the French residences and resulted in the death of 58 paratroopers.

My deep-held thinking is to keep the lines of communication open for any titbit of information, even with the most despicable scum in the world. This is what human intelligence delivers. Especially so for the natural deep cover NOCs like I was. We befriended the enemy in the name of peace when it was our own precious life that was on the line. Satellite photos and electronic intercepts are not the answer. Neither is murdering them from drones or torture chambers.

If Elias Nimir was kept alive I have always felt that he would have provided crucial information about the other two suicide attacks that followed. *The biggest clue was that he had stated unprompted from the beginning that three drivers had been chosen to be martyrs.* On a bad day I have even pondered that his death was ordered so the war could be kept going and the arms industry could benefit from increased sales. But that will always be denied.

* * * * * * * * *

Epilogue

People grow tired of a confusion whose end is not in sight.
— Alexis de Tocqueville

Regarding the fact that nothing I wrote can be verified as fact was deliberately designed by the powers that be. It is exactly the same as unsubstantiated stories being used to substantiate an unsubstantiated story…labelling it as fiction then is *more truthful* these days and less libellous.

You can appreciate it's not easy to carry something loaded inside your head. It gets heavier as the years go by. Eventually you have to either let it wing free or bury it. I chose to let it escape for my own closure. But it took decades just to figure out what happened in the fine print and a good many more years to formulate it into font form that others could fathom.

Here I am finally writing about it but not enough language can fill the ripped tears between the pages and the raw tears in my eyes to adequately express my emotions. But my worst fear was that my memory would fade and cause an injustice to the victims.

The unspoken rule then was to survive so that I could, and that I did, did I not?

Look, I'm just giving you the reader the facts as I know them to be. I am not drawing any conclusions to avoid the appearance of an agenda. You have to arrive at your own realties yourself, that is if you desire to do so. I can't do that for you. But don't succumb to *la politique de l'autriche* (the politics of the ostrich) by willingly putting your head in the sand and ignoring these disclosures altogether.

The peoples of the countries that do strangle the truth it seems then that they refuse to understand their past mistakes and in doing so are committing to a future that is likely to repeat itself.

Truth emerges in today's western mainstream media in the form of an interpretative mixture of appeasement to power and the received conforming view. It results not in the thinking section of the story being delivered but rather an unthinking selection of the story that they want you to know, ie: the punch line is missing.

Based on what I found out in Bulgaria and Lebanon all the players, including me, were suckers into the biggest perception management tricks ever devised and periodically reactivated since.

So I left the employ of SIS without giving notice. Now in "overcover" (life after deep cover) I am a permanent conscientious objector of UK and US foreign policy. So many of our leaders are bona fide war criminals today. Still getting away with murder.

My SIS passing out report that I eventually got to read stated: "…has an ability to under-estimate danger, takes risks that are not always necessary plus habitually exceeds the task at hand, which subsequently places himself in life-threatening situations. As a result of his fearless action his SCI (sensitive compartmented information) has a higher than top secret level of security clearance that will have to be observed in perpetuity." This translated also means that *my image and likeness cannot be seen in public.* Sensible given that so many would seek revenge if they could find me.

That was the viewpoint of those likeminded seniors at SIS. Those who sought progress and freedom. Regrettably we also had the un-likeminded from within that started their internal campaign. They were known as the defenders of the realm.

In the months following my sudden resignation my parents forwarded several telegrams onto me that they'd received. They were ordering me to voluntarily report to a special unit within the Naval Detention Quarters at Berechurch Hall Camp in Colchester, Essex, which was northeast of London.

I ignored them and got on with integrating myself into civilian life.

In the years since I quit without notice in January 1983, I have run into some former intel lads I knew who did this 'n' that in their careers and when I brought up some event I know they were involved in they each looked blankly at me as if to say, 'Don't remember that at all.' Three times out of three over decades this has occurred and I'm fascinated that I can recall our involvement but they can't. So I began to think that they actually did undergo what we'd heard about in the grapevine early in our careers, which was they showed up at said establishment and underwent what was then called ECT (electro-convulsive therapy).

To those like me who suspected the existence of this possibility, whenever the subject came up in our younger days we would jokingly reverse the acronym with our own code and with a wink 'n' nod describing it as 'a telling cognitive (after) effect' ('a TCE'). Now I'm not so sure the practice wasn't true. But how could I remember and they didn't?

Had I reported in as ordered I probably would have been placed in custody awaiting the outcome of a sham investigation and while there I would have been administered with treatments to have permanent memory loss…or as the UK government described it in legalese in those days "psychoanalysis for complex patients in difficult settings".

Just for good measure, to be sure of my own sane judgement, I went to see a private psychiatrist on my own steam. Mainly with the intention to check that I wasn't suffering from post-traumatic stress disorder. Her verdict was that I wasn't. Neither did I suffer from a condition known as deception of memory, which means that I was not somebody who could not differentiate between truth and fact. Most encouragingly she proclaimed that I had an above average recall for detail and there was nothing wrong with my retention.

Nevertheless, it took me many years to unravel my experiences with a clear head and I now finally have jumbled it into some logical order. But I would not have had done so if I'd undergone this illegal medical procedure.

As a result of my experiences I'm not tempted to airbrush my memoirs. I just want to tell it without a seatbelt across my heart and editors hereinafter wishing to change the colour of my paint. I implore the reader to try and read between the lines much like I am forced to write it that way. Thank you from the bottom of my heart.

* * * * * * * * *

THE END